BUILDING A CO-OPERATIVE COMMUNITY IN PUBLIC HOUSING

The Case of the Atkinson Housing Co-operative

JORGE SOUSA

Public housing projects were the original form of government-supported housing for low-income residents. Over the last fifty years, however, many of these projects have struggled with high crime rates and other social problems. One solution proposed to address these ongoing issues is to convert public housing projects into co-operatives, thus empowering residents to make their own decisions affecting their community. *Building a Co-operative Community in Public Housing* follows the journey of a Toronto public housing complex as it was converted into a resident-operated co-operative, a first in Canada.

Jorge Sousa traces the story of Alexandra Park, which became the Atkinson Housing Co-operative in 2003 after a ten-year conversion process. Sousa, who himself was raised in the community, looks at various factors that influenced its decision to pursue community-based control, as well as the experiences of both residents and government officials engaged in this process. Finally, *Building a Co-operative Community in Public Housing* offers both inspiration and an empirical framework for members of other such communities facing similar circumstances who want to learn how to go about undertaking this process.

JORGE SOUSA is an associate professor in the Department of Educational Policy Studies and director of the Work and Learning Network at the University of Alberta.

Building a Co-operative Community in Public Housing

The Case of the Atkinson Housing Co-operative

JORGE SOUSA

UNIVERSITY OF TORONTO PRESS
Toronto Buffalo London

© University of Toronto Press 2013
Toronto Buffalo London
www.utppublishing.com
Printed in Canada

ISBN 978-0-8020-3862-3 (cloth)
ISBN 978-0-8020-3803-6 (paper)

Printed on acid-free, 100% post-consumer recycled paper with
vegetable-based inks

Library and Archives Canada Cataloguing in Publication
Sousa, Jorge
Building a co-operative community in public housing : the case of the Atkinson
Housing Co-operative / Jorge Sousa.

Includes bibliographical references and index.
ISBN 978-0-8020-3862-3 (bound)   ISBN 978-0-8020-3803-6 (pbk.)

1. Atkinson Housing Co-operative (Toronto, Ont.) – Case studies.   2. Public
housing – Ontario – Toronto – Case studies.   3. Housing, Co-operative –
Ontario – Toronto – Case studies.   4. Alexandra Park (Toronto, Ont.) –
Social conditions – Case studies.   I. Title.

HD7305.T68S68 2013   363.5'8509713541   C2013-901392-X

All royalties from this book will be donated to the Co-operative Housing
Federation of Toronto Charitable Fund to support communities seeking
community-based control.

University of Toronto Press acknowledges the financial assistance to its
publishing program of the Canada Council for the Arts and the Ontario Arts
Council.

Canada Council   Conseil des Arts
for the Arts   du Canada

ONTARIO ARTS COUNCIL
CONSEIL DES ARTS DE L'ONTARIO
50 YEARS OF ONTARIO GOVERNMENT SUPPORT OF THE ARTS
50 ANS DE SOUTIEN DU GOUVERNEMENT DE L'ONTARIO AUX ARTS

University of Toronto Press acknowledges the financial support of the Government of Canada through the Canada Book Fund for its publishing activities.

To those who believed in the conversion and to those who continue to persevere in strengthening a wonderful community

Contents

Illustrations

Acknowledgments

The completion of this book represents one further step on a very personal journey of supporting efforts to improve the physical and social conditions faced by public housing communities. At times, the challenge of completing this book would have been insurmountable were it not for the belief and support of different individuals. Everyone mentioned here was crucial in assisting me in the task. My appreciation can never be sufficiently expressed, but the following words represent my attempt to do so.

I want to start by thanking the members and tenants of the Atkinson Housing Co-operative. Without their trust and patience this work could not have been finished. Although I was involved in the early stages of the conversion process, their continued commitment to pursue Sonny Atkinson's dream has ensured that other public housing projects can benefit from their efforts. I recall Sonny publicly stating that he helped me to keep out of "trouble," which I thought was silly. Many years later, however, I can honestly say that part of his legacy has indeed been to get me to stay out of trouble. Thank you, Sonny, for being you. The leaders of the Alexandra Park Residents' Association and the Atkinson Housing Co-operative worked with me in varying capacities over the years and were pivotal to the completion of the conversion process and to my research. A special thank you goes to the property manager, Don White, and the former president of the co-operative, Fathi Sheik Hassan. I have appreciated your trust and kindness, and I could never thank you enough.

My research and the conversion process were possible because of very knowledgeable and dedicated individuals, who include Alina Chatterjee, Albert Koke, Tom Clement, Donna Harrow, David Hulchanski, and Mark Goldblatt. Their efforts remind me that a cause is always worth pursuing in spite of persistent obstacles. The strength of the co-operative movement lies in the dedication of its elders. A special thank you goes to Ian MacPherson, whose passion and commitment to co-operative studies helped me to understand their valuable contribution to the improvement of society.

This book was also made possible because of the commitment of those at the University of Toronto Press. Thank you, Virgil Duff and Doug Hildebrand, for your patience and understanding over the last few years. I also want to thank the reviewers for their insights and comments. While the comments were a bit bruising, they made for a much better final product, and I hope I did them justice. I also express sincere thanks to Stephan Dobson for his tireless and careful editing of the manuscript. It takes a particular kind of person with such skill and sensitivity to find gems in the repetition and other shortcomings associated with the early stages of the writing process.

Since the completion of my doctoral studies and in my current position as associate professor I have gone through many personal and professional changes. I wish to express deep gratitude to my loved ones: Eduardo, Eduard, Ginnie, Gaby, Daniel, and Xiao Jing. Their unwavering support and everyday interest in my life reminded me of the need to appreciate the challenges and delights that occur outside of the context of research. A special thank you goes to my mother, Virginia Sousa, who unfortunately passed away before she could see the fulfilment of both the conversion and her dream of seeing her children complete their formal education. To her I say, "It is done." However, the learning does not stop. In advancing my path towards becoming a bona fide academic, I have been humbled and inspired by the work of dear friends. I have been blessed with knowing and learning from two authentic and committed scholars, J.J. McMurtry and Dip Kapoor. We share the belief that all research is social and political. Taking a stand is something that we do with pride because of the trust given to us.

I reserve the final statement for my academic mentor and friend, Professor Jack Quarter. It was fortuitous that I met him at a time of indecision in my life. I was given opportunities that other students can only dream about. His clear way of thinking about research was a driving force for me at all stages of my development into an academic. Working with him helped me to realize that community work involves real practice and real patience, and our discussions have always been inspiring. Jack's belief in me and my work opened many doors for me which would have been unseen otherwise, and for that I thank him. Fortunately, my work with Jack continues in different forms. His ongoing encouragement and caring about me and his other former students is exceptional among professors. I am a better human being because of knowing Jack Quarter. He patiently waited for me to complete this book but every now and then would ask, "How is your manuscript?" Well, Jack, I am now able to say that it is done.

BUILDING A CO-OPERATIVE COMMUNITY
IN PUBLIC HOUSING

Introduction

Public housing was originally heralded as one solution to the problem of low-income earners' not having access to high-quality, affordable housing. Government and housing advocates believed that public housing would improve the lives of a vulnerable population (Bacher, 1993) and could in turn assist in efforts to revitalize those urban areas characterized as slums (Rose, 1980). While a significant amount of public housing was built from the mid-1940s to the mid-1970s, that housing model has become the housing of last resort – a space in which residents live not out of personal choice but because of economic circumstances. This reduction in choice has had a profound effect on the residents living in these communities as well as on the way in which the general public views the communities.

The common perception is that public housing projects are rife with crime and that the individuals living in them do not care about their community or their role in society. While it can be argued that residents bear some responsibility for many of the underlying problems associated with public housing, there is ample evidence to suggest that the management practices are equally at fault; they engender the helplessness and apathy that result in the residents' feeling disconnected from their community. While many public housing authorities and residents have worked towards improving the communities by adjusting management practices and providing more supports to meet the residents' needs better, those efforts have failed because they tended to be more cosmetic than substantive; these practices and supports do not address the core systemic issues associated with living in public housing.

Persistent government neglect in maintaining a housing project in downtown Toronto during the late 1970s and into the 1980s led its frustrated residents to take it upon themselves to explore alternative management arrangements, arrangements aimed at improving their living conditions by their increased involvement in the decisions affecting their community. Many residents of Alexandra Park shared the belief that this improvement would require a new vision. Supporters from the co-operative housing movement who were working with the community leadership believed that this vision involved the community taking control of crucial decision-making practices and their implementation. If the vision were to be realized, the community needed to build on its activist tradition and high levels of resident engagement.

Becoming a co-operative was the preferred arrangement because of its emphasis on community development, member participation, and successful management approaches. The co-operative housing model was seen as the means by which residents' decision-making power could result in actions that reflected the community's desire to implement local solutions to the challenging social problems that had afflicted the community since the 1970s. Among government officials from the Ministry of Housing there was both disbelief and hesitation as to whether public housing residents could effectively manage a housing property as de facto owners. Further, the government officials failed to recognize that the residents' desire for a change was a reaction to problematic management practices. In spite of the reservations, the residents' leadership worked with members of the co-operative housing sector for over ten years to build community support for the conversion process and to negotiate with the government to relinquish its control over the community.

In April 2003 the residents of the Alexandra Park community in Toronto completed a ground-breaking process to convert the project into Canada's first tenant-managed, public housing co-operative, called the Atkinson Housing Co-operative. This case is unique in Canada in that the process was initiated locally in order to combat the sense of helplessness felt by the residents in the face of the increased violence arising from profound social problems and systemic government neglect. Thus, the impetus of the conversion was the belief that improvement of the living conditions commonly experienced within public housing projects could be achieved through local control over management and decision-making processes. Many residents welcomed the opportunity to have a say in how their community was managed, with the hope that a healthier community would result. For them, health meant a security of tenure, free from the unreasonable scrutiny of government officials who treated them with little dignity and disrespect. However, other residents opposed the conversion because they were concerned that the change would lead to uncertainty regarding their responsibilities as members of a co-operative. For instance, they were convinced that their rents would increase and they would be forced to do their own maintenance. Moreover, many residents indicated that they were fearful of having a neighbour make decisions that might have a negative impact on their home life. As will be shown in this study, the conversion process encountered many unanticipated challenges, largely because such a process had never been undertaken before and there were no clear reference points or strategies to which the stakeholders could refer; this was new terrain for everyone involved.

The story of the creation of the Atkinson Housing Co-operative demonstrates the complexity of trying to improve established public housing projects when different interests are at stake. The aim of this book is to describe the history of the Alexandra Park community, identify the key lessons learned from the conversion process, and provide potential strategies for addressing unanticipated challenges. The intent is to influence community developers, public housing residents, and policymakers who are interested in nurturing the transition of government control to community-based control in a vital need like housing. To that end, there are two specific objectives associated with the exploration of the Atkinson experience. The first objective is to address the fundamental question of how the Alexandra Park community was able to organize in such a way as to convince a government housing authority to transfer significant control of a significant public asset to residents. The second objective is to provide a framework – the Framework for Community-Based Control – for other public housing or low-income communities that want to undertake a process towards attaining control. The theoretical and conceptual underpinnings of the framework are a synthesis of related bodies of knowledge as well as the lived experiences of the members of the Atkinson Housing Co-operative. While the framework presented is intended to explain after the fact the steps by which the community gained control of its housing, there are practical ways in which the framework can be applied in different contexts, as will be shown in the concluding chapter.

This study analyses the conversion process from a variety of perspectives. First, the content is an empirical exploration of the contributing factors that influenced the community's decision to gain greater control. Second, while the Atkinson Housing Co-operative represents a single case of such a conversion occurring in the Canadian context, the absence of a plan or blueprint presented many challenges that need not occur in future conversions; therefore, it was crucial to include the experiences of both the residents and the government officials engaged in this process. Third, from a community-development perspective the key issue at this juncture is what can be learned from this case that can be applied to similar settings in a non-prescriptive way. Throughout the text the obstacles associated with a community's journey to become a co-operative are also highlighted.

The contents are presented as a form of ethnography that demonstrates a concerted effort to provide the reader with an empirical account of the conversion process. However, this work also comes from a very personal place. It has been my privilege to document a unique process, one that had not previously occurred in Canada, which resulted in changes to a public housing project. Over the years, I spent a significant amount of time within the community as both a resident and a researcher. As someone who had grown up in the community, I participated in the events that led to the conversion and lived there until 2000. As a former resident, I provide some of the stories told to me by my neighbours and friends, as well as including personal reflections of growing up in this community for over twenty-five years. The stories clearly reveal the commitment and dedication of regular folks wanting to improve their community on their own terms. Gaining community-based control is the result of residents taking specific actions to challenge the social structures that cause the stigma associated with living in public housing. I had the privilege of witnessing and participating in ground-breaking community work, and part of the research process was the challenge of shifting between the roles of resident and researcher. In a number of instances I was deeply enmeshed in the community dynamics, while in others I was a beneficiary of the community-building initiatives.

Originally my knowledge and understanding remained at the local or emic level. In my early role in the community, as a member of the board of directors of the Alexandra Park Residents' Association in 1995 and of the Atkinson Housing Co-operative in 1999, I was involved in decisions that would not only benefit the community but also affect potential research findings. In my role as one of the decision makers, I promoted the conversion ideal as the best option for the community. For instance, in 1995 I primarily worked with the residents who wanted to learn about co-operative housing and the change that attaining it could mean for the community. However, since I was not working with the residents who opposed the conversion, I saw only one side of a developing picture.

At different times I took part in various facets of the conversion process, during which I noted many factors and observations. In all instances, I maintained detailed records in order to keep track of particular events occurring in the community. However, I did not develop a systematic understanding of the factors associated with the conversion until I had resigned from the board of directors. For instance, I was able to recognize that the conflicts of 2001 were not spontaneous but had been brewing among the residents for many years.

In 2000, I started to understand from a research or etic perspective the efforts that were being undertaken to convert the property into a housing co-operative. In that year the board of directors recognized the need to research the conversion process , and I received official support and encouragement at a board meeting. The board believed that I was able to see aspects of the process and understand the context within which they emerged. Through taking the role of participant observer since the mid-1990s, I have been able to grasp an understanding of the factors associated with the conversion. That understanding informs my research in terms of design, that is, the ways in which the data was collected and the events were selected for further analysis. My intention was to develop a methodology whereby the residents and their voices (albeit from archives) are sharing rather than giving information. At different points of the information-collection process, individuals stated that they experienced a form of catharsis because they felt that they were being listened to. This very act of being heard enriched the data but also had therapeutic elements, which is consistent with Murray's (2003) assertions of the benefits of conducting qualitative research. These experiences informed my development of the theoretical lens used to explain the conversion process.

Throughout the research process it was well known that I favoured and actively supported the co-operative alternative. This bias presented different challenges, not least of which was the need to continually re-establish trust with different members of the community. The greatest challenge, which will be elaborated in the discussion section, presented itself when I witnessed decisions being made that could have adverse affects on the community's journey to becoming a co-operative. In those instances I would be faced with the dilemma of acting and participating as an insider or tempering my involvement to that of an outside resource or researcher. This distinction would consistently inform my participation in the conversion and my interpretation of the findings. In a few instances the residents and members of the board of directors reminded me of my role.

Chapter Overview

The journey towards achieving community-based control needs to be understood within the socio-historical context of the development of public housing as well as the development of the community itself. The content will provide the reader with an analysis that is grounded in theory as well as in the lived experiences of those involved in the conversion process. I achieve this objective by situating Alexandra Park in a housing-policy context and by providing a historical overview of the factors leading up to and occurring during the conversion process.

The first chapter reviews the different government programs that created public housing, which was later referred to as *social housing*; however, in this study the terms are seen to be distinct. The chapter focuses on the development and operations of public housing projects in Canada. I discuss how the programs that created public housing projects were seen as the solution to the lack of affordable housing for low-income individuals (Streich, 1993). However, instead of balancing the financial hardships faced by many residents with the development of a sense of community in public housing, the original programs prioritized the goal of providing affordable housing at the lowest possible cost to the taxpayer; in other words, fiscal concerns overrode the goals of helping and protecting the most vulnerable and, in particular, of creating a sense of community (Bacher, 1993; Rose, 1980; Wolfe, 1998). The neglect of building a greater sense of community and the fostering of a dependence upon government administration have perpetuated the stigma and the oppressive nature of public housing projects.

In the first chapter I also show the way in which the 1973 amendments to the National Housing Act, which established partnerships between the government and non-profit organizations (NPOs), implicitly encouraged the building of communities. These partnerships were intended to address several issues by providing an affordable housing alternative, maintaining affordable housing stock without social problems, and encouraging a sense of community in social housing developments (Dreier and Hulchanski, 1993; Wolfe, 1998). They developed mixed-income communities with an autonomous governance system that encouraged a sense of ownership and pride among the residents (Cooper and Rodman, 1992).

Included in this chapter is a description and comparison of the different social housing models, using three dimensions: the management and governance process, the impact of a mixed-income community on community building strategies, and the impact of the size and design of the developments on the lives of residents. The policies and programs outlined in this chapter form a foundation for explaining the conversion of Alexandra Park housing project into a housing co-operative. I conclude with a description of the tenant management movement and relate it to the efforts of the residents of Alexandra Park to acquire community control.

In the second chapter I develop a theoretical lens by which to understand both the reasons for the conversion and how it was made possible. The lens is developed from an exploration of different literatures and bodies of knowledge that can explain the manner in which the conversion process was completed. This theoretical exploration is the basis for a synthesis into a single conceptual framework comprising seven attributes: community assets, forms of social capital, styles of community leadership, community consciousness, the role of government, cultural change, and resource mobilization.

The third chapter begins with a historical overview of the Alexandra Park housing project, including a description of the original structures in the area and the events that led to the decision to build a large housing project. Since 1969 the residents have made use of the best characteristics found in the co-operative housing model in order to transform their community, thus making the conversion a natural progression. In addition to the historical context, I discuss the key characteristics of the community, including the demographics, the physical design, and the quality of life in public housing. I also provide a description of both the circumstances and the advocacy that led to the efforts to create a stronger, healthier sense of community through conversion into a housing co-operative.

Both this chapter and the fourth chapter are organized around a set of pivotal events that triggered community activism and participation. The events are separated into two general themes across the two chapters: those that led to the conversion process and those that occurred during the conversion process. The events are structured according their background and significance to the community's development, and each description ends with an explanation of its relevance to the conversion process. In the fourth chapter I describe four events that reflect some of the key policy and community-level issues that became important in the latter stages of the conversion process. The information gleaned from these eight events will be used to understand empirically the factors associated with the process of converting a public housing project into a co-operative. These two chapters are arranged in chronological order, but some background information will be provided to clarify the last two events.

In the fifth chapter I build on the description of the key events by interpreting them through the theoretical lens described in the second chapter. In the sixth chapter I introduce a framework for community-based control. The framework consists of five components that are the result of a reconfiguration of the seven elements explored in the previous chapter. In this chapter I argue that the framework for community-based control can be a valuable development tool for individuals or groups seeking to attain greater control over the decisions that affect their public housing project. I conclude with a discussion of the policy implications, while providing the reader with a series of lessons learned that are worth considering in future conversion undertakings.

The afterword describes the current status of the Atkinson Housing Co-operative. I utilize aspects of the framework for community-based control to assess the impact of the different events and activities that took place from April 2003, when the Atkinson Housing Co-operative officially took control of the property, to April 2012. Although it is premature to state with authority whether the new community has been successfully transformed into a co-operative, the information reveals that there is a developing sense of satisfaction in some vital areas within the community. However, the ways in which these areas relate to an emerging co-operative identity have not always been clear, and factors such as self-reliance and co-operation should be developed and instilled during a conversion process.

1 Canadian Public Housing Policy and Programs

Throughout the twentieth century the competitive nature of the private housing market made it difficult for lower-income individuals and families to acquire affordable housing. In many Western countries, governments have intervened in the housing market in a variety of ways to ensure the availability of such housing. The typical approach has been to introduce policy and programs that are designed to finance housing for lower-income earners. Policies generally serve as platforms, guidelines, or regulations that governments, organizations, and individuals follow to ensure that social order is maintained. In the context of government, policy is synonymous with laws, statutes, or acts. In a social democracy, governments develop policy that is intended to provide a cushion for those individuals who are most vulnerable to market forces (Howlett and Ramesh, 2003). In essence, public policy "is an action usually undertaken by government, directed at a particular goal and legitimated by the commitment of public resources" (Dobelstein, 1993, 16). The development of public policy starts with a problem and a statement related to goals, with strategies that can be applied to their achievement (Brooks and Miljan, 2003; Dobelstein, 1993). It is important to distinguish between public policy and social policy and to recognize the relationship between the two. According to McKenzie and Wharf (2010), social policy is the branch of public policy that relates to the human services.

Canadian housing policy is an example of social policy that serves both regulatory and social functions. The regulatory function is primarily associated with the private housing market (Anderson, 1992; Bacher, 1993), while the social function relates to housing people who are economically disadvantaged (Prince, 1995, 1998). The social function is associated with the provision of housing for low-income earners through public housing programs. The efficacy of the social function, which is the focus of this chapter, has been questionable given consistent shortages of an adequate and affordable housing stock and that cyclical changes in government can result in changes to a housing system, changes that are based on ideological stances rather than on addressing a public need.

In Canada the development of social housing policy has been sporadic because there have always been tensions as to whether government should be involved in providing housing for society's most vulnerable or whether the market should be allowed to address the needs of the most vulnerable without government involvement (Bacher, 1993). In spite of the tension, government intervention has resulted in a large stock of public housing; however, management approaches and funding programs have been in jeopardy because, as new governments come to power, priorities and commitments shift to reinforce the ideology of a new administration.

According to Rose (1980) and Bacher (1993), Canada has always grappled with the issue of developing the best approach to ensure that all citizens have access to affordable, high-quality housing, by either renting or owning. Bacher (1993) states that instituting Canadian housing policy has been an ongoing battle, one that aims to balance the autonomy of the private market and the principles of the welfare state. In other words, there is an irresolvable tension grounded in ideological positions wherein private sector investment in the housing market is given primacy over the provision of a "cushion" for individuals who cannot afford to participate in the private market. Needless to say, strategies that have attempted to balance the needs of the private sector to profit from the housing market and those of low-income earners to access affordable housing have always been controversial.

To keep the private sector involved, government programs offer financial incentives or guarantees for developers to invest in housing (Anderson, 1992; Bacher, 1993; Rose, 1980; Van Dyk, 1995). To meet the need for affordable housing, governments have launched special programs, often operating outside the market for low-income earners (Bacher, 1993; Dreier and Hulchanski, 1993). In Canada in the 1940s the federal government enacted the National Housing Act to formally establish partnerships with the two other levels of government to build and manage large housing developments, known as public housing. The literature provides two reasons that Canada developed affordable housing programs:

to ensure adequate housing for returning war veterans (Anderson, 1992; Rose, 1980) and to fulfil the social objective of providing affordable housing for low-income earners. After the Second World War, housing was provided for veterans through federal support, and large housing projects for those less fortunate also were initiated (Rose, 1980).

The National Housing Act (passed in 1944) is the primary legislative policy that regulates all housing development and agreements between the various governing bodies that participate in managing or financing housing in both the public and the private sectors (Sewell, 1994). The act is intended to "promote the construction of new houses, the repair and mod-· ernization of existing houses, and the improvement of housing and living conditions" (National Housing Act, 1985, p. 1). Since 1944 the National Housing Act has formally outlined the federal government's role in providing affordable housing as well as programs to encourage private sector development (Dennis and Fish, 1972; Rose, 1980). The act has undergone many changes since its creation; some were intended to clarify the government's position on affordable housing, while others reduced the role of the federal government in providing affordable housing (Bacher, 1993). The original formulation of the National Housing Act was vague in terms of specifying the type of housing developments that government programs would fund, a vagueness that caused many delays in the building of new housing. Subsequent amendments to the act were more specific (Dennis and Fish, 1972; Wolfe, 1998). For instance, cost-sharing arrangements with the provincial governments for developing public housing were formally established in the 1949 amendments (Rose, 1980).

The 1944 version of the National Housing Act established a government agency to oversee the building and financing of housing developments (Rose, 1980). Formerly known as the Central Mortgage and Housing Corporation and now referred to as the Canada Mortgage and Housing Corporation (CMHC), the agency would play a significant role in initiating different housing programs as well as developing policies and practices that would guide the operations of many housing properties. CMHC worked in partnership with different levels of government to build public housing.

Building Public Housing

In most North American cities that provide large-scale public housing the housing projects replaced areas characterized as "slums" (Rose, 1963; Sewell, 1993; Social Planning Council of Metropolitan Toronto,

1970). Public housing refers to developments that are owned and administered directly by a level of government and built for the exclusive use of low-income earners, with government providing subsidies to offset any financial hardship. Accordingly, all properties consist entirely of low-income individuals and families. Although housing the poor was a genuine concern for many leaders and politicians throughout the twentieth century, there was a reluctance to have any form of government involvement in an area normally left to the private sector (Friedman, 1968). In post-Depression Canada most of the poor in urban centres were living in housing stock that had fallen into serious decay (Rose, 1958). Consequently, people's health became a prominent concern that required urgent action on the part of all levels of governments (Sewell, 1993, 1994). There was broad consensus that these city areas had to be redeveloped and that opportunities should be provided to improve the quality of life for individuals living there (Rose, 1963; Sewell, 1993; Social Planning Council of Metropolitan Toronto, 1970).

The concept of public housing became more widespread in the United States with President Roosevelt's 1933 New Deal (Friedman, 1968), the objective of which was to kick-start a sagging economy after the Great Depression. Following the Second World War, American government investment in housing was primarily geared to housing veterans and to rehabilitating the slum conditions in which many poor families were living (Friedman, 1968). In Canada the federal government, faced with similar concerns, began to consider greater involvement in the housing sector. Urban redevelopment occurred because citizen groups and community activists placed pressure on the three levels of government for "slum clearance" programs (Bacher, 1993). Albert Rose documented these endeavours in his seminal piece *Regent Park: A Study in Slum Clearance* (1958); he describes the efforts to build Canada's first public housing project as well as the residents' experience of living in that community.

Initially the building of public housing projects did not have support within government and the public at large (Dennis and Fish, 1972; Rose, 1980; Sewell, 1994). The main opponents were conservative ministers and also the housing developers who considered such programs to be an intrusion on their ability to profit from the housing market (Anderson, 1992; Bacher, 1993; Van Dyk, 1995). Several researchers have stated that a lack of political support hardened the government's resolve to limit its involvement in the housing market and led to its decision to leave housing to the private sector (Bacher, 1993; Dennis and Fish, 1972; Wolfe, 1998).

Despite the strong opposition, the government funded programs that built several public housing projects of varying sizes in Canada from the mid-1940s to the mid-1970s (Sewell, 1994). The Regent Park housing project in downtown Toronto, for example (the first major housing project in Canada, completed in 1949), was the result of CMHC involvement as a partner with the municipal and provincial governments (Canada Mortgage and Housing Corporation, 2004; Rose, 1980, 1958). These public housing projects were intended to address the objective of ensuring that low-income earners had access to affordable housing (Streich, 1993). However, the absence of equitable policies related to management and eligibility would have a devastating effect on the ability of many of these projects to take into account the long-term needs of residents.

In the 1960s and early 1970s CMHC established a series of principles to guide the housing's appearance and management (Dennis and Fish, 1972). As suggested by Bacher (1993), these principles reflected an ideology that perceived the poor as marginal to society and as people who needed to be motivated to make a contribution to the economy. Consequently, the government's raison d'être for participating in the building of housing was to support citizens' transition from poverty to the middle class (Dennis and Fish, 1972). In essence, the residents should not remain wards of the state, and the governing practices of these public housing projects should focus on getting people to live in the private market, through either renting or owning. Public policy consistently emphasized that the housing was intended to be temporary in that it would be transitional housing for new immigrants and temporary affordable housing for low-income families (Dennis and Fish, 1972; Rose, 1980; Sewell, 1993). The result was projects rife with social problems, and the subsequent policy changes to battle those problems were largely unsuccessful.

Housing Policy and Social Problems

In spite of the government's efforts to provide high-quality affordable housing, the physical and social conditions found in many public housing projects had deteriorated by the mid-1960s. In many locations residents were eager to leave as these communities became known as sites of pervasive social problems, such as vandalism and drug trafficking, and of questionable management practices. The existence of these problems was unanticipated, reflecting the governments' policy of focusing on "bricks and mortar" development rather than social development. Explanations of the causes of the social problems have included the concentration of poverty in a single geographical location (Prince, 1998) and the promotion by large communities of impersonal and weak attachments between residents (Epp, 1996; Prince, 1998). In fact, the concentration of poverty has resulted in the stigmatizing of those living in public housing. While these explanations are feasible, a review of the literature and policies associated with building public housing suggests that the history of public housing in Canada demonstrates systematic disenfranchisement and paternalism.

According to Dennis and Fish (1972), structural and political causation in the social problems are the result of a conservative, "almost religious" ideology that guided the early development of strategies associated with the building of the housing developments. Dennis and Fish describe the way in which CMHC established a series of principles that ensured the building of public housing at the lowest possible cost to government. Those principles mandated that the design of the projects should discourage residents from remaining in the community for an extended period of time (Sewell, 1993). The criteria can be divided into three categories: the individual housing units, the overall design of the housing project, and the relationship to the wider neighbourhood.

According to an internal CMHC position paper, the individual units should be built in such a way as to make them functional but "less socially desirable" (Dennis and Fish, 1972, 175). Dennis and Fish present the features that describe CMHC's intention: a minimum room size, a cement or cement-and-brick interior, a uniform colour, and durable and functional appliances. These criteria were applied at the project level in order to ensure that costs were kept to a minimum (Dennis and Fish, 1972). The effect has been to stigmatize public housing residents, in part because of the institutional appearance associated with such projects. The overall design of the public housing project itself also followed principles of uniformity. According to Dennis and Fish (1972) and Hellyer (1969), the larger housing projects are often isolated from the surrounding community and are identifiably less attractive than that neighbourhood. Hellyer (1969) states that the design made the residents feel alienated from each other and from the surrounding community.

Public housing projects consist of a variety of housing forms, including row houses and high-rise buildings, which can be different from those of the neighbouring community. Most often, the units look alike on the exterior, and there is little physical separation between the houses. For instance, when Alexandra Park was built in 1968, there were no fences dividing the individual yards, and any fences that were provided were in stark contrast to those of the neighbourhood. The design of the Alexandra Park housing project often resembled a maze that would keep residents in and the neighbourhood out. According to one of its original architects, the intention behind the lack of fences or dividers was to promote interaction among the residents rather than separation (Jerome Markson, personal communication, 15 March 2004). While the plan to encourage social interaction among the residents was worthwhile, the end result was a lack of privacy, which discouraged interaction among residents (Klein, 1969). The lack of privacy and clear separation between the houses created an absence of what Newman (1972) refers to as defensible space, an absence that he argues is a primary contributor to criminal activity within low-income communities. Newman argues that tenants need to be able to have some control over that space that immediately surrounds their home. This control can take the form of a fence, a lawn, or a parking space (Newman, 1996). To provide some separation between the houses, walls were erected to separate particular sections of the project from each other (Sewell, 1993). In many instances, both inner roads and pathways were cut off from major streets in order to be used for residential purposes (Sewell, 1993).

It would be misleading to suggest that the design of the housing projects was the primary cause of the pervasive social problems. Although physical surroundings can have a significant impact on the incidence of crime and a sense of connection to the community, the social-psychological environment is equally important. In addition to the problems associated with the design, there was a persistent lack of social services and of activity space for the residents. Where there were services and activities, access was limited to those living in the project; the surrounding community was not included. For example, swimming pools and basketball courts were used only by the youth living in the housing project, thereby reinforcing the separation from the neighbourhood. The consequence of the design was segregation of the residents from their neighbours, resulting in a ghetto of low-income earners.

With respect to the management of public housing, the administration was and remains top down in that the decision-making process does not involve the residents in a meaningful way. Until 2000, provincial housing corporations (for instance, Ontario Housing Corporation) administered public housing projects, and local housing authorities or municipal government agencies were responsible for direct manage-ment of the properties (Van Dyk, 1995); however, the local authorities were accountable to provincial government through a provincial crown corporation – not to either the municipal government or the residents (Smith, 1995).

The governance structure of most housing authorities includes a board of directors operating as an arm's length agency of the govern-ment, where the government is the sole shareholder. In the majority of cases all board members are government appointees and are therefore neither independent of the government nor accountable to the residents (Sewell, 1994). Such a board structure does not afford the possibility for residents to have a direct say in the development and management of their communities. This structure ensures that policies serve the pur-poses of management rather than the needs of residents. Some of the key decisions made by the board of directors include specifying eli-gibility for housing, setting market rent levels, and determining man-agement practices. This approach was justified on the grounds that the residents were perceived as wards of the state, incapable of making decisions because they live in public housing.

Eligibility Criteria

Public housing projects have always been intended for low-income earners (Dennis and Fish, 1972). Indeed, as we have just seen, the expectation was that those who qualified would live in the project tem-porarily, that is, until they were able to move into the private market; at this point they were expected to leave (Rose, 1980). In effect, a culture of "turnstile" tenancy was created to encourage a change of residents, and this culture worked against the building of a sense of community. The expectation of departure created a sense of transiency that resulted in the residents' feeling disconnected from their community. In fact, resi-dents generally felt discouraged from becoming involved in the devel-opment activities that were intended to foster greater cohesion among the community.

A system for determining eligibility was created soon after the first public housing project was built in Toronto. Referred to as a *rental scale*, it has two components. First, prospective tenants must have low income as determined through a household income means test. Sec-ond, rent is geared to income (technically called *rent geared to income*, or

RGI), meaning that the rent for qualified households would be approximately 25 to 30 per cent of their total income (calculated using the gross amount rather than the net amount). A household's income can change from one month to the next because of employment availability; therefore, the rent can fluctuate, which makes it difficult for a renter to stop receiving government support. In some cases, the rent exceeds what is paid in the private market because a household's rent is based on income rather than market price, which fact was recognized as early as 1973 by a provincial task force examining the effects of various housing practices within the Ontario public housing system (Ontario Advisory Task Force on Housing Policy, 1973). These fluctuations in rental prices can be problematic for tenants and also for the project as it can strain their budgeting practices and create a tremendous administrative burden (OECD, 2008).

The rents within a project are based upon those in the private market of nearby neighbourhoods. The underlying assumption is that there is a maximum potential revenue for each unit, referred to as the *economic rent*, which is analogous to the rents of similar size units in adjacent neighbourhoods. Since fluctuations in residents' incomes can affect the revenue for the housing project, any shortfall is met by the government in the form of a subsidy (for example, the RGI subsidy). Thus, it is in management's best interests to ensure that residents have a level of income that can reduce the amount of household subsidy or limit the government's financial liability. However, the absence of social services to help individuals improve their income potential ensures that the government continues to provide significant funding to these housing projects, all the while never addressing the many social issues faced therein. Consequently, owing to government subsidies, housing authorities strictly enforce a system of eligibility that closely scrutinizes the incomes and assets of households, including their bank accounts and inherited properties (Toronto Community Housing Corporation, 2012a).

The Ontario Advisory Task Force on Housing Policy (1973) summarizes several consequences of the scheme of establishing rents on the lives of residents. First, the RGI scheme creates disincentives for the residents to improve their economic circumstances because all increases in income will be absorbed by an increase in rents. For instance, a family member may want to work extra time in order to generate more income for the household, which may conceivably improve their economic situation. However, the resident's economic situation may not actually improve since a percentage of his or her financial gain will be absorbed in the recalculation of the rent, thereby locking the resident into a system where any economic improvement is minimal. Second, the RGI scheme means that a household's rent can change from month to month. The uncertainty in knowing the amount of rent makes it difficult for residents to save any funds and for them to improve their economic position (Sewell, 1994). Finally, if the rent increases, the increase bears no relationship to the quality of the housing and to the living space. It is conceivable that a family could be paying a higher-than-market rent, yet the quality and size of its housing would be below market standards.

Management Practices

Metropolitan Toronto Housing Authority,[1] the government agency responsible for public housing in Toronto, manages rent collection, maintenance and repair, hiring and supervision, occupancy standards, and unit allocation. The management of an individual project is responsible for the implementation of relevant policy decisions made by the housing authority. These functions are necessary to all housing developments, but the way in which they are administered tends to have a greater impact on public housing residents than on individuals living in private rented housing.

In addition to the physical design and the eligibility criteria, the management of public housing developments of all sizes has always been an area of concern for both government and residents (Franklin, 2000; Haworth and Manzi, 1999; Tunstall, 2001). According to Haworth and Manzi (1999), the management practices in public housing have historically been normative, with a moralistic undertone. In most instances, residents have been discouraged from participating and are powerless when problems related to the running of the property emerge; in effect, learned helplessness becomes part of a resident's concept of self. Since at least the early 1970s (Ontario Advisory Task Force on Housing Policy, 1973) government and managers have argued that these practices are a reflection of budget constraints, yet management practices have also been shown to contribute to the stigma associated with public housing residents (Dennis and Fish, 1972).

In Canada the larger developments are managed on site, while the smaller ones have off-site management (Sewell, 1994); however, in both instances major policy decisions continue to be made off site in a central office. Having local management was seen by government as a better way to address the needs of the residents (Sewell, 1994), yet, according to Sewell, residents in the larger housing developments find the management practices more problematic because the decision makers do not necessarily understand the complex needs of the residents.

Residents of public housing projects are not expected to be involved in developing the policies and implementing the practices that can directly have an impact on their lives. Management cites the lack of expertise of the residents as an explanation for this (Dennis and Fish, 1972; Rose, 1980; Sewell, 1994). Another reason given is the residents' alleged lack of intellectual ability, which is an unfortunate perception because it encourages the stigmatization and marginalization of public housing residents. The residents have attempted to overcome the stigma associated with living in public housing; however, it is very difficult to overcome perceptions held by people in positions of authority. Prince (1995) states that changes to management practices are required in order to improve the public's and residents' perceptions about the condition of public housing properties.

A key concern of many residents and housing advocates has been the unresponsive nature of the management (Carder, 1994), which can make public housing residents more vulnerable than individuals renting in the private market. For instance, the lack of choice and realistic opportunity to move into other housing because of their low or fluctuating income leaves residents powerless; this, in turn, perpetuates a unique vulnerability because they are forced to acquiesce to any regulations imposed by management's neglect. Residents have cited the extended response time for minor repairs as a major concern, as well as management's accusatory approach – that residents are trying to defraud the housing system.

Owing to the complexity of the social problems, the residents and the government typically focus on individual households and have opted to neglect the state of the community as a whole (Koebel and Cavell, 1995). A variety of researchers have suggested that the lack of control and power over their housing has had a detrimental effect not only on the residents' ability to feel pride in their community but also on their willingness to participate in actively changing their environment. As early as 1969 (Hellyer, 1969) and also in later research (Koebel and Cavell, 1995), one finds the argument that increased resident control in the management of these communities is a way to improve the negative living conditions and image of public housing.

Addressing the Limitations of the Public Housing Model

It is not my intention to suggest that all public housing is fraught with social problems. In fact, there have been examples of successful public housing projects; however, these projects tend to be small in size and better integrated into the surrounding communities (Dennis and Fish, 1972; Hellyer, 1969; Smith, 1995). As discovered by many authors and researchers well before me, problems have been most evident in the large developments where the concentration of poverty is greatest (Prince, 1998) and the properties are unwieldy, complex, and difficult to manage. Consequently, these properties have been seen as a symbol of urban blight and have come to represent what is wrong with housing policy (Dennis and Fish, 1972; Rose, 1980).

With the increased recognition of both the myriad of problems within large public housing projects and the unwieldiness of management, a number of task forces, committees, and initiatives over the past fifty years have attempted to determine the best approach to addressing these issues. Prior to building public housing projects, the federal government explored the questions of what is an appropriate approach to financing low-rental housing and what model should be used. In 1944 the *Final Report on the Subcommittee on Housing and Community Planning*, also known as the Curtis Report (Government of Canada, 1944), recommended a greater federal presence in low-rental housing by the provision of loans to municipalities for the building of new housing stock (Bacher, 1993). In addition, the report recommended replication of the successful European example of co-operative housing as the primary means to provide low-rental housing that would not concentrate the poor in the outlying areas of large cities (Dennis and Fish, 1972). The Curtis Report continues to be a pivotal document in the history of Canadian housing policy because it was the first attempt to offer a progressive approach to the difficulties found in public housing projects; however, the federal government was reluctant to act on the recommendations because of financial constraints and philosophical differences largely based on political ideology (Bacher, 1993; Dennis and Fish, 1972). Consequently, large-scale public housing projects continued to be built into the 1970s. Ironically, once government changed its approach to the funding of housing for persons with low incomes – from public housing to other forms of housing that included individuals and families from different incomes – the non-profit housing co-operatives recommended in the Curtis Report became a successful model (Wolfe and Jay, 1990).

Another key step taken by the federal government was to establish a task force in 1968, headed by housing minister Paul Hellyer (Dennis and Fish, 1972; Rose, 1980). Members of the task force met with bureaucrats, housing advocates, and public housing representatives in order to arrive at a complete sense of the problems associated with the public housing programs. According to Hellyer (1969), there was compelling qualitative and quantitative evidence that public housing programs were not the panacea to the housing problem, as had been originally hoped. The final report detailed the poor state of the public housing stock and made a series of recommendations for improving the federal government's response to housing the poor.

One of the significant recommendations made by the Hellyer task force was the undertaking of a comprehensive review of the social and psychological problems associated with living in public housing (1969). According to Hellyer, until a review was completed, "no new large housing projects should be undertaken" (1969, 55). Another recommendation was to replace the funding of new public housing projects with a more socially oriented approach to providing affordable housing (Hellyer, 1969). The approach was to create smaller forms of non-profit housing, including co-operatives, which were more fully integrated than public housing into the surrounding communities (Hellyer, 1969). It was this recommendation that ushered in a new era of housing policy and practice in which low-income housing came to be referred to as social housing, and new projects were supposed to be run as non-profit and in partnership with government. However, the existing public housing stock remained within government control.

Partnering with Non-profit and Co-operative Groups: Moving towards Social Housing

In order to implement several recommendations of the Hellyer task force, amendments to the National Housing Act were initiated in 1973 to direct funding away from new public housing developments to the building of social housing, including co-operative housing (Van Dyk, 1995; Wolfe, 1998). These changes effectively started the process of abolishing the public housing model. The revisions focused on new government programs that were aimed at encouraging non-profit organizations, including municipalities, to build smaller developments that contained individuals and families of different income levels (Carter, 1997; Van Dyk, 1995), and to commence neighbourhood-improvement initiatives (Dreier and Hulchanski, 1993). It was believed that non-profit organizations could better manage the housing and ensure its integration into the surrounding communities (Anderson, 1992; Dreier and Hulchanski, 1993). Further, it was understood that non-profit organizations were better able to account for the needs of residents on a local level by encouraging the sense of community as well as providing high-quality housing (Wolfe, 1998). As a result, partnerships with non-profit development groups became the primary vehicle for delivering social housing. It was also believed that such partnerships would be best suited to managing the smaller properties in order to create vibrant and diverse communities, something that was absent in the original public housing programs.

The federal government stopped building public housing by the mid-1970s and focused the new funding programs on developing small properties through partnership agreements with the non-profit sector. The new programs, referred to as Section 61 and Section 95 of the National Housing Act, involved the federal government in the provision of direct mortgage financing (which was below market levels) of newer and smaller housing developments, in which 90 per cent of the mortgage had to be repaid by the property and the remaining 10 per cent was considered a capital grant that was "earned over the life of the mortgage" (Carter, 1997, 5).

Models of Social Housing

In Canada co-operatives and non-profits have traditionally constituted the two forms of social housing (Skelton, 2002). As both forms are not oriented towards the accumulation of profit, they are often referred to as non-market because the units cannot be sold on the open market (Dreier and Hulchanski, 1993). The purpose of each housing model is to provide high-quality, affordable housing and to promote a sense of community, but the main difference from public housing lies in the governance structure and the level of resident involvement.

The majority of the co-operative housing stock is non-equity, which means that the housing is for use only and the resident does not hold a financial or equity stake in the resale of the property. In the case of non-equity co-operatives, the units are geared primarily for low- and moderate-income families (Co-operative Housing Federation of Toronto, 2003; Dreier and Hulchanski, 1993). While there are equity housing co-operatives in the United States and to a lesser degree in Canada, non-equity co-operative housing is common in both Canada and Western Europe (Quarter, 1992; Skelton, 2002). Co-operatives are generally more diverse and vibrant than are most low-income communities because they are small in scale and are designed to fit into neighbouring communities (Co-operative Housing Federation of Toronto, 2003). What made the co-operative model congruent with the desires of the Alexandra Park residents was the focus on democratic control through purposeful participation and, further, the fact that the co-operative operates for the benefits of its members and not state appointees.

Integral to living in a housing co-operative is the notion that members have security of tenure, meaning that households choose to live in the community for as long as they wish. This is in stark contrast to the situation encouraged in public housing projects. Co-operative housing communities are owned by a co-operative corporation that represents and comprises its members, who are the residents. Each member has one vote in the decision-making process, in contrast to public housing projects wherein the residents are disenfranchised from the decision-making process. Since the members collectively control the co-operative, they are motivated to ensure that their housing is well managed and affordable. The members must adhere to community-established by-laws and housing charges , charges that are analogous to rent. Most important, co-operative members have a voice in the decisions that could affect their home, thereby increasing a sense of belonging to their community.

In housing co-operatives, participation can take many forms – in fact, it is an expectation associated with membership – and has the common purpose of sustaining the community for the benefit of present and future members. Normally the members participate in committees that assist in the operations of the community, for example, the hiring of staff, the maintenance of the property, and the selection of new members. In addition, there is a democratically elected board of directors that is made up of the members and is legally responsible for the organization. A housing co-operative is more likely to have members of mixed income, meaning that one household may be receiving a government subsidy while its neighbour may be paying market price. Since there is a greater diversity of people, there will be a greater mix of specialized knowledge with a greater likelihood of there being individuals with the appropriate experience to participate in community processes (Cooper and Rodman, 1992).

One feature that sets the co-operative model apart from other forms of social housing is its inclusion in a global movement that is grounded in principles espousing equity, equality, self-help, democracy, and solidarity (International Co-operative Alliance, 2013). The primacy of solidarity ensures that co-operatives are based on the shared goals and values that reflect efforts to improve society through movement building. Being part of a movement guarantees that resources and expertise are available to support an individual co-operative. In essence, solidarity is grounded in the International Co-operative Association's sixth principle, co-operation among co-operatives (International Co-operative Alliance, 2013). As will be shown in the description of the conversion process, the involvement of the Co-operative Housing Federation of Toronto (CHFT) and the Co-operative Housing Federation of Canada (CHFC) with individual housing co-operatives reflects this principle of solidarity and demonstrates a commitment to actively develop new co-operatives. Such a commitment by a third party to supporting new housing co-operatives is in stark contrast to the participation in non-profit housing and public housing.

In Canada there are two types of non-profit housing providers: private non-profits, which are owned and administered by independent groups such as churches, service clubs, seniors' organizations, unions, ethnocultural groups, and co-operatives; and municipal non-profits, which are administered by municipal governments or their designates (Ontario Nonprofit Housing Association, 2002). The fundamental difference is that in private non-profits the administering group and decision-making body is a corporation comprising the members, whereas in municipal non-profits sponsors control the decision-making practices. It is important for the reader to note that the success of each model will vary according to a community's particular circumstances; representative decision-making practices may not be feasible or desirable within some housing properties.

As with co-operatives, both private and municipal non-profit housing communities tend to be small scale (under one hundred units), fit well with surrounding neighbourhoods, and have residents of various income levels (Rose, 1980; Van Dyk, 1995). Non-profits receive two forms of government subsidies: a rent-geared-to-income subsidy to assist low-income households in affording the rents and a "bridge" subsidy to fund any budgetary shortfall or to defray the cost of capital projects and other development costs. In addition, non-profits maintain their own waiting lists for all units, and approval of new members by the board is not necessary. In general, there are shorter waiting times for market units. These organizations have the option of dividing their lists according to special-needs households, for example, for seniors or victims of abuse, which are granted priority access to available subsidized and non-subsidized units.

Municipal non-profits operate at arm's length from all levels of government, but they receive funding from the municipal government. The size of municipal non-profit communities varies from under one hundred units to over one thousand units. The government normally appoints the board of directors, which can mean that residents often lack a voice in the development of their community. In private non-profits, residents may have a say through the board of directors in the management of the community, but the directors are neither accountable to the members nor representative of the residents. In some cases, however, there are community elections for the board.

Transforming Public Housing

Social housing programs have provided a supply of affordable housing for citizens who are most in need, but the negative impact of the policies that had created and maintain the public housing programs is still present. The implementation of the different programs and policies connected to the three models of social housing has been a source of confusion among the three levels of government owing to a lack of definition of the jurisdictional and managerial responsibilities (Sousa and Quarter, 2003). Taylor (2003) suggests that problems with the public housing model largely resulted from the failure of administrative and managerial systems. Specifically, systems associated with public housing programs continue to discourage the building of community pride because of the community design, policy constraints, and the lack of security of tenure (Dennis and Fish, 1972; Sewell, 1994).

As described above, there has been ample evidence that has led policymakers, politicians, and housing advocates to declare that improvements are needed for public housing projects, but the absence of a feasible plan to address the social and structural issues has made improvements difficult to achieve. Housing advocates and researchers who have proposed improvements to the existing public housing system suggest that the focus of any such improvements should fall within two areas: first, adjusting the practices of management, and second, rehabilitating the physical stock. Researchers have suggested that many housing projects will continue to have high incidences of social problems and will continue to deteriorate as a consequence of the management and rehabilitation concerns not being adequately addressed (Peterman, 1996; Somerville, 1998). However, it has rarely been asked what the residents themselves are prepared to do to deal with the social problems. As already noted, residents of public housing have developed a profound sense of helplessness, and they do not have a strong sense of belonging and of connection to a community; therefore, a cycle and pattern of neglect is perpetuated by all stakeholders (Peterman, 1996; Somerville, 1998). Nevertheless, this is no reason not to ask the residents what they could do even though the circumstances that created the social problems are often outside their control.

Over time, public housing residents have become very familiar with the potentially negative impact of decisions made about their communities, but their ability to influence or make decisions that affect their community – which is a key ingredient in creating a sense of community (Kingston, Mitchell, Florin, and Stevenson, 1999) – is limited because the decision-making process remains outside the project. It is commonly believed that allowing the residents some form of control will empower them to improve their community as well as their lives (Rohe, 1995). This strategy has been strongly promoted by housing advocates, government task forces, and public housing residents themselves. During the 1960s a tenants' movement emerged in both Western Europe and the United States that called for increased resident participation in the operations of government-assisted housing properties (Hague, 1990) because it was widely believed that government policies and practices were contributing to the deterioration of many of these communities (Bauman, 1994).

Evidence has shown that the involvement of residents in managing their housing has led to improved satisfaction with their housing conditions. Van Ryzin (1996) found that satisfaction increased with improved maintenance, management strictness (such as screening potential residents), and the provision of supportive services. For instance, improved maintenance produced a greater sense of pride and in turn had an impact on residents' sense of security. Interestingly, resident involvement in security matters was not as strongly correlated to overall resident satisfaction. One explanation is that resident involvement in improved security efforts is a goal rather than a means to achieve satisfaction (Van Ryzin, 1996).

The notion that resident empowerment resulting from the control of decision-making processes can solve the social problems found in public housing is not entirely a consensus among housing researchers.

Peterman (1996) questions whether empowerment attained through complete resident control is the solution as claimed by housing advocates. He states that residents ultimately desire high-quality affordable housing, which they were not always receiving under government-funded programs. Sewell (1994), for another, questions whether conversions are the panacea to the social problems found in public housing. Although evidence is mixed about whether the lives of individual residents can be enhanced in this way, housing researchers believe that the development and implementation of different forms of resident management arrangements can lead to improvements in the community as well as better relations with the wider neighbourhood.

In Canada there are no examples of conversions away from public housing, so one must refer to literature and examples found internationally in order to find parallels. A common approach for involving residents in decision making has come in the form of tenant-government partnerships, which are found in the United Kingdom in the form of tenant-management organizations (TMOs) (Best, 1996; Hague, 1990; Miceli, Sazama, and Sirmans, 1994; Tunstall, 2001) and in the United States as resident-management corporations (RMCs) (Koebel, Richard, and Robert, 1998) or tenant-management corporations (TMCs) (Vale, 2002; Epp, 1996; Koebel and Cavell, 1995). In this arrangement the government retains some control of decision making in partnership with the residents, but the residents gain greater control than they do in typical public housing projects. The partnership takes the form of a contract that outlines the responsibilities of the tenants in maintaining the property (for example, hiring a property management company), maintaining a rent-collection process, and making repairs to the property. Ultimately, a housing authority maintains ownership and is accountable for the property. According to Lane (1995), these partnerships have produced successful cases demonstrating that increased tenant participation in all facets of management can improve the overall conditions of the property and the tenants' lives. The intention is to develop stronger managerial skills, enhance a sense of ownership among the tenants, and, most important, create a greater sense of community.

The challenges faced by resident-managed corporations in the United States have largely been related to the training and development of the tenants towards becoming responsible managers. When making difficult decisions (for example, regarding evictions or rent arrears), tenants have found that being under the same scrutiny once given to government managers makes them feel isolated from the rest of the community

(Koebel and Cavell, 1995). In addition, a resident-managed corporation is normally managed by tenant volunteers, which can lead to burnout. In spite of these shortcomings, Koebel and Cavell (1995) provide vivid examples of community empowerment activities initiated by different resident-managed corporations. Thus, forms of resident management need to be complemented with resources provided by different social service agencies (Lane, 1995). A variation of the resident-managed corporation model has been the establishment of tenant compacts, as developed in the United Kingdom. According to Steele, Somerville, and Galvin (1995), tenant compacts are agreements made between tenants' associations and the local housing council that provide residents with an opportunity to be involved in the policies that affect their community. Although tenants have some influence over policies, they are not responsible for the actual operations of the housing properties. Another conversion model for public housing is the outright sale to tenants, a model that Taylor (2003) states has produced mixed results because of the substandard condition of these properties and because low-income homebuyers cannot afford the cost of renovation. As a result, these individuals continue to live in deteriorating conditions but without the cushion of government support (Taylor, 2003).

The closest approach to outright conversion from public housing to resident control is found in individual or group homeownership opportunities and is commonly found in the sale of public housing properties to individuals or tenant groups. Incidences of the sale of these properties are famously found in England and, to a lesser extent, in the United States. The sale of this housing has resulted in the development of the limited equity co-operative, which operates like other housing co-operatives in that the co-operative corporation is directly responsible for the governance and management of the housing community; that is, this model requires member involvement (Miceli, Sazama, and Sirmans, 1994). However, the members of a limited equity co-operative have an ownership stake, and a unit can be sold on the market, although there are constraints on the amount of profit (Leavitt and Saegert, 1990; Miceli, Sazama, and Sirmans, 1998). Although the limited equity co-operative has some parallels to the Atkinson co-operative, in the latter case the members do not have an ownership stake.

The evidence is mixed on the effectiveness of limited equity co-operative conversions for improving the quality of the communities, a pattern that parallels the experiences of resident-managed corporations. Leavitt and Saegert (1990) and Peterman (1996) are critical of the management and planning by the members; however, Rohe (1995) is more positive and suggests that increased member involvement has created vibrant and diverse communities because there was a feeling of ownership. According to Rohe (1995), successful cases had support from a sponsoring organization, and proper planning principles were applied to management decisions. Koebel and Cavell (1995) state that without external training, attempts at increasing tenant participation are not effective. Koebel and Cavell (1995) add that residents must believe that they are making a difference to their community, and, if needed, external resources should be available to them.

In Canada, approaches to improving the public housing system by increasing tenant participation have been much more conservative. There have been no examples of successfully completing the conversion of public housing properties into any of the alternative management arrangements described above. The general pattern within Canada has been to either neglect these properties or simply start anew in what has become known as "revitalization." In fact, there are two examples of communities within Toronto that are undergoing efforts at revitalizing the neighbourhood by the demolition and rebuilding of the housing property (Toronto Community Housing Corporation, 2011). As these properties, Regent Park and Don Mount Court, have always been known as sites with severe social problems and were considered to be beyond social repair, the desire was to implement strategies that reflect a bricks-and-mortar approach to solutions.

According to the Toronto Community Housing Corporation (2011), efforts to revitalize these communities involve rebuilding the properties with new housing that will include social housing as well as private sector options such as condominiums. Although it is widely known that the properties were facing exorbitant rehabilitation costs because of the years of neglect, the efforts to revitalize by razing the buildings do not address the core systemic issues associated with public housing. A bricks-and-mortar approach will continue to mask the inequity and disrespect perpetuated by both government and the residents themselves (for example, Rose, 1980) and only fuels the stigmatization associated with public housing. Silver (2011) provides an important critique by suggesting that the revitalization approach reflects a neoliberal project and that genuine efforts to improve these communities should start from within.

The view that public housing residents can manage themselves is still a foreign notion to government housing bureaucrats and politicians, and, as such, government regulations and policies limit the ability of residents to be involved in decision making. Aside from the dedication of a few individuals, residents within such communities tend to become apathetic owing to the "we know what's best" nature of government administrators who operate in distant – and sometimes not so distant – bureaucracies. As will be shown in the subsequent chapters, a key difference found in the Atkinson Housing Co-operative (AHC) is that there is greater tenant control in managing the property than that called for in the changes to Ontario housing policy (Sousa and Quarter, 2003).

Fortunately attitudes are changing, and governments are looking for innovative ways to increase tenant involvement. However, as will be shown, the Atkinson experience is a fundamentally different approach than the one taken by the Toronto Community Housing Corporation. In fact, the approach is so different that TCHC does not even acknowledge the innovative nature of the Atkinson Housing Co-operative, primarily because the Alexandra Park conversion emerged from a tradition of seeking community control through tenant self-management and not from the deficit-focused approach used in the razing and rebuilding of public housing.

2 Constructing a Theoretical Lens to Understand the Conversion Experiment

Public housing programs were not conducive to building a sense of community, because management practices fostered the exclusion of a group of people who were economically disadvantaged (Randolph, Rumming, and Murray, 2010). Community building was not a factor since the housing was intended to be temporary; the residents were expected to move once they were financially able to participate in the private housing market (Dennis and Fish, 1972; Rose, 1980). The absence of features that create a sense of community is best seen in the lack of resident involvement in decision making, often characterized as a barrier to community growth and accountability as well as resident responsibility to their community (Bacher, 1993). Public housing programs created a class of citizens who were not informed about the way in which their housing operated. Fiscal conservatism governed the design and aesthetics of public housing (Bacher, 1993; Dennis and Fish, 1972). In essence, public housing creates a population that is disengaged from the property as well as from society (Randolph, Rumming, and Murray, 2010; Taylor, 2003).

As noted in the previous chapter, the problems with the public housing model are well documented, and serious efforts have been made to overcome the many shortcomings; the absence of a sense of community was highlighted as a major flaw, within various government reports (for example, the Hellyer Task Force in 1969) and by housing advocacy groups (Bacher, 1993). The Hellyer report (1969) highlighted the weaknesses but neglected to recommend improvements to the existing projects. In effect, it ensured that the status quo with respect to the management practices of existing public housing stock was maintained.

Changes to housing legislation in the 1970s (for example, the National Housing Act, 1973) was a reflection of an explicit intention to move away from the public housing model and direct resources towards non-profit and co-operative housing because of their focus on community building. The new housing projects were intended to be smaller, and decision-making power was to be located at the community level. The discontinuation of public housing in favour of non-profit and co-operative housing that was more in touch with local needs illustrates an ideological shift on the part of government; however, this shift only applied to new co-operative developments and was not extended to the existing public housing stock.

Individuals and families residing in public housing projects across Canada have a significantly lower quality of life than do those residing in co-operatives (Cooper and Rodman, 1992). Public housing projects have a lower-quality physical environment, characterized by a homogeneous aesthetic and an above-average range of social problems, including vandalism and drug use. This reality has contributed to the stigma associated with public housing. Also, because of the dependence upon government, the residents of public housing projects are vulnerable to changing policies that can result in reduced support.

In the mid-1970s, calls to reform public housing became the focus of advocacy groups and community-based agencies (Bacher, 1993). In most cases, the residents worked with local agencies to build a greater sense of community. Integral to this was the recognition that building a sense of community must become part of all government housing initiatives, including existing ones. The primary goal was to remove the stigma associated with the public housing model by seeking alternative management arrangements. However, without government support in the form of funding and new policy initiatives, substantive improvements were short lived.

The stigma associated with public housing results from the failure to provide the residents with a meaningful degree of ownership of, responsibility for, and control over the place in which they are living. Control of public housing in terms of its management and decision making is located with the housing corporation that is appointed by, and solely accountable to, local political leaders. These administrators are a class apart from the residents who must live with housing conditions that may be detrimental to individual and community health (Sennett, 2003).

An analysis of power enables us to understand the way in which public housing management practices perpetuate the exclusion of society's most vulnerable. Policies and practices related to public housing have created a cycle of exclusion that breeds segregated communities and maintains poverty. In the next section I review the way that the social distance that residents have from the decision-making process contributes to the deterioration of public housing projects by perpetuating the systematic disenfranchisement of a vulnerable population.

Power and Policy Development

The discourse on power relationships within society is long and varied. Weber (1947, 152) defines power as the "probability that one actor in a social relationship will be in a position to carry out his [sic] will despite resistance." A person or group with this ability to control can overcome obstacles and establish processes that will ultimately benefit that individual or group (Giddens, 1984; Sennett and Cobb, 1972). According to this view, power is finite (it is in short supply), and the struggle involves taking some at the expense of other actors (Taylor, 2003), which is to say that it is conceived of by these thinkers as a zero-sum game. Alternatively, a pluralist analysis of power demonstrates the impact of changes in social practices (Taylor, 2003) and is predicated on the assumption that power is more fluid and unlimited (Dahl, 1961).

According to Giddens (1984), power structures comprise social practices that are produced and reproduced over time. These structures become embedded in a level of bureaucracy; for example, in public housing, policies exclude the residents from becoming integrated within the broader society. In the context of public housing, power is located within a system that involves politicians setting key priorities (for example, starting or cancelling a housing program) and a government bureaucracy that must operationalize and practise these priorities on a day-to-day basis. In both cases, the individual politicians tend to be out of touch with the impact that their policy priorities will have either on vulnerable populations or on the strengthening of local communities. For instance, eligibility regulations can be politically driven to target low-income families. Moreover, these regulations can often have the effect of discouraging community building because, should a household's financial circumstances improve or even stabilize, the household can become ineligible to receive a rent subsidy and therefore cannot remain in the community (Sewell, 1994). This last issue is an example of the lack of security of tenure that many public housing residents face.

Government's approach to public housing is the upholding of an administrative arrangement in which those in power can affect the lives of those who cannot access that power base through active participation. The dominant ideology defines the legitimate forms of knowledge and meaning, which inevitably defines the reality of living in public housing (Sennett, 2003) and, in effect, becomes a form of hegemony. Gramsci (1971) used the term *hegemony* to describe the process by which a dominant ideology is internalized by citizens through the production and reproduction of social practices. Residents living in public housing can be seen as internalizing the dominant ideology of government practices that reinforce the deficits of the residents rather than building on their existing strengths. As a result, the residents come to believe that they are unable to participate effectively in managing the development in which they reside because all the practices and structures ensure that they are never able to develop or exercise those skills.

Government officials suggest that the primary reason for situating decision making within government is that the management of public housing is infinitely complex and that the residents are unable to manage by virtue of their need for government support in the first place. In effect, a hegemonic ideology justifies the exclusion of a role for the residents who can potentially and constructively inform decision making in the development where they reside. According to Gramsci (1971), celebrating social differences is essential to countering the hegemonic forces manifested in the dominant practices and social structures. Within co-operative housing communities the impact of hegemonic forces has the potential to be softened or even reduced because such a community has the power to not only define its own needs but also actualize them; in this case, the decision-making practices reflect the community and not the position of government bureaucracy.

Research in critical social theory reveals the extent to which individuals and groups internalize the hegemonic practices that oppress and subjugate them (Giddens, 1994). Public housing is a case in point: the political position taken by government was an attempt to ensure that low-income earners had access to adequate housing; however, the type and level of assistance were not defined by those who needed it but by those in a position of power. For a community to emerge within public housing, residents have to be active participants in decision making, a procedure that is absent in traditional management practices.

The residents of the Alexandra Park housing project recognized that powerlessness was a contributing factor to the limitations of what could be done by the community to address entrenched stigma and social problems. In spite of the elements of strong leadership and community activism, this feeling of powerlessness was preventing the community from living in a setting free from violence and the escalating drug trade. The decision to convert to a co-operative was intended to shift the locus of decision-making control and to wrest control away from government administrators because they were seen as neglecting the residents' need to live in a safe and secure environment. Moreover, the residents had potential solutions to many of their social problems, most of which were discounted owing to bureaucratic inertia or an unwillingness by government to act on proposals put forth by the local leadership. While it is impossible to identify one sole reason for the deterioration of public housing properties, solutions to social problems were seen as requiring bureaucratic interventions because resident initiatives were discounted; they were often deemed to be the source of the problems in the first place – or, worse, the problem itself.

According to Taylor (2003), it is important to recognize the way in which the social processes perpetuating social exclusion can inform an understanding of the factors that contribute to the problems and to the solutions found in managing low-income housing. Room (1995) states that social exclusion is the process whereby individuals become "detached from the organization and communities of which the society is composed and from the rights and obligations they embody" (5). Room argues that such detachment will hinder individuals from securing their social rights, thereby undermining their participation as citizens and leading them to suffer persistent disadvantage (6). In essence, if individuals are unable to participate as part of the broader society because of conditions beyond their control, it is not very difficult to understand that there is an absence of a feeling that one belongs to a group; in other words, hindering one's agency can reduce social cohesion.

Public housing policy reflects a residual approach to social policy, that is, a policy that is intended to address a social issue that has already occurred, rather than being preventative. This approach implies that the residential population requiring public housing is in some way deficient, unable to participate in mainstream society, and, as such, needs special considerations. The development of public housing was intended to provide a safe, secure, and affordable arrangement for families of low to moderate income, but instead of being integrated into mainstream society, they have remained on the margins. The asymmetrical power relationship between government agencies and public housing residents creates and perpetuates the notion that residents cannot control their lives and therefore could not possibly be expected to control the operations of their community. In this sense, social inequalities are reproduced in and by the very structures that are meant to help people.

Initiatives to counter this perspective have been successfully applied in many countries, including Canada, in the form of co-operative and non-profit housing – developments that have fewer social problems than does public housing. In non-profit and co-operative housing, the residents are better integrated within the community – indeed, within the community *as* community – even if they depend upon social assistance from government sources. While the absence of social cohesion has been cited as a contributing factor to the problems found in many public housing projects, Sennett (2003) argues that a lack of respect on the part of project administrators towards the residents works against building social cohesion, and he illustrates this point through a description of his own experience of growing up in Chicago's infamous Cabrini Green housing project. As a means to address the power differential that exists within public housing projects, Sennett suggests that participation can be seen as a form of ritualistic exchange: "had we been allowed to participate in the running of the housing project, we would at least have been given back our participation, our time" (220). In other words, as an outcome of an exchange, increasing participation can result in the residents' making a significant contribution to the management of their community, thereby ensuring that they develop a stronger sense of belonging to and ownership of their community, all of which were driving forces behind the Atkinson conversion.

Sennett is not alone in arguing that participation by residents in management can lead to improvements in the overall quality of life of the community. According to Somerville (1998), the empowerment of residents through participation can be purposeful and beneficial. Taking control challenges the dominant ideological forces, particularly those that perpetuate social inequalities through social hierarchies (Sullivan, 1990). The goal of empowerment is to integrate an excluded citizenry, a process that, according to Taylor (2003), contains three elements. First, people must become politically aware of the impact that the practices of power have on their ability to make decisions that affect their own lives. A second element is the availability of options or choices that individuals can make, should their needs and desires not be adequately satisfied. The final element is that one's rights, responsibility, and citizenship are not unduly blocked. In the context of public housing, these elements are largely absent because the dependency on government support is linked to the relinquishment of some rights, such as the maintenance of savings or the ownership of property, either of which could help a family wishing to leave public housing.

The disempowerment of residents in public housing has created a class of citizens without a sense of belonging to their community. On the surface, residents appear not to care about their community, but it is difficult to gain an appreciation for one's community when one is continually living under intense scrutiny in order to remain eligible for government support.

Developing a Sense of Community

A sense of community represents an emotional or other connection that individuals have with the place in which they live and towards the relationships that they have established (Prezza, Amici, Roberti, and Tedeschi, 2001; Van Laar, 1999). A sense of community refers to the characteristics of a community that create cohesion and stability (Chavis and Pretty, 1999; Kingston, Mitchell, Florin, and Stevenson, 1999), characteristics that emerge from the feeling of belonging to a group and the type of interactions that occur therein (Van Laar, 1999).

In a neighbourhood, developing a sense of community is premised on the inherent human need to relate with others in a secure and healthy environment (Kingston, Mitchell, Florin, and Stevenson, 1999; Van Laar, 1999). A sense of community is demonstrated by individuals who reside within a particular geographical location, who share common values that reflect community cohesion, and who participate in activities that have a common goal of improving the community (Kingston, Mitchell, Florin, and Stevenson, 1999; Van Laar, 1999). However, the challenge is to understand the way in which a sense of community develops and the factors that must be present to sustain it. The raison d'être of the Alexandra Park conversion process was to build upon, and indeed to transform, the existing sense of community by empowering residents and having government administrators relinquish some control over decision making.

In many places, citizens achieve a sense of community by virtue of the amount of control that they have over their living conditions (Hancock, 1996; Kingston, Mitchell, Florin, and Stevenson 1999; Peterman, 1996). Control can be manifested in the degree to which individuals participate in various activities that are integral to the operation of their community, for example, governance in housing co-operatives (Co-operative Housing Federation of Toronto, 2003). Within social housing communities, the degree of resident control varies from housing co-operatives, where it is substantial (Wolfe, 1998), to public housing projects, where it is minimal (Sewell, 1994). In many public housing communities the feeling of connectedness is not easily achieved, owing to the organizational environment (Freeman, 1998; Somerville, 1998).

In a very broad sense, the diverse backgrounds (for example, of ethnicity and experience) of community members can contribute to the creation of a sense of community (Kingston, Mitchell, Florin, and Stevenson, 1999). A key benefit of a mixed-income community is that it enhances the residents' base of knowledge because individuals are more likely to have varying levels of insight and experience (Dreier and Hulchanski, 1993; Wolfe, 1998). If the goal is to create a public housing community in which the residents can feel a stronger connection to one another and a greater sense of belonging, and to create a context in which all are socially included, we need to factor difference as an asset rather than a problem that requires a solution. The field of community development has produced a significant body of research that has helped communities to grow, by establishing processes that create and augment community capacity.

Models of Community Development

The purpose of community development is to initiate strategies and activities that can strengthen existing community capacity and empower disenfranchised citizens, thereby creating a greater sense of community (Christenson, Fendley, and Robinson, 1994; Hustedde, 2009; Minkler and Wallerstein, 1999; Phillips and Pittman, 2009). According to Henslin (2003), one way to empower residents is to create social structures and practices that foster a sense of belonging to their community. Research has outlined various models and frameworks that have enabled ordinary citizens to improve their lives and to also be involved in activities that benefit their community – and arguably the common good (for example, Jacob, 1999; Fisher, 1999). In this section I describe four models that strive for social change at the local level, a description of which will help the reader to understand the activities and mindsets that contributed to the conversion process of the Atkinson Housing Co-operative. The strength of these models is that they provide guidelines for individuals and groups seeking to improve the social and economic conditions of their community.

The first model for community development is sometimes referred to as the Alinsky approach. Saul Alinsky based his approach on mobilizing grassroots organizations in order to empower a poor and disenfranchised citizenry (Alinsky, 1971). He initially gained fame for organizing the Back of the Yards campaign in Chicago in the 1930s (Alinsky, 1971), one of many Alinskyan examples of creating coalitions within communities of the unemployed and low skilled. According to Alinsky (1971), social change can only be achieved through the mobilization and organization of people who are victims of institutions whose interests are often in conflict with the interests and needs of local communities. Alinsky's reputation for confrontation arises from his advocacy of particular organizing tactics that are based on his belief that the poor are not just poor in resources, such as money, jobs, or social services, but they lack the power to affect the distribution of these resources. In spite of this, Alinsky discovered that numerous organizations in even the poorest of neighbourhoods could be organized as long as there was a common interest linking these groups.

The Alinsky approach was distinctive in that he helped to mobilize individuals and community organizations for radical action through existing institutions such as union locals, churches, and service clubs. His primary purpose was to get people to combine and act together at the local level in order to become powerful enough to redress social and economic grievances. The critical step towards building effective community power was developing the psychological power of individuals through the discovery of common interests that could be turned into strategic political action.

What the poor lacked in resources they made up for in numbers. Whether an organizing goal was a new traffic light or a neighbourhood health clinic, a victory strengthened the sense of both individual and group potency and the importance of organization. These concepts, now loosely referred to as *empowerment strategies*, have had immense influence on contemporary thought about community organizing.

The Alinsky approach is considered controversial because the tactics and strategies focus on targets as enemies that are both visible and local. According to McKnight (1995), this approach is difficult to implement in complex modern communities because the targets tend not to be local and are therefore less visible. In the context of the Alexandra Park conversion, the Alinsky approach can explain why resident mobilization was a key ingredient in combating external forces, but it does not provide useful strategies when confrontation is no longer a necessary tactic.

A second model for community development is associated with the Rothman approaches to community organizing (Rothman, 2000, 1995, 1968), which consist of locality development, social planning, and social action. Locality development utilizes a process approach to social change that is based upon the broad participation and initiative of as many people in a community as possible. It involves building capacity through co-operation, voluntarism, and education in order to implement community initiatives, initiatives intended to achieve community-determined goals that are accomplished through consensus-building strategies. Thus, locality development strengthens social relations and builds community structures that can foster local change (Rothman, 1995, 2000).

Social planning is normally associated with the involvement of external agencies and resources, such as government ones for beginning the development of problem-solving strategies aimed at some form of social change (Rothman, 1968). Social planning relies on developing an objective and a subjective understanding of the problems that a community is facing (Rothman, 1995). The outcome is the provision of institutional support through the implementation of specific projects or programs (Rothman, 1995). Policy planners and analysts guide complex change processes through interventions supported by government agencies. A concern with this approach is the significant reliance on professional expertise to frame problems and develop solutions. Often the short-term solutions to complex problems produce longer-term problems for a community (Taylor, 2003).

Social action, however, is intended to organize disadvantaged populations towards their making demands for increased resources or treatment in accordance with the principles of social justice (Rothman, 1968). The objective is to readjust power relations in society so that a community is on an equal footing with the rest of society. Community members are identified as victims of power structures, and they need to engage in conflict with the oppressor. Thus, Rothman's conception of social action is similar to Alinsky's in that the use of conflict or confrontation creates institutional change by shifting resources and altering relationships among individuals. Rothman's (2000) typology of community development approaches – locality development, social planning, and social action – can be a useful guide to understanding how social change can result from building political capacity and working with outside groups in order to rectify the asymmetrical power relationships faced by low-income communities. However, a weakness of the typology is the disconnect between the different approaches, which results in the efforts to build community capacity being focused on developing solutions for short-term projects.

The third framework, represented by the work of McKnight and Kretzmann, is called community regeneration. It overcomes the weaknesses of other community development models by building *sustainable* community capacity through understanding that all communities have gifts, referred to as assets that can be called upon to strengthen communities. According to McKnight and Kretzmann (1999), community development initiatives tend to take a deficit approach to capacity building; that is, they address a community's needs by focusing on what it lacks. A deficit approach solves a community's problems through introducing services, thereby perpetuating a dependency on external resources to help meet needs. McKnight and Kretzmann state that an "alternative is to develop policies and alternatives based on capacities, skills, and assets of low-income people and their neighbourhood" (158).

Kretzmann and McKnight (1993) believe that community assets are resources provided by individuals and by organizations to build capacity for community control. An asset-based approach to community development focuses on mapping and strengthening existing assets as the means to achieve sustainable social change. In the context of the Alexandra Park community, the assets are the resources and experience brought by residents and supporters to contribute to development and change. Community developers using this approach believe that community assets are enhanced by building upon existing resources – through the introduction of new opportunities – and using the additional resources that come from learning (Hustedde, 2009; McKnight and Kretzmann, 1999; Phillips and Pittman, 2009).

The final model refers to the framework developed by Wilkinson and Quarter (1996) to assess community development through the formation of co-operatives. The framework is based on three elements, and each has specific components that balance the internal and external goals of individuals within a community. The first element, community consciousness, focuses on the underlying reasons and actions that led members of a community to call for changes. One component of community consciousness is community attachments, which refers to a "connection that people feel to each other and to the location of their community" (129). For example, an individual's willingness to attend a public meeting that is aimed at protecting or enhancing the community is the result of a connection felt to a place. The outcome may not be the individual's preference, but, at the very least, the participation was significant.

Another component of community consciousness is a movement perspective, which is characterized by the precedence of community good over private interests. For example, the residents of a housing co-operative may be keen on such self-interested objectives as a low housing charge, but if there is strong community consciousness, they should also care about the co-operative housing movement as a *movement*, extending the opportunity for that form of living to others who view it as desirable.

The second element of Wilkinson and Quarter's framework accounts for the "activities that empower the members of the co-operative or the community at large" (126). This element refers to the need to develop strategies that "encourage member involvement" and promote "self-reliance" (129). This element speaks to the volitional aspect of community development, and in order for a community strategy to be effective, leaders have to find mechanisms to galvanize community involvement in initiatives.

The third and final element focuses on the key supports involved in establishing strong supportive structures. The first component is the impact that community-based organizations have upon community development activities, and the second involves assessing the role and impact of external support organizations. External support organizations can have a positive impact on community development. However, according to Wilkinson and Quarter (1996), the impact can be mixed if support or funding organizations create unrealistic expectations (that is, ones that a community cannot meet), for example, by providing funding for an initiative with conditions attached that are beyond the capacity of the community to meet.

The four models for community development focus on social action and capacity building to improve the conditions found in different low-income communities. It is important to note that there is a significant limitation associated with trying to implement known community development models as a generalized prescriptive strategy because doing so often results in unsustainable social change (Berkowitz and Cashman, 2000). At bottom, what has worked in one community may not work in another because the socio-historical context is likely different and the patterns of behaviours that led to particular actions will have had different origins. For example, the Wilkinson and Quarter (1996) framework was developed in a tiny Acadian community in Prince Edward Island; it may not be directly applicable to an urban housing community, because the local contexts and needs of the latter are likely different from those that informed the development of the original framework. In spite of this limitation, features of a community development model that can be generalized into a framework should be adapted to different contexts as long as the development strategies account for the idiosyncratic nature of a community. The analysis here adapts and synthesizes features of the four community development models and critical elements from different bodies of academic literature (for example, co-operative studies and political sociology) into a framework that explains the process leading to the creation of the Atkinson Housing Co-operative.

Identifying the Critical Factors

A significant factor in community development is the presence of community assets. The presence and use of different assets is indicative of a community's strength and of differing supports (Taylor, 2003; McKnight and Kretzmann, 1999). The conversion of the Alexandra Park housing project into the Atkinson Housing Co-operative was possible because of the combined efforts of the residents and of the co-operative resource group, the Co-operative Housing Federation of Toronto, to identify and utilize the resources that form the foundation of the community's assets. In some respects, Alexandra Park was typical of public housing projects, but its tradition of resident activism, a tradition going back to 1969 when it became the first public housing project in Canada to form a residents' association, made it different. This tradition was an important factor in the community's ability to convert itself into a housing co-operative.

The increasingly critical discourse on social capital focuses on examining the way in which societal structures are produced, or not produced, at the community level (Taylor, 2003), which is particularly relevant to understanding the Alexandra Park conversion process. The concept of social capital is derived from social networking theory and is commonly used to describe the quality of relationships among actors within a network, in particular how they engage each other and the degree of reciprocity and trust they have in their interactions (Saegert and Winkel, 1998). Bourdieu (1986), for example, looks at social capital as a social theory that focuses on the way in which an individual's position within a social network is used to maintain status in the group, while Coleman (1988) emphasizes that networks form social capital as the means of building trust and reciprocity. The literature on social capital reveals a lack of an agreed-upon understanding of the way in which social capital functions to support communities. For instance, individuals with access to social capital foment and consolidate resources for acquiring power and status (Taylor, 2003; Bourdieu, 1986). Alternatively, social capital functions to build relationships and establish social processes through networks of trust, and also to create norms of reciprocity to encourage community growth (Taylor, 2003; Putnam, 2000). Although the two variants appear incongruent, they are actually not mutually exclusive of the goal of achieving community-based control. Thus, I use social capital as a means to explain the ways in which the social processes functioned to both consolidate power and build trusting relationships among the residents of Alexandra Park, all with the goal of attaining control over their community.

Although the research using social capital theory can be blind to power relations (Fine, 1999), it can lead to a better understanding of the ways in which people can work together and the benefits that result. Robert Putnam's (1998, 2000) popularization of the concept of social capital focuses on the social interactions between members of a community and across communities. His conceptualization is influenced by Coleman (1988) and, in particular, by the strength-of-weak-ties theory presented by Granovetter (1973). According to Granovetter, relationships can be characterized as ties that link people, and those ties – which can be either weak or strong – operate together as a network of interaction that is part of a series of social networks located in different communities; membership in such a series of networks is correlated with people feeling a greater attachment to their geographical location.

Putnam (2000) asserts that community cohesion is best maintained through weak ties because they represent a more resilient type of interactive system and are suitable for building links between people of different interests and backgrounds. Putnam refers to social capital as being the glue that binds together the members of social networks, and identifies it as being one of the key elements in creating stronger cohesion within a community. According to Putnam, there are two main forms of social capital: bonding and bridging. Bonding refers to the value of relationships or networks assigned within a given group; bridging refers to the links to heterogeneous groups normally from outside a community. bridging has a variety of benefits, including making links outside the community to promote the interests of the community. The bonding and the bridging social capital refer to the important function of social networks, but their relative role varies according to the link being made and its purpose.

Although social capital can serve positive functions in community settings, it is important to consider the underlying motivations that help to create new norms and social processes. The consolidation of power through networks of trust can perpetuate systems of inequality as well as serve as a mechanism for reducing inequality. Therefore, in relation to community development, social capital can be viewed as a double-edged sword. Although relatively little of Putnam's research focuses on public housing, he does state that housing policy must encourage the building of social capital in low-income housing communities (Putnam, 1998, 2000). According to Putnam (2000), norms of reciprocity and trust can be a determinant of an individual's sense of belonging to a community. Cohen and Prusak (2001) view social capital as an aggregate of resources or a stock of trust, shared values, and behaviours that promotes "active connections among people that bind the members of human networks and communities and make co-operative action possible" (4). In other words, social capital can support a sense of community (Lomas, 1998) when it serves the function of exposing the values and acceptable behaviours shared by the members of a community.

Leadership is another important factor in community development. Although the utopian notion of community development is a grassroots phenomenon, almost spontaneous in character, evidence suggests that community development initiatives require effective leaders who can contribute to the mobilization of the residents. The field of leadership development has focused on such issues as understanding the processes of social influence and understanding the personality attributes of an effective leader (Dahl, 2000). Researchers have found that there are two forms of leadership that influence the successful outcome of group action (Bennis and Nanus, 1985; Kanungo and Mendonca, 1996). First, there is transactional leadership, which involves a leader maintaining authority by giving rewards for loyalty and imposing sanctions for disobedience (Kanungo and Mendonca, 1996). Second, there is transformational leadership, where a leader's actions are intended to promote behavioural and attitudinal change (Kanungo and Mendonca, 1996).

The presence of a committed leader had an important role in the Atkinson conversion process. However, as will be discussed in chapter 4, there were instances when the form of leadership became an obstacle to the conversion. Although the need for strong community leadership is a necessity for effective community development, a community may not always have the capacity to encourage new leaders; moreover, a community may not have the wherewithal to train and develop them.

Not uncommon in community development initiatives is the important role that external leaders, individuals referred to as *change agents* (on which see Hughes, 1998), may take in actively supporting the growth and change of a community. In the Atkinson conversion, change agents who emerged from the co-operative sector took on an important role in support of the community's leadership. Throughout the process they helped members of the community to understand the benefits of converting to a co-operative and some of the challenges in managing such an organization.

Community development is compatible with co-operative formation because the co-operative movement emerged in response to the social and economic inequalities that existed in nineteenth-century Europe and North America (MacPherson, 1979). According to Melnyk (1985), the movement represents the desires of marginalized groups to pool resources with a focus on the common good. Research on co-operative formation has focused on describing and implementing the strategies for empowering disadvantaged and oppressed groups.

Over time, co-operatives have become a viable alternative to institutions that perpetuate social inequalities, and there is a growing body of research that has revealed the relative effectiveness of co-operative housing. For instance, Ley (1993) suggests that several factors have contributed to making housing co-operatives successful. These include keeping the housing charge affordable; creating management and governance structures that are local and include members in positions of leadership; having an accountability arrangement between the co-operative and the government; and feeling part of a movement with accepted principles that are ingrained in the community's social consciousness and that promote the common good.

I ground my study of the conversion process in a theoretical framework in order to identify the underlying factors that help to explain how and why the residents of the Alexandra Park public housing project assumed control over their community by converting it to the Atkinson Housing Co-operative. On the surface it appears that the conversion was merely a shift from central management to co-operative management. While that may be the case, upon deeper analysis of the community's development and the conversion process one finds that the residents had to acquire a skill set that called for a level of critical analysis, financial literacy, and conflict resolution. Rather than using these skills against a neglectful landlord, the residents eventually employed them in managing the property co-operatively.

As shown in this chapter, a synthesis of housing policy and community development theory reveals key concepts that can be used as a basis for understanding how the Atkinson community was able to gain control of its housing and become a co-operative. I believe that one must apply a community development mindset in order to make sense of the barriers placed by social housing policy on community building. Using a community development approach to inform a lens for understanding the Alexandra Park conversion can reveal some of the core beneficial characteristics that the community possessed and that allowed it to become a co-operative. In addition, it can identify the critical factors involved in converting public housing into co-operative housing. Furthermore, this approach allows for an awareness of the aspects of community development that should be in place to enable a low-income community to assume greater control over its management. The theoretical synthesis provided in this chapter can also be the basis for a framework that can be used in other low-income communities that may be considering gaining control over their community or are in the process of doing so.

3 Exploring the Circumstances That Led to the Conversion Process

Alexandra Park opened in 1968 and remains one of the largest developments in the social housing system. It is located in a downtown Toronto neighbourhood in which immigrants have traditionally settled (Social Planning Council of Metropolitan Toronto, 1970). Before the construction of the housing project the area included an unusual blend of industrial, commercial, and residential land use purposes. The local residential population comprised mainly low-income groups from Eastern and Western Europe, and at that time they were mostly concerned with high unemployment rates, access to good education, improvement of the slum-like dwellings, and the prevalence of crime (Social Planning Council of Metropolitan Toronto, 1970). Safety was also a key issue for families in the neighbourhood, including concern for children playing in an area that included heavy traffic because it was predominantly occupied by commercial activities, such as warehouses (Lapointe and Sousa, 2003).

The planning of the urban redevelopment that created the Alexandra Park housing project emerged from a 1956 City of Toronto urban renewal report, which stated that 44 per cent of the housing in the area was uninhabitable and had to be replaced and that the remaining 56 per cent of the housing was upgradeable and could be rehabilitated (Social Planning Council of Metropolitan Toronto, 1970). According to the original architects and planners, the final design incorporated crucial lessons taken from the failures of other large public housing projects, which had been built in the 1940s and the 1950s. For instance, the new development was intended to be integrated better into the surrounding neighbourhood in order to avoid the stigma encountered at other projects (Klein, 1969). The architects stated that keeping many of the existing structures in place would ensure that the new project blended well with the surrounding area (Klein, 1969). However, as the development proceeded, preservation of the older buildings became more difficult and costly; consequently, none of the original structures exists within the housing project. Furthermore, walls were erected to separate particular sections of the project from one another and from the surrounding community. The walled areas inside the property and along parts of the perimeter created dark, isolated spaces. In the end, the property was both aesthetically distinct and physically isolated from the neighbourhood.

The final design of the project eliminated the original grid pattern that had both inner roads and pathways cut off from major streets. There was a conscious effort to create crossways that would allow people to get from one side of the project to the other (Klein, 1969). According to Jerome Markson (personal communication, 15 March 2004), one of the original architects of the Alexandra Park housing development, the aim was to build a housing project that resembled a pedestrian-friendly European community, where children and their families could walk safely without fear of any traffic.

The development has two apartment buildings (one six-storey and another eight-storey) and 270 townhouses, for a total of 410 dwelling units. The apartment buildings have one- and two-bedroom units, and the townhouses are three-, four-, and five-bedroom units. There is very little green space in front of residents' homes, and the dwellings are built right up to the paved walkways that connect the units. According to Jerome Markson (personal communication, 15 March 2004), the architect of the project, the property appears more institutional in character than was intended. Over time, the design has made it difficult for residents to interact with one another and to build a sense of community. Figure 1 shows a layout of the property.

Selecting the Key Events

As with all communities, different events and activities bring community members together, while others become a source of conflict. In spite of the challenges, the Alexandra Park community remained committed and motivated to see the conversion through to completion. In order to make sense of the conversion process, I decided to focus attention on the way in which particular historical events, henceforth referred to as *key events*, served as triggering points in some instances to establishing

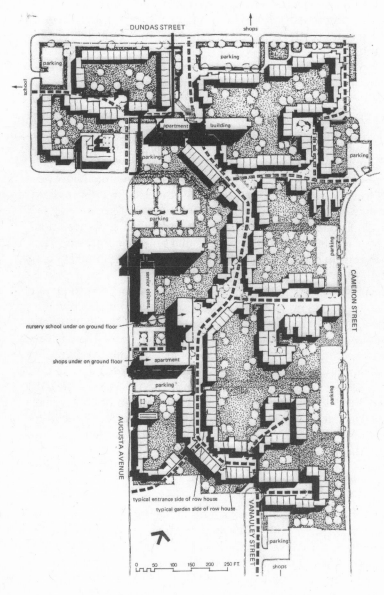

Figure 1. Layout of Alexandra Park Housing Development. In this map of the original property, which appeared in an article by Klein (1969), the pathways snaking through the property were intended to resemble a European pedestrian walkway. Notice how the property was enclosed from the rest of the neighbourhood. Image courtesy of *Canadian Architect*.

stronger resident relationships as well as bringing to the surface ongoing conflicts within the community. These key events serve as pivotal points to empirically understand the factors associated with the conversion into a co-operative. An analysis of these events forms the basis for identifying the factors that have contributed to the growth of this community, from inception to conversion.[1]

A final list of key events was not determined prior to the collection of information because of the hope that more events would be revealed during the collection process. The determination of events as key was derived from the study of documents (for example, minutes of board meetings), observations (for example, community events), interviews, and my own reflections as a resident. The primary criterion for inclusion of an event was the presence of records of repeated discussions and other documentation of the events. Eight events represented pivotal points in the community's development into a housing co-operative:

1. The formation of the Alexandra Park Residents' Association in 1969
2. The opening of the Alexandra Park Community Centre in 1978
3. The community security march in 1992
4. The community meeting to introduce the conversion into a housing co-operative, in 1993
5. The referendums in which the community overwhelmingly supported the proposed conversion, in 1995 and 1998
6. The passing of a leader and change agent, Sonny Atkinson, in 1997
7. The election of the Alexandra Park Residents' Association's board of directors in the fall of 2001
8. The transference of management authority in 2003

These earlier events reveal the formation of the residents as activists, which became critical for the conversion process to maintain momentum during some challenging times. In fact, the level of resident activism served to instil a sense of community ownership that is not normally expected in residents of public housing projects. Further, in spite of the numerous unexpected challenges that would affect the momentum towards the conversion, the community remained committed and motivated to see it through to completion. Therefore, the resident activism that led to the conversion of Alexandra Park into the Atkinson Housing Co-operative is founded in events that occurred over a thirty-year time span. Each event will be explored in this chapter as well as in chapter 4.

Using the key events as the basis for analysis certainly demonstrates the developmental trajectory associated with converting into a co-operative. In addition to the content, the important consideration in examining key events is to understand the impact that events can have on a community's growth. This book is an opportunity to understand not only the content of the events but also their impact on the conversion process.

Event 1: The Formation of the Alexandra Park Residents' Association, 1969

A key feature of the Alexandra Park Housing community has always been the presence of an active residents' association, the Alexandra Park Residents' Association (APRA). According to its original 1971 constitution (Alexandra Park Residents' Association, 1988), the APRA was created to improve community relations, to further a good relationship with the Metropolitan Toronto Housing Authority, and to "provide social, recreational, and educational activities for the community" (1).

According to all stakeholders interviewed and confirmed in relevant documentation, the existence of the Alexandra Park Residents' Association was a unique and integral feature of the housing project. APRA worked with the residents to make Alexandra Park a strong and cohesive community. Residents refer to helping one another, socializing outside their homes and at community events, and forming lasting friendships because of the association's efforts. In addition, throughout the history of the community, and especially during the conversion process, the community centre remained the focal point of APRA's endeavours. The APRA board initiated the process of converting into a co-operative because this model was regarded as a response to the systemic absence of voice within the decision-making processes of the housing authority. As will be shown later, the strength of the Alexandra Park Residents' Association became a crucial factor, one that demonstrated the community's capacity to manage its affairs, as well as highlighting the need to have accountable and transparent decision-making practices. Thus, the formalizing of the board of directors of the Atkinson Housing Co-operative was a natural evolution of the Alexandra Park Residents' Association.

Background of the Key Event

Shortly after the Alexandra Park housing project opened in 1968, the problems typically found in other public housing projects began to emerge, including vandalism and alienation (Smith, 1968). According to Jerome Markson, building a sense of community was not foremost in the minds of the planners, but he knew that problems would persist if support was not provided to residents. In an earlier interview, Mr Markson acknowledged that "the project was intended to be innovative by providing a safe place for families. We learned our lessons from other housing projects, and Alexandra Park was supposed to reflect that education. However, CMHC did not provide the expected resources for community building. They wanted to see new homes, and that is all they got" (personal communication, 14 November 2003).

Shortly after the project had opened, Mr Markson's concern came to be shared by the residents. One particular concern was the lack of activities for the community's youth, which encouraged rowdy behaviour (Smith, 1968). According to one resident, "when we moved into the community in 1969, we knew that there were problems, but we did not know what to do about them. The teens had nothing to do, and the management and the police [were] starting to see us as troublemakers and lazy" (Faye, personal communication, 12 April 2003).

In addition to concerns about youth, the residents were worried about the negative image portrayed by the media and the local police. For instance, when a fight between two groups occurred in Alexandra Park, it was invariably reported as a "negro" against another group that was referred to by its culture, for example a Portuguese youth (for example, see Maier, 1969). According to Barbara, a resident since 1969 and one of the founders of the APRA, this negative portrayal brought residents together for the purpose of improving the community by looking for solutions to the existing problems as well as improving the community's image (personal communication, 13 April 2003). The residents considered that a good place to start was having a group discuss and act on issues emerging within the community. However, no one from outside the community, such as the police or representatives of government housing, was involved or even expressed a willingness to help them deal with the emerging needs. As a result, the residents felt that the housing authority did not understand the problems facing the community, which was an entrenched sentiment that arguably influenced the desire to pursue the conversion option.

Initially, the residents' attention was mainly focused on providing activities for the youth, but they then recognized that their issues could best be addressed by organizing a common voice through an association that would give them legitimacy with the property management.

Thus, the birth of the residents' association within Alexandra Park emerged during a time in which the residents felt that being proactive would allow them to improve both the image and the quality of life of the community (Alexandra Park Residents' Association, 1988). According to several residents, the Alexandra Park Residents' Association was created because some residents felt that the community's needs were being neglected by the housing authority. According to Barbara, there was interest among the residents to take it upon themselves to make a community: "The housing in the community was always OK. From the day we moved in, we were comfortable with the housing that we had, but we also knew that something was missing. As neighbours we would ask ourselves, 'What is there for the kids to do?' The pavement was dangerous for the kids to play on, and many were getting hurt. We did not have a community centre to provide a space for the kids to play. There also were no playgrounds for the kids to play in. So when we moved into the community we had good housing, but there was something missing, and a few of us felt that we needed to do something about it" (personal communication, 12 April 2003).

Edie, another founder of the association, had a similar description: "I moved here in 1969 and I was wondering what my kids could do. I was told that there were no programs for children because there was no money. As residents we were not satisfied with those comments, so we did it ourselves. We started with activities in front of each other's houses. The idea was working, and so we decided to come together as a group of parents because we cared about the future of the community and about having something for our children to do" (personal communication, 12 April 2003).

The Alexandra Park Residents' Association was formed in 1969, shortly after the development had opened, as an attempt to address the needs of the community, and its mission was focused on "promoting the general welfare of the residents of Alexandra Park" (Alexandra Park Residents' Association, 1988, 3). Although the association was not an advocacy group per se, it did participate in consultations on a number of the decisions made by the housing authority, for example, around parking and security (Alexandra Park Residents' Association, 1988). Further, promoting the general welfare of the residents involved advocacy and implementing a variety of programs and services; however, when it came to making crucial decisions that would have a direct impact on the community (for example, who would provide the security service, hire a property manager, or establish occupancy guidelines), the APRA had very little impact on any final decisions made by the authority. The community leadership was frustrated with its negligible influence over real decision making, but there was little that it could do to force the housing authority to include them in the process.

Shortly after the association was formed, a significant issue emerged that helped motivate the residents to become organized and more activist. The issue was the building of the promised community centre. The APRA wanted to meet on a regular basis in order to exchange ideas and plan activities that would build a sense of community among the residents; however, the members of the original association did not have a place in which to meet regularly. They met in the basements and kitchens of individual households: "We did not have a place to meet so we talked in our homes until we had a regular place to meet" (Faye, personal communication, 12 April 2003). The group would also meet at the St Christopher House community centre, which was located outside Alexandra Park and was the sole source of youth activities at the time; it would come to have a significant impact on the activities of all residents within Alexandra Park.

In 1972, Ontario Housing Corporation gave the Alexandra Park Residents' Association access to a house that became its home base for the next six years. In this location the association undertook activities that reflected the community's ability to self-organize in order to address resident concerns, including the operation of a co-operative convenience store, homework clubs, and a board with committees.

APRA's governance structure consisted of six executives and ten members at large. The executive comprised five officers in the following positions: president, first vice-president, second vice-president, general secretary, and treasurer, with the immediate past-president as the sixth (Alexandra Park Residents' Association, 1971). According to the constitution, the influence of the president was far greater than that of the remaining executives in terms of the day-to-day business of the association. For instance, the president was the sole signatory and represented APRA on all business matters. However, and interestingly, the president did not cast a vote unless it was a deciding vote (that is, to split a tie). The community held elections every three years for the different positions in the association. The APRA also had a committee structure that assisted the board in various community activities and in addressing the areas of need within the community. According to the members' handbook, the committees included recreation, public relations, senior citizens, ways and means, and the newsletter. The executive appointed an individual chair to each committee, and these individuals reported to the board and provided oversight for the association's daily operations and initiatives, for instance meeting with media or planning programs for seniors or youth. According to several residents, the system operated well until a president undertook tasks in a unilateral manner, without the consent or knowledge of the executive (personal communication, 16 November 2002).

Sonny Atkinson, who had moved to Toronto from Nova Scotia, was the first president of the Alexandra Park Residents' Association and the person after whom the Co-operative was later named. He stepped down from his role as president in 1971 when another resident wanted to "become more involved" (Barbara, personal communication, 16 November 2002). During Sonny Atkinson's tenure, he consistently advocated on behalf of the residents – or, to borrow the descriptor that focus-group participants commonly used in reference to his style, he would "get under the skin" of the housing authority (personal communication, 12 April 2004). Many agreed that Sonny Atkinson had the community's best interests in mind in any decision he made. A few individuals described his leadership style as confrontational, but with a good heart. His primary focus was to ensure that the community was well maintained and safe. He would not accept a negative response to a request that he made to the housing authority, and he wanted to ensure that the voice of the community was heard. Subsequent presidents built upon the foundation of community building established by Sonny Atkinson, but their strategies were always less confrontational (Barbara, personal communication, 16 November 2002).

Beginning in the mid-1980s, drug activity and other social problems (such as prostitution and vandalism) became pervasive in the community (Sewell, 1994; White, 1996). These problems forced the Alexandra Park Residents' Association to take a more proactive approach to improving their community. There were two chief concerns for the residents with respect to the drugs: first, it was believed that the perpetrators of these crimes came from outside of the community and were taking advantage of the community's design and vulnerability to carry on their activities; second, some of the residents were indeed also selling drugs. Law-abiding residents felt powerless to deal with these issues for fear of reprisals from their neighbours, and they also felt that their concerns were not being heeded by the housing authority. Furthermore, there was a tense relationship with police officers as they were not seen as making an effort to understand the underlying reasons for the social problems that existed within the community.

To combat the increased incidences of vandalism and violence that began to permeate the neighbourhood, the APRA increased the availability of community-based programming (for example, recreation activities) and organized festivals and block parties that created constructive outlets for youth. During a focus group meeting a number of residents looked back with fondness to the days when neighbours were talking and having fun at the different parties. One resident stated during a focus group meeting, "I used to see more kids outside and the parents laughing together. We used to have more parties, but now we don't have that. Maybe it's because of the Nintendo, but this is not the same place" (personal communication, 13 April 2004). Although the community-based programming continues to the present day, when the APRA's priorities became focused on the co-operative conversion in the early 1990s, youth programming and community festivals were either reduced in frequency or discontinued altogether.

Another initiative of the Alexandra Park Residents' Association, which started in 1971 with the purpose of improving security in the community, was the implementation of a system of "block representatives" (Seeking Volunteers, 1971). In this program the community was geographically divided into twelve areas, and volunteers agreed to serve as the "eyes and ears" of each area. According to Barbara, these volunteer representatives were on call for twenty-four hours a day and were supposed to observe and report any problems. Reports were made monthly to the Alexandra Park Residents' Association, and the executive provided the reports to the property management. The housing authority did not explicitly support the system of block representatives, because they were seen "as a bunch of vigilantes"; however, representatives of the housing authority did recognize the utility of the block representatives, and they would later want to formalize the system (Linda, personal communication, 12 May 1998). In fact, similar initiatives, such as the Neighbourhood Watch program, were in vogue in middle-class neighbourhoods at this time, which was possibly a factor that made the government housing authority look sympathetically upon the initiative.

According to many long-time residents, the block representatives program was very successful because the residents were working together (focus group, 13 April 2004). The block representatives worked closely with the Alexandra Park Residents' Association executive, who, in turn, worked with the local police and housing managers to monitor and address problems (Vakili-Zad, 1993).

Although the Alexandra Park Residents' Association existed from 1969, it was only legally incorporated as a non-profit group in 1976 (Alexandra Park Residents' Association, 1988), which reflected the organization's increased stature outside of the community. In a few interviews, it was mentioned that in the APRA's formative period, passion and commitment drove the association, and skills followed later. One local agency, St Christopher House, operated in partnership with the APRA, helping to build capacity among the resident leaders through leadership training and youth programming. According to a former program director of St Christopher House, "the resident leadership was clearly focused on meeting their needs, and concerns for the wider neighbourhood were not top of their agenda. They could be referred to as isolationist, but we supported their goals and objectives" (personal communication, 15 March 2004).

Ontario Housing Corporation, the government agency responsible for the social housing system in Ontario, recognized the successful efforts of the Alexandra Park Residents' Association and proposed to develop a formal working relationship with it. The formalization of the relationship, in 1976, was recognition that local initiatives could be quite successful in combating social problems (Vakili-Zad, 1993). Ontario Housing Corporation entered into a shared-management arrangement with the Alexandra Park Residents' Association, the second of its kind in Ontario. The agreement was intended to establish a governance process so that the residents would have a meaningful opportunity to voice concerns and contribute to solutions (Alexandra Park Residents' Association, 1975; Ontario Housing, 1977), and it also served as a foundation for the conversion into a co-operative. As per the agreement, a management board was created, with equal representation from the housing authority and the Alexandra Park Residents' Association. This board addressed different resident-related issues, including rent default, antisocial behaviour, resident transfers, budgetary matters, and residents' complaints.

Another key area of the agreement was the creation of a formal process to supervise and select the block representatives (Vakili-Zad, 1993). Up to that point, block representatives had been volunteers who were keen on improving the community; however, the agreement stated that the representatives were to be hired and paid an honorarium. According to Barbara, the hiring of block representatives and the payment of their honorarium negatively affected the motivation for the task. These new positions led to competition between individuals who wanted to earn the extra money in order to improve their livelihoods. "Sonny believed that people should receive money for their services, but he failed to recognize that the value of the system was questioned once money and competition was part of the way things worked" (Barbara, personal communication, 23 April 2004).

This arrangement between the Alexandra Park Residents' Association and Ontario Housing Corporation was formalized in 1976 but only lasted for three years because of a lack of tenant participation (Vakili-Zad, 1993). Although the agreement stipulated some financial support for its implementation, it was unclear whether the housing authority would adhere to the decisions emerging from this process; to the residents, it was unclear whether the best interests of the wider community would be served by having such a formal agreement. Some residents started to view the Alexandra Park Residents' Association as an extension of the housing authority, and, as a result, the recruitment of new members and new block representatives became more difficult. Residents complained that the association was no longer working within the framework guided by the original principles of community building and programming. In addition, resources were not in place to ensure proper training of the representatives on the management board who were making decisions that would affect the lives of the residents. According to one source:

> The agreement didn't last because we didn't know what to do. It is like asking someone to fix a house without having the tools to fix it. Back in 1977 there were different problems here, and we wanted to do more than listen to peoples' reasons of why they shouldn't be evicted. APRA was there to help the whole community and not just one family at a time. So, the agreement folded and we were glad that it was over because the community changed quite a bit because of that. You could ask anyone who was there; they probably don't remember what was happening, but if you ask them about the festivals, they would know what you are talking about. That's what I mean when we had some say but we didn't know what to do with it. (Barbara, personal communication, 12 April 2003)

The demise of the shared agreement in 1979 did not mean that the Alexandra Park Residents' Association was unwilling or unable to take on a more active role in management responsibilities. According to Mark Goldblatt, who would come to play an important role in organizing the conversion to a co-operative, "The management agreement served a particular function, and that experience planted a seed for greater involvement. As a co-operative housing developer I met Sonny in 1978 when he told me that 'the community needs to have more meaningful participation in the operations of the project.' Sonny claimed that 'APRA brings credibility to the community, but not necessarily [the same feeling] to the housing corporation because of the income factor'" (personal communication, September 2002).

Goldblatt was suggesting that Alexandra Park was stigmatized and that this hindered APRA's efforts in organizing on behalf of the community. Even though the end of the agreement diminished the voice that the Alexandra Park Residents' Association had with the housing authority, the association's skills were transferred to running the community centre, to which I return in describing the second key event below.

Significance of the Key Event to the Conversion Process

The success of the Alexandra Park Residents' Association in building a greater sense of community became a key factor in commencing the process to becoming a co-operative. Sonny Atkinson would build on the experiences from the 1970s and 1980s in his call for greater control in the decisions that affected the community. He became very concerned with the increased incidence of drug activity during the 1980s. He believed that the community was good; the problem "was the people from outside selling the drugs" (White, 1995).

When Sonny Atkinson resumed leadership of the Alexandra Park Residents' Association in 1991, he began actively seeking increased resident involvement in all decisions affecting "his community," as he commonly referred to Alexandra Park. At this point, the Alexandra Park Residents' Association became more *activist* in its orientation as the impact of the housing authority's negligence became greater. Problems were related to poor response time to maintenance requests and the way in which the housing authority responded to the "antisocial" behaviour that had increased among the community's youth. To address these concerns, the APRA worked with different third parties, including the housing authority and local community centres. With regard to the poor response time to maintenance requests, Sonny Atkinson maintained records of information provided to him by different residents on the length of time it took before a unit was repaired. Sonny then presented his analysis to the property management. According to Laura Mark of the housing authority, "this approach would work with us early on, but Sonny did not understand that lack of funds and other administrative processes were the source of delays and it was not because we did not care" (personal communication, 5 August 2001).

The one crucial limitation of the Alexandra Park Residents' Association was the lack of a mechanism to include youth as part of a succession plan. The leaders of the time, including Sonny Atkinson, relied on their track record when running for re-election, and for residents who were outside of the APRA's executive, there was a perception that it was difficult to become involved. Moreover, the youth of the community perceived a great social distance between themselves and the leadership of the association. I recall asking friends over the years why they were not involved in the APRA, and they asked me in turn, "Why should I?" Another typical response was, "Sonny is a tyrant." The perception of the APRA's leadership as closed, especially on the part of the youth, was not particular to perceptions of Sonny Atkinson but was generalized to the different presidents over the years. In time, the association came to be seen as a clique that was unable to address the needs of the community.

I was curious about that perception and whether it was justified. Discussions with different residents and a review of previous minutes of meetings both suggest that the ongoing problems with security within the community led in part to the perception that the Alexandra Park Residents' Association was ineffective. For instance, at a community meeting a resident questioned the executive: "What are you doing about the maintenance problems? I mean, how long does it take to get a ceiling fixed? I have waited for over a year" (Alexandra Park Residents' Association, 1986b). The executive replied, "We know it's a problem."

People lost faith in the association, but that faith was revitalized when Sonny Atkinson began taking firmer action to deal with the pervasive drug problems and making the initial steps towards the co-operative conversion. However, at the same time, the closed and authoritarian leadership created a sense of mistrust among the residents as they wondered why they would let the leaders of the APRA control their community. As will be seen in the discussion of subsequent key events, the formation and utilization of social capital in the form of trust in the leadership became particularly relevant to the events leading up to the completion of the conversion process.

Beginning in 1991, Sonny Atkinson initiated different activities that were intended to enhance a sense of safety among the residents. He worked with the local police to begin foot patrols in order to deter criminal

Figure 2. Entrance to the Community Showing Remnants of the Dividing Walls. Fences later replaced the walls that were knocked down by the residents. Image taken in 2006 by the author.

activity (White, 1993, 1996). These foot patrols were deemed to be moderately successful, but many of the perpetrators of crime would take advantage of the neighbourhood's design to hide from the foot patrols behind the large concrete and brick walls that were located at entrances and around the courtyards. These walls also intensified the institutional appearance of the project and created a symbolic barrier to the wider neighbourhood. Figure 2 shows the remnants of the original walls.

In conclusion, the Alexandra Park Residents' Association originated because a group of residents attempted to address the needs within their community. It was a driving force for improving the community, both the quality of resident life and the condition of the property. As will be shown in the discussion of the next key event, there was a strong tradition of activism that is not common in public housing projects. It was the energy from this activism that helped to initiate the process of converting into a co-operative. As stated earlier, one of the APRA's key responsibilities was the local community centre. In the next key event, I describe the efforts undertaken by the Alexandra Park Residents' Association to build a community centre, one that would house the association and serve the needs of the residents.

Event 2: The Opening of the Alexandra Park Community Centre, 1978

One of the first actions taken by the Alexandra Park Residents' Association was to lobby successfully the housing authority to build a community centre that would include the association's offices. Named the Alexandra Park Community Centre, it was opened in 1978 and represented the first partnership between the residents and the housing authority.

From the inception of the centre the association took an active role in its construction, including design, and later in its management. It provided a place in which the Alexandra Park Residents' Association could meet, and the residents had a leading role in defining its programming. Furthermore, the community centre ensured that the Alexandra Park Residents' Association was fulfilling its primary objective of providing services for the community. Over time it has given residents and community leaders access to recreational and educational activities and a hub for activism.

The presence of a community centre within a public housing project is not unique to Alexandra Park. What is unique is that a resident body has always managed this community centre. Although APRA's leadership started as inexperienced managers, their commitment to improving their community led them to obtain the resources and learning opportunities needed to operate the community centre. Moreover, the centre not only offered programming for the local residents but also provided a means of employment for many of the residents, including the youth.

According to a review of the Atkinson board's minutes from 1998 to 2002, managing the Alexandra Park Community Centre was the topic that consistently dominated the meetings. The centre was a symbol of successful resident mobilization, and the notion that a different resident group might take over operations was frightening to many long-time residents. The management of the community centre divided the residents. For this reason, the building of the community centre in 1976 and its subsequent role within the community is considered here to be a key event in the conversion process. I provide a description based on interviews, board minutes, and newspaper articles of the events leading up to the construction of the centre, and I conclude this case with a discussion of the current status of the Alexandra Park Community Centre, including the role it had in the conversion process.

Background of the Key Event

The Alexandra Park Housing development and neighbourhood redevelopment was touted by the Social Planning Council of Metropolitan Toronto (1970) and the development department of the City of Toronto (City of Toronto Development Department, 1971) as the solution to the planning deficits and significant social problems pervasive in the area. For instance, the Social Planning Council found that "the most pressing problems in Alexandra Park were brought about by unemployment, the strange ethnic mixture of its population – mainly British, Polish, Ukrainian, French and Italian with smaller groups of Germans, Portuguese, Hungarian and other European and Asiatic groups, school drop-outs, multi-problem families and a prevalence of crime" (City of Toronto Development Department, 1971, 2).

The City of Toronto Development Department (1971) described the overall redevelopment as a "first attempt at a fully comprehensive project consisting of a mixture of renewal, conservation and rehabilitation" (3). However, beyond hiring a social worker "to deal with any social problems" (3), little effort was made to deliberately address the social problems that had influenced the redevelopment in the first place. According to the architect, Jerome Markson, the new development was intended to introduce innovations for a vulnerable population: "The alienation found at the Regent Park development set the stage to make the Alexandra Park community welcoming to children and families. The main problem was associated with the fact that [provincial] government support was tied to federal funding, which meant that we could not do everything we wanted to. So what you see today is a fraction of what we had hoped would be in place at the time" (personal communication, 10 May 2004).

Mr Markson was referring to the building of community space where children could play safely and where adults could congregate. Although there were social agencies in the neighbourhood, it was felt that more was needed to meet the unique needs of a vulnerable population (Smith, 1968). Thus, the new project was supposed to attend to the wants of children by providing a community centre and recreation programs; the centre would also be a meeting space for the adults (Markson, personal communication, 10 May 2004). However, the final project did not include the promised community centre, but a tennis court and a basketball court were constructed.

The Alexandra Park Residents' Association recognized the need for improved services and began in 1972 to call for the community centre to be built, as promised in the original plan for Alexandra Park. According to Barbara, a former board member of the APRA, the St Christopher house "was great, but it was not open during the hours when the children needed it most, which was after school." Local social services agencies were not accountable to the Alexandra Park community and were not always open at appropriate times, as noted by Barbara: "They could do whatever they wanted, and we could not say what that was" (Barbara, personal communication, 14 April 2004).

Arguably the community centre became a resident-led initiative once it became clear that the provincial government was not going to keep the promise of building one. The leading role played by the Alexandra Park Residents' Association in the community centre was recognized by government officials, as stated in an interview with Laura Mark, a former housing authority employee: "The community centre was unique in that it was operated by a residents' association that was quite active and vocal. They knew what their needs were and they were best able to articulate them. Sonny [the president of the APRA at that time] was always a guiding force, but the following presidents provided key leadership to see the centre built" (personal communication, 14 April 2004).

Ms Mark acknowledged that the lobbying efforts of the Alexandra Park Residents' Association were critical to the decision to proceed with constructing the centre: "Sonny was persistent, as were other leaders." Therefore, from the centre's inception, there was an activist tradition at Alexandra Park, one that continued in the community centre's management. Conceivably, this tradition was a forerunner of the subsequent activism. An unofficial groundbreaking ceremony for Alexandra Park Community Centre occurred in 1976 and involved adults and children from the community. The ceremony was unofficial because it was held to demonstrate the frustration that Ontario Housing Corporation had not followed through on the promise to build a community centre (Thomas, 1976). According to the president of the APRA, Frances Bruce, "everyone hears about the bad things here at Alexandra Park. But there are more than 500 teenagers here who've never had a place to go. We want to tell people why these children get into trouble" (Thomas, 1976). However, two days later, on 12 July, the local Member of Provincial Parliament Larry Grossman announced at a public meeting that funds were now available: "If you want it, it is yours" (Praeger, 1976). The audience seemed astounded and started shouting "no, no" in disbelief. But Mr Grossman provided assurance by saying that a letter was on its way. Frances Bruce was certainly surprised and said that the building would be used to house a food co-operative and a clothing exchange (Praeger, 1976).

The Alexandra Park Community Centre opened in 1978, almost ten years after the start of the housing project itself. Children were invited to the ceremony, as were other dignitaries According to a resident who was present at the opening, "there was such excitement at the potential gains for the community" (personal conversation, 14 November 2001); this view was expressed by many who recalled that seminal event.

Over time, the community centre – managed and organized according to the residents' desires and direction – has served as a hub of community activity and community mobilization. External support for the centre's operations came from different agencies and government departments, but the resident role in management has always been central. According to the constitution of the Alexandra Park Community Centre (1985), the operations of the community centre were directed by the executive of the APRA as a management committee; however, greater decision-making power was given to the president to oversee the operations. According to the APRA minutes (for example, see Alexandra Park Residents' Association, 1985, 1986a), this arrangement caused difficulties between the staff of the community centre and the executive of the Alexandra Park Residents' Association.

Funding the centre was always a key area of concern, but as will be seen below, residents also took an active role in securing it. From its inception the community centre was poorly funded, but this challenge proved a blessing for the community because it forced them to learn how to raise funds and to mobilize volunteers to provide the necessary services. Furthermore, efforts to raise funds required individuals to develop an understanding of government and non-government processes. According to a grant application to the City of Toronto Department of Parks and Recreation (personal communication, May 1979), the centre had 100 volunteers who provided 8,000 hours of community service in 1978. According to Barbara, "we were not always able to have activities for the kids that always worked. What we had going for us was that we cared, and that helped motivate us to go on" (personal communication, 14 April 2004). The role of volunteers would remain integral to the life of the community centre; the residents ran the programs because they did not have the resources to hire people. By 1994 the number of volunteers and volunteer hours reported to the City of Toronto Department of Parks and Recreation had increased to 200 and 20,000, respectively (personal communication, March 1994).

Once the community centre had been built, the housing authority expressed concern about whether its programs could be sustained on such a limited funding base. According to Laura Mark, "we knew that the community was strong, but they wanted to do so much for each other. We could not provide all of the funds they needed, so they had to rely on their own ways to get money. We were worried about that, but our hands were tied" (personal communication, 14 April 2004).

To supplement the government funding, the association organized programs and services with the purpose of raising the funds needed to operate the community centre. Activities included weekly bingo for seniors and renting space within the community centre for outside events. The association's financial statements in 1986 show that the revenue for operating the centre was $160,000, of which $30,000 came from bingo and rentals. However, from the mid-1980s to the early 1990s, government funding was scaled back across the social service sector. By 1993, government funding for the community centre had decreased from 80 per cent in 1985 to 66 per cent, or $90,000 of the association's budget, but the community's contribution was unchanged at $40,000.

Additional efforts to raise funds involved more sophisticated strategies, including seeking grants from diverse sources. After much effort the Alexandra Park Residents' Association was granted charitable status in 1985 in order for it to be able to raise funds for recreational and educational programs in the community centre (Alexandra Park Residents' Association, 1987). Per Sherman Middleton, a former president of the association, the charitable status was tied to "our need to maintain our programming" (Alexandra Park Residents' Association, 1988). Although the uses of charitable status have broadened over the years, it was highly unusual for the residents' association of a public housing community to pursue such an application – another indication of Alexandra Park's uniqueness. According to the agreement, the APRA would maintain charitable status for the purposes of running the centre (Alexandra Park Community Centre, 1985). As stated by Sherman Middleton, linking the charitable status to the centre ensured accountability and underlined the fact that the funds were to be used to support its programs (the Alexandra Park Residents' Association meeting minutes, 14 November 1985).

Significance of the Key Event to the Conversion Process

The community centre was a symbol of the Alexandra Park Residents' Association's activism, and once built, it became the hub of the community for its day-to-day social interactions, social events, and initiatives that required community mobilization. Activism and mobilization always started in the community centre, so it was not coincidental that the community centre would later house the initial discussions related to the conversion to a housing co-operative.

The community centre continues to be managed by the residents' association and thrives as a meeting place. When the conversion to a housing co-operative was underway, the hope was that the association and the Atkinson Housing Co-operative's board of directors would work together since there was overlap in the composition of the two groups, but as will be described in a subsequent case, this did not happen. In fact, the community centre became the focal point of conflict among some residents (primarily those who did not support the conversion process), rather than being the hub where the residents mobilized to support the process. As will be shown later, those dissenting residents felt that the Atkinson Housing Co-operative's board of directors was trying to dismantle the presence of the APRA, which was in fact true. However, the new Atkinson board of directors did not explain the need to reduce the confusion associated with having two representative bodies for the community. The issues were complex, but one issue included allegations of mismanagement of community centre funds. These differences will be discussed further in the next chapter.

Event 3: The Community Security March, 1992

Since Alexandra Park's founding in 1969, illegal activities such as drug dealing, prostitution, and vandalism shaped the public's image of the housing project as a dangerous place in which to live. Although these problems are a significant part of the community's history, there was a notable increase in drug activity towards the latter part of the 1980s, largely conducted by individuals who did not live in the community (Alexandra Park Residents' Association, 1990b). The residents became concerned about the impact of the illegal activity on the image of the community as well as on their quality of life. Thus, community and police actions targeted those entering the community to buy or sell drugs, as well as those drug dealers who operated crack houses within the neighbourhood and the project.

The anger towards the drug activities climaxed in the summer of 1990 when the Alexandra Park Residents' Association organized a community security march in response to a vicious assault on a mother and son. The march was intended to raise awareness of the community as a place that does not tolerate criminal activity, as well as a place where people protect one another. Furthermore, the message was conveyed that the residents were not alone in dealing with these issues (Alexandra Park Residents' Association, 1990a, 1990c). This march forced the housing authority to initiate changes to the design of the property (for example, the tearing down of the barrier walls) and to forge a stronger relationship with police with the purpose of improving security practices.

Background of the Key Event

While the residents were living in fear of the known drug dealers living in the community, they were primarily fearful of those who entered the community to buy and sell crack cocaine, the drug of choice at that time. There was a general feeling that the housing authority was not doing enough to shield and protect the residents from the rampant drug activity and associated antisocial behaviour (Alexandra Park Residents' Association, 1989). Members of the Alexandra Park Residents' Association executive took it upon themselves to emphasize the importance of reporting problems to the housing authority and to the police. For many residents, the reporting strategy created apprehensions because of possible retribution by the drug dealers (Papp, 1990). Sonny Atkinson said that "the residents lived in fear, so stronger measures had to include changes to the physical property, and we needed to increase the police presence. The design of the property protects the drug dealers because there are many places to hide" (White, 1993). Sonny believed that security could be improved by instituting seemingly simple actions (White, 1996), including evicting tenants known to be drug dealers, removing a series of barrier walls, improving the street lighting, and removing trees that served as hiding places for illegal activity.

Local politicians were invited to a community meeting on 12 March 1990 so that they could see how the residents were coping with the daily dangers of living in Alexandra Park. The residents made the following and similar statements: "Drug deals take place right outside my home," and "She rarely gets any sleep because there are drug deals right outside her window every night" (Alexandra Park Residents' Association, 1990b). A recurring complaint made by many residents was that the police knew the identities of the drug dealers but were not arresting them (see Appleby, 1990a, 1990c); the residents were convinced that the inadequate security practices were exacerbated by the fact that the police and the housing authority knew which dealers were causing the problems and appeared to do nothing about it. One resident stated, "If it is clear who the pushers are, then it should be clear what we do about them: get rid of them." Another resident questioned priorities: "[The housing authority] finds it easy enough to do something about tenants if they don't pay the rent."

It was resolved at the 12 March meeting to establish a security/drugs committee, chaired by Sonny Atkinson, with representation from local politicians and residents. Some residents, including a former treasurer of the Alexandra Park Residents' Association, were sceptical about the utility of a committee (personal communication, 16 September 2003). However, subsequent actions demonstrated that the work of this committee would be integral to the community's movement towards self-management. Members of the Security/Drugs Committee worked with the local police and the housing authority's security division to carry out safety walks through the neighbourhood. However, from the perspective of some residents, the walks were pointless (Appleby, 1990a, 16). Nevertheless, the walks continued, and they highlighted the design flaws that made apprehension of the criminals difficult.

An obstacle that hindered police efforts and prevented any improvements to communication between the residents and the police was the fear of reprisals. A resident observed one night that after twenty police officers had spent an evening walking through the project, he felt that "what they're doing is a total waste of time unless they get some of those kids talking, which is unlikely" (Appleby, 1990a, 16). A profound sense of fear was expressed on a radio talk show devoted to the crime in Alexandra Park, in which a resident stated: "Police don't do anything about it, and they don't stop to catch them. I have seen this happen. The police don't do anything. We have formed a group. Why don't they arrest them? The police say they can't unless they have more evidence. People deal right in front of them. I am afraid of my safety, so you can't just go out and report them. There are so many dealers around that it is hard to know exactly who is doing what. I have seen many fights" (CFRB radio show, 12 July 1990).

The level of frustration within the community came to a boiling point when a mother and son were assaulted in front of their home on 7 July 1990; the mother was physically assaulted, and the son was stabbed six times by unknown assailants (Appleby, 1990b). The mother and son were well known and liked in the community; according to one resident, "they were not involved in any illegal activity." Unfortunately the culprits were never found, and the police determined that the incident was a bungled robbery attempt. However, the experience helped to fuel a feeling within the community that something immediate and drastic had to be done to resolve the drug problems. A resident characterized that time as "living in a jungle and having to behave war-like" (personal conversation, 16 September 2003).

Residents began to protect themselves through a variety of means; for example, they established a neighbourhood watch group to monitor the entrances to the project and to warn intruders against entering the area if their goal was to deal or buy drugs. In the spring of 1990 residents placed APRA signs in their windows that read: "WARNING. ALEXANDRA PARK is being monitored by residents and police. Anyone seen buying or selling cocaine will be photographed and reported to the police. Any cabs or cars engaged in coke pickups or deliveries will have their plate numbers reported. YOU HAVE BEEN WARNED."

Some groups of residents resorted to violence and used baseball bats to confront both drug dealers and users. The media referred to these groups as "resident organized vigilante groups" (Appleby, 1990b). A local radio program devoted an entire afternoon to the issue of vigilante groups emerging at Alexandra Park (Hawton, 1990). Among those interviewed was Sherman Middleton, the president of APRA, and in response to the question of whether or not these residents should be regarded as vigilantes, he stated:

These are not vigilantes. This is a concern by community people who want to raise their families. They don't want their children involved in drugs. We want a safe and quiet environment. Living in Metro housing is enough, so we don't need these problems. We do not have any vigilante gangs here. We have a concerned community who want to live in a safe environment. It is only normal to protect yourself, but we are not out for retaliation. The reaction is to defend. The buyers come from outside the community. The dealers are not approaching certain people inside the community. They walk away when told to leave. I tell them to take this garbage and leave. Now people know we mean business. I repeat that it is not vigilante gangs at work here.

The level of frustration was not only targeted at the drug dealers and buyers; there was also a general dissatisfaction with the way in which the local police and the housing authority responded to the fears expressed by the residents. The Alexandra Park Residents' Association executive believed that persistent calls to improve the security presence had to be coupled with changes to the design of the community so that the police could arrest the drug dealers who normally hid behind the walls. Thus, tearing down the barrier walls became a target for immediate action.

On 14 July 1990 a "Take Back the Streets" community security march was organized by the Security/Drugs Committee of the Alexandra Park Residents' Association and led by Sherman Middleton and Sonny Atkinson, at that time the president of the association and the chair of the Security/Drugs Committee, respectively. Over 120 residents and supporters attended, collectively chanted, "God hates crack," and sang "We Shall Overcome" (Papp, 1990). The supporters included housing advocates and politicians, and Toronto Mayor Art Eggleton called for a 24-hour police foot patrol, which was cheered by the crowd (Papp, 1990). According to a *Globe and Mail* article, "the marchers marked walls they want torn down. The walls frame narrow twisting alleyways, which form a haven for drug dealers" (16 July 1990). Although the event lasted for only one hour, it was an empowering experience for the community. The housing authority became more responsive to it, and the APRA assumed an air of increased credibility within the community and felt able to engage in other forms of community mobilization.

The successful response to and support for the march caused Sonny Atkinson to continue with the foot patrols until the drug problem was ended (Alexandra Park Residents' Association, 1990b). Remarkably, there was evidence of rapid improvements within the community regarding incidents of drug activity. Minutes of a meeting of the Security/Drugs Committee on 2 August 1990 state that "the drug problem has cooled down." Further, at a committee meeting on 10 September 1990, it was reported that the night foot patrols had continued to bring out residents, arrests of trespassers had increased, and significant improvements had been made to the lighting of the sidewalks. By December 1990 Sonny Atkinson stated that after a walk through the project with a government housing security officer and local police, he had a sense that there was "general satisfaction with response and improvements" among the residents (Alexandra Park Residents' Association, 1990c).

As the drug activity declined, the housing authority displayed willingness to consider the redesign of the neighbourhood. According to the minutes of the Alexandra Park Residents' Association's board meetings held in July and August 1990, definite decisions were made with respect to the walls being torn down. At the August 2 and 13 meetings the property manager outlined the process to tear down the walls in and around the community, and finally it was decided to tear down twenty-five walls.

A public ceremony was held on 30 August 1990, during which local dignitaries, including Mayor Art Eggleton, each took a turn at using a sledgehammer on one of the walls. The chair of the housing authority at the time, Jean Augustine, stated that "the residents at Alex Park are reclaiming their neighbourhood from the drug dealers," and the Mayor confirmed, "This is a message to the drug dealers that we want them out of Alexandra Park and out of the city" (Moloney, 1990). At the ceremony Staff Sergeant Darcy Keller felt that the removal of the walls would make patrolling easier, but ultimately "if we don't have the backing and support of the people, our efforts are fruitless. In this case, the citizens decided they wanted something done" (Moloney, 1990).

The community security march was quite successful in raising awareness that the illegal activity was being perpetrated by outsiders.

Perhaps it also symbolized the potential for self-governance by the residents in solving their community's problems. However, the housing authority's response was too slow for the residents; fourteen months after the ceremony to tear down the barrier walls only six of the twenty-five walls had actually been removed (Toughill, 1991). In a *Toronto Star* article Sonny Atkinson expressed the community's frustration: "I've been hollering like a dog about this. But it seems the louder you holler, the less gets done" (Toughill, 1991). In response to Sonny's claims, the general manager of the housing authority, Byron Hill, blamed the residents for the delay because "a year-long consultation process was needed. I think you'll find the majority of residents are very pleased with our progress" (Toughill, 1991). Sonny Atkinson disagreed with Byron Hill and stated that the residents themselves were prepared to tear down the walls if the housing authority continued its delays: "If dignitaries with their tiny muscles can knock down a brick wall, surely hard-working people like us can do that too" (Toughill, 1991). However, the housing agency responded, and in a follow-up *Toronto Star* article, Huang (1992) reported that twenty-one of the twenty-five walls had been torn down and most of the crack houses had been closed.

For Sonny Atkinson and the other leaders of the Alexandra Park Residents' Association, their action in driving out the drug dealers was an empowering experience and led to increased expectations. According to Sonny, the community still had a long way to go. "They should give us more say in running the project. We feel they're using us for a dumping ground," he said (Huang, 1992).

Significance of the Key Event to the Conversion Process

The community security march can be regarded as a transformative experience for Alexandra Park as it gave the residents a sense that their voice mattered. From 1989 to 1992 the residents' pleas to improve their community became louder. The community's success in tearing down the walls and driving out the drug dealers did not silence the residents; in fact, it had the opposite effect. The Alexandra Park Residents' Association executive began to broaden its interests and to mobilize the residents to realize greater autonomy.

The march was successful because of a coalition of residents, other supporters, and politicians. With this coalition intact, calls for increased autonomy were taken seriously. While the residents were working as an organized group, the local municipal councillor, Liz Amer, was corresponding with Jean Augustine to express her support for co-operative conversions specifically and self-management efforts generally (Amer, 1990). Unfortunately there is no public record of Jean Augustine's response, but in previous correspondence she had agreed that improvements to design and management were required (Augustine, 1990).

The activities associated with the security march represented a turning point in the community's development. The march helped the residents to realize that it was possible to successfully organize an event to raise awareness and initiate meaningful change. The tearing down of the walls was a symbolic action to end the separation of the community from the wider neighbourhood. With Sonny Atkinson's determination, the backing of the Alexandra Park Residents' Association, and the external support that was mobilized to drive out the drug dealers, a dynamic was in place that would create the basis for the conversion to a housing co-operative.

Event 4: The Community Meeting to Introduce the Conversion into a Housing Co-operative, 1993

The success of tearing down the barrier walls that had provided protected areas for criminal activity motivated the Alexandra Park Residents' Association to address the broader issue of the housing authority's management practices because they were perceived as not effectively addressing the security and housing needs of the residents. Furthermore, the housing authority acted in an ad hoc manner and did not resolve systemic problems faced by residents (White, 1993, 1995, 1996). Sonny Atkinson felt that involvement by the residents in the hiring of a security company was essential as they would be knowledgeable and sensitive to the needs of the community. Such resident involvement was unheard of in public housing. As expressed by Sonny Atkinson, the drug activity was a key factor in the call for more resident control of decision making, but the general lack of satisfaction with the housing authority's strategies laid the foundation for a more fundamental shift in the community's management. Furthermore, the absence of meaningful resident involvement in decision making was also cited as a reason the residents initiated a process for greater control of the community.

Another issue that helped mobilize the residents was the recognition that there was a greater likelihood that residents would remain in the community if they felt they had security of tenure. As residents increased their income, they were encouraged to move out of the community – and often those who exited were community leaders – or they would see their rents exceed those in the private housing market (White, 1996). A related issue that galvanized residents was the requirement that they would have to move to another community if they were under- or over-housed owing to a change in household composition and if an appropriately sized unit was not available in the community. This was particularly difficult for older residents whose children had moved out (Sewell, 1994).

A third concern of the Alexandra Park Residents' Association was related to the continuing slow response to maintenance requests, in some cases several months. Sonny Atkinson wanted tenants to take on some of the repairs and be paid for their efforts, but management resisted. As a result of these concerns, in 1992 Sonny Atkinson started calling for local control over key management functions (Wright, 1994a), something that he believed would minimize drug activity and create a greater sense of community pride. Initially, the housing authority resisted greater control, but matters started to change once housing advocates and members of the co-operative housing sector began to align themselves with the APRA.

Owing to the convergence of the interests of the Alexandra Park residents and those of the broader co-operative sector, Alexandra Park became a pilot project for the first conversion of a public housing project into a housing co-operative. Residents wanted more control over local management, and the co-operative sector had a vision of creating co-operative housing out of public housing projects. Other important stakeholders became interested in this conversion, particularly municipal and provincial politicians who had concerns about the public housing system. Coincidently, the APRA executive was independently exploring alternative management options for improving the community's health (Goldblatt, 1991).

In summary, the impetus for the conversion of Alexandra Park into the Atkinson Housing Co-operative revolved around a combination of concerns. The residents decided to pursue the conversion in order to improve the following:

- safety and security
- responsiveness to maintenance requests
- sensitivity to their needs
- consultation on major decisions
- security of tenure

The community security march had helped bring to the surface a deep dissatisfaction with the housing authority's unreasonable and lengthy responses to maintenance requests and the general demeanour of the property office's staff. As a result, there was a willingness to investigate innovative ways to improve the community through the Alexandra Park Residents' Association. Over many years the association's executive had been urging the housing authority to address these issues, but members attributed the lack of success to their not having a say in the actual management decisions and practices. This argument was shared by local politicians and housing advocates.

A review of minutes from meetings held by the Alexandra Park Residents' Association and by the housing authority, correspondence between the Alexandra Park Residents' Association and local politicians, and personal interviews reveals that calls for involvement in decision making started in 1990. After almost four years of private discussions and lobbying efforts, a meeting was held on 13 October 1993 to formally gain the community's support to explore the possibility of becoming a self-managed property. This meeting is considered to be a key event because the outcome provided the association's executive with the formal support to educate the community about seeking autonomy from the housing authority through conversion into co-operative housing. The actions that preceded and followed the meeting illustrate the community's capacity for self-determination, as well as the level of external support that the community had for the conversion.

Background of the Key Event

The pursuit of increased control over management responsibilities originated in a meeting of local politicians and the community in early 1990. Two municipal councillors, Dale Martin and Liz Amer, who had been invited to attend, encouraged the residents in their introductory remarks to seek self-management in order to deal with the complex issues that they faced daily (Alexandra Park Residents' Association, 1990a). According to Linda, a former treasurer of the Alexandra Park Residents' Association, "the remarks made by the politicians made us think about taking control of the property. But at that time we were thinking self-management and not co-op. Co-op did not even enter our minds. It was Sonny who pushed for it. Sherman [Middleton] was concerned with other things, but Sonny wanted power" (personal communication, 21 November 2002).

Between 1990 and 1991 the Alexandra Park Residents' Association was trying to address many property management issues. The minutes of different board meetings demonstrated a high level of frustration as well as the obstacles to purposeful involvement in the decision-making process. There was a sense that the APRA's initiatives were being taken for granted, a view that was expressed bluntly by Sonny Atkinson at a board meeting on 21 April 1991: "We are doing [the housing authority's] work for them and they get the credit. What we do, we feel is not acknowledged, for example, the community garden. MTHA took the credit for this ... appointment to the [housing authority's] board, the tenants will not have a majority. We have saved the community money. If any savings are achieved, it should stay in the community. The community wants to be self-managed. We need money for community development and board training." Atkinson's words illustrate that the Alexandra Park Residents' Association saw the need to change how they functioned within the community. This statement is the first formal reference to the community seeking self-management and is a precursor to the formal goals and objectives of converting the property into a housing co-operative.

There was genuine concern that the exploration of tenant self-management would have a negative impact on the community because the Alexandra Park Residents' Association would be shifting its focus from community programming towards consultation with the government housing authority about the outcome of the conversion efforts, which could be complex. Sherman Middleton did not share Atkinson's desire for greater responsibility, because "it involved more work, and his focus was on the community centre" (Donna Harrow, personal communication, 16 April 2003). However, according to Donna Harrow, who volunteered in the community and taught at the local public school, "Sherman would support exploring the management alternatives because he shared the same frustrations with the housing authority's inactions."

An important incident that shifted the focus of the association was the decision by the housing authority to take the keys to the community centre away from Sherman Middleton (Alexandra Park Residents' Association, 1991a), allegedly because of poor management and questionable accountability. The residents shared the APRA's anger with this incident as they had a strong sense of ownership of the community centre. One resident, for example, stated, "My mother helped create the centre." The outcome of the meeting was the passing of a motion by the residents to get back the centre.

The housing authority's efforts to prevent the Alexandra Park Residents' Association from managing the community centre caused a great deal of acrimony between the association's executive and the housing authority. At a February board meeting a board member stated that the "community lost confidence in [the housing authority]" (Alexandra Park Residents' Association, 1991b). Members of the APRA's executive took the issue personally in that they could not understand why access to the centre had been removed. For the executive, something very meaningful to them was being taken away by the same people who administered their community, and they were powerless to do anything about it.

From the perspective of the housing authority, legitimate concerns regarding the way in which the centre was functioning had precipitated their actions. According to a representative of the housing authority, their "response was related to access to programs and maintenance" (Alexandra Park Residents' Association, 1991b). Although the issue was resolved rather quickly (within a month), damage to the relationship between the residents' association and government management seemed irreparable. Although there were times that followed when the association would still be consulted, the housing authority's attempt to take control of the community centre instigated the call for a new landlord.

While the residents were seeking alternative management arrangements, other factors would both directly and indirectly influence Alexandra Park's movement towards conversion to a housing co-operative. Independent enquiries and efforts were taking place with the intent of improving the condition of public housing projects in general through greater tenant self-management. One report released by a 1991 task force established by the Canada Mortgage and Housing Corporation recommended greater tenant involvement in the management of Alexandra Park's community (CMHC, 1991). This report energized both residents and housing advocates alike to pursue alternative management arrangements. In 1992 the Ontario Housing Corporation would seek to implement policies that would set the conditions for tenant self-management (Alexandra Park Residents' Association, 1993a).

Frustrated by the lack of leadership around solving the chronic problems of many housing projects in Toronto, a group of leading housing advocates and activists responded to CMHC's report by putting together a plan to convince the provincial government to change the way that public housing was managed; this involved the conversion of existing properties into housing co-operatives (Goldblatt, 1991). The emergence of this group of housing advocates represented an interesting effort by citizens to challenge the status quo with respect to the years of neglect of the public housing stock. They established a working group, called the Public Housing to Co-op Conversion (PHCC), at the same time that new scholarly literature suggested that a change of organizational form was a crucial step towards improving the living conditions found in public housing projects (for example, see Peterman, 1989; Chandler, 1991; Vakili-Zad, 1993). The group laid out a plan that focused on ten objectives (Goldblatt, 1991):

1. To create healthy and safe communities
2. To promote tenant education and community development
3. To initiate substantial physical rehabilitation
4. To increase resident control or professional management
5. To preserve public control of project land
6. To maintain existing income mix
7. To guarantee tenure for existing residents
8. To provide economic incentives for cost control
9. To focus on needs defined by the community
10. To seek tenant approval for conversions

With these objectives in mind, the working group called on the newly elected New Democratic Party provincial government to authorize a demonstration process in order to assess the viability of converting public housing projects into co-operatives. Mark Goldblatt prepared a proposal that combined research and pilot projects for such a process (Mark Goldblatt, personal communication, 18 September 2001).

The PHCC working group received political support from the provincial government. In fact, the group met with the then Minister of Housing, Evelyn Gigantes, and the chair of the Ontario Housing Corporation (the provincial housing agency), Nancy Smith; both expressed interest in the proposal. The next step was to determine whether there existed a community that would support such an initiative. Unfortunately government support remained in principle only, a commitment to implement the proposal never materialized, and the PHCC working group discontinued its work. However, Mark Goldblatt believed in the concept of conversions and decided to pursue the idea independently. Further, according to Goldblatt, "there had not been a feasible group able to take on this monumental task until I met Sonny" (personal communication, 18 September 2001).

While the PHCC group was finding its legs, the housing authority formed a resident advisory council (Resident Advisory Council,
1993), which contained representatives from different housing projects,
including Sonny Atkinson; Atkinson was later elected chair of the
council (Resident Advisory Council, 1994). It was through his participation on this council that Atkinson and Mark Goldblatt initially met
(Mark Goldblatt, personal communication, September 2001). Goldblatt
had heard about the interest of Alexandra Park Residents' Association
in tenant self-management, and he contacted the association via Sonny
Atkinson in order to explore the possibility of conversion into a housing co-operative. Sonny had been researching models that allowed
for resident control, and Mark Goldblatt informed him that the co-
operative model allowed for not only greater resident participation but
also greater autonomy from the housing authority (Atkinson Housing
Co-operative, 1996).

Sonny Atkinson liked the co-operative conversion proposal and
started to wonder whether this would be a realistic and feasible option
for Alexandra Park. He invited Goldblatt to attend the board meeting
of Alexandra Park Residents' Association in February of 1993 to explore
the idea of tenant self-management or co-operative conversion (Mark
Goldblatt, personal communication, 18 September 2001). The notion of
co-operative management appealed to them both because of their common interest in resident control and because of the model's emphasis
on the importance of reducing government intervention in the daily
lives of residents by providing them with opportunities to exercise
greater autonomy.

Shortly after the meeting, Sonny Atkinson sent a letter to the local
NDP Member of Provincial Parliament, Rosario Marchese, who then
expressed his interest in the co-operative conversion idea. In his letter
Atkinson formally requested his support for the community's desire
for control over decision making because the proposal "seems to have
been supported by Housing Minister Evelyn Gigantes and the chair of
the Ontario Housing Corporation" (Atkinson, 1993). Atkinson invited
local politicians such as Rosario Marchese, and advocates from the non-
profit housing sector with expertise in co-operative housing and tenant
self-management, to a community meeting on 13 October 1993 to discuss housing co-operatives and the conversion of Alexandra Park into
a co-operative. Attached to the invitation was a letter from Atkinson in
which he stated: "I am writing to invite you to an important community meeting at which we will talk about the possibility of Tenant Self

Management in Alexandra Park. I am sure you have a lot of questions about how it can work to your benefit and how it can be done. At the meeting there will be people who can answer your questions."

Alexandra Park Residents' Association minutes (1993a) show that there were approximately fifty residents present. The presentations by the invited guests described the factors that would change and those that would remain should they become a housing co-operative. In summary, "the residents would become the landlord, and each member of the co-op would have a say in the running of the co-operative. The Provincial financial assistance would continue so that tenants would continue to receive assistance with their rent. The main difference would be that there would no longer be an automatic increase in rent with an increase in a person's income; instead there would be a rent ceiling above which rents could not rise. Tenants who choose not to become part of the co-operative, would have a guaranteed right to remain [as tenants of] the co-operative. Any cost savings resulting from their self-management would flow back to the community to be used for improvements."

It was noted that being tenants of a co-operative meant that the residents would have to adhere to the same policies and practices that applied to public housing projects. Those present at the meeting embraced the idea of becoming a co-operative, but according to the minutes of the community meeting (Alexandra Park Residents' Association, 1993a), a number of questions were asked, including:

- "Will I lose my subsidy?"
- "How will repairs and maintenance be paid for?"
- "Who will pay for the conversion process?"
- "Will my neighbours know about my private affairs?"
- "Who will work in the co-op?"

Although the presenters answered some of the questions, understandably there was still confusion regarding the benefits of becoming a co-operative. One of the guests, Tim Maxwell from a local community legal clinic, pointed out, "This was only the beginning of the process, and a lot of education was still required prior to any vote among tenants regarding Alexandra Park converting to a co-operative." One resident felt, "What was presented seemed too good to be true. How could things not change but also change? I left feeling that it was hard to believe what they were saying. I knew Sonny, and I am sure he had something up his sleeve" (Linda, personal communication, 21 November 2002). As indicated by Linda's statement, there was some scepticism among the residents and some mistrust of Atkinson, and these attitudes reinforced the need to ensure that the residents had access to thorough education and community development activities.

The community demonstrated enough interest to pursue the idea, so Sonny Atkinson began working with Mark Goldblatt to develop a proposal to convert the Alexandra Park housing project into a housing co-operative. At this time the Alexandra Park Residents' Association formally contacted the housing authority to seek its support of the conversion proposal (Atkinson Housing Co-operative, 1996). While the Ministry of Municipal Affairs and Housing supported the initiative, there was no program in place to provide the financial resources that the community needed for the conversion. However, the association and the co-operative representatives were undeterred by the lack of financial resources and attempted to raise funds while completing the conversion process.

Since the process was new, government housing representatives and the Alexandra Park Residents' Association were unsure of the procedures to follow. With the help of Mark Goldblatt, it was determined that the initial step to building a strong case for converting into a housing co-operative was to assess the level of community support for the initiative, which could be done through a referendum. A series of community development activities was undertaken with the help of the co-operative sector and some government funding.

Significance of the Key Event to the Conversion Process

The October 1993 community meeting was considered a success by the Alexandra Park Residents' Association executive because it then had a mandate for approaching the housing authority about converting into a co-operative (Alexandra Park Residents' Association, 1993b), and this led to the planning of a referendum. The notion of converting to a co-operative changed from being only a fanciful idea to being a serious proposal that required the creation of a process that involved lobbying the government and surveying residents' support.

Since a conversion from public housing to co-operative housing was unfamiliar territory for all stakeholders and supports, the organizers had to rely on expert resources for member education and negotiation, at both the level of the community and that of the housing authority.

The conversion process was going to be complex, and a primary challenge was to get funding. Thus, the early stages involved developing a work plan that built on existing support as well as new links outside of the community. However, the October community meeting was seminal in that it marked a change in resident attitudes from that of being focused exclusively on their households to one involving a greater focus on their community. This change was already in progress, as indicated by the mobilization to drive out the drug dealers, but with the meeting of 1993 this perspective became more entrenched.

The different stakeholders involved in the process have been pioneers in developing an innovative model that empowers residents. As one of the organizers from the co-operative sector stated, "there was no blue print. Every step had to be created based on existing conversion experiences and accepted practices." A significant outcome of the conversion process was a new model of social housing that combined aspects of the public housing and co-operative housing models. In retrospect the steps taken by the community and supporters to become Canada's first public housing co-operative seem planned and systematic. However, it was the dedication of members of the co-operative housing sector and of key residents that maintained the momentum for the conversion process in the face of numerous obstacles, including bureaucratic inertia in a changing political landscape, and residents who did not always understand the implications of the conversion. In the end the individuals constructed a process that reflected experiences from other conversions that had occurred in mixed-income communities, as well as fundamental community development principles.

4 Formalizing the Conversion Process

The community's desire to convert to a housing co-operative seemed to be a natural development of the level of activity and activism described in the first four key events. Although it appeared that the foundation had been laid, much more work needed to be completed before the provincial and municipal governments would formally recognize the conversion process. Any effort to formalize the community's call for more control required that the residents demonstrate explicit support for the conversion option, shown through a referendum. However, as will be shown in the following key events, a series of additional actors and unanticipated factors had a profound impact on the movement of the conversion process beyond desire to negotiation and then to completion. In this chapter I will describe five key events that followed the community's endorsement of the efforts by the Alexandra Park Residents' Association to purse self-management by converting into a housing co-operative.

Event 5: Community Referendums, 1995 and 1998

The support that the Alexandra Park Residents' Association received at the 1993 community meeting started a new chapter in the community's journey to form Canada's first public housing co-operative. The residents sought to live in a healthier, safer community by ending years of government neglect and ineffective strategies. They decided to seek control over the decision making because of the adverse impact that government decision making was having on their lives and on the community generally. The residents realized that act of becoming a housing co-operative would not result in a decrease of their rents or a significant redesign of the property; however, they believed that greater control over decision-making practices would result in the members feeling a heightened sense of community and greatly improve their quality of life.

Since there were no prior successful cases of converting public housing into a co-operative to follow, the stakeholders were breaking new ground by creating a conversion process that was unique to public housing. According to Tom Clement, executive director of the Co-operative Housing Federation of Toronto, "there was no blueprint that we could follow because this had not been successfully attempted before" (personal communication, 15 June 2000). The stakeholders referred to the experiences of conversions of private properties into co-operatives, and it was decided that holding a community referendum was the appropriate way to gauge the community's support for the conversion (Mark Goldblatt, personal communication, 14 November 1999). As will be described below, the overwhelmingly positive resident response in favour of converting into a housing co-operative represented a turning point in the community's desire for greater control.

Background of the Key Event

The endorsement for the conversion proposal that came from the community meeting in October 1993 was quickly acted upon by the Alexandra Park Residents' Association. The next step was to determine whether there was broader community support for converting into a co-operative, which was accomplished through a referendum. The challenge associated with this step was the lack of financial resources and a blueprint to effectively conduct a comprehensive community consultation process. Whether there would be financial resources was uncertain, but the historic level of community engagement was deemed to be integral to a successful referendum result. The activities preceding the referendum involved substantial efforts by the residents and members of the co-operative housing sector to provide education and training opportunities for all residents. Moreover, it was necessary to appropriately describe how the changes would benefit the community. The referendum represented the first time that public housing residents had been asked to determine the fate of their community. In the APRA's 1993 annual general report, Sonny Atkinson's tone in describing the association's new direction was one of excitement and focus: "The most exciting and challenging task that the Association has undertaken is the Co-op Tenant Self Management. On October 13, 1993 at a meeting, the

Association received community endorsement for the initiative ... [and] is now embarking on intense community consultation and lobbying. We believe there are sufficient responsible, skilled and willing people living here who, given the training, could manage the housing project. It will allow the residents to be in control of the housing project and thereby more able to make it a better place to live" (Alexandra Park Residents' Association, 1993a, 1).

As the statement illustrates, the desire and support was in place to initiate the conversion process; however, the means to gauge the overall support and to conduct extensive community consultations was a source of concern for the association. According to Mark Goldblatt, "we were not sure where the money was going to come from. I had to be paid, as well as anyone else who was to be involved in the process" (personal communication, 14 November 1999). A strategy was developed that involved lobbying government for financial and political support and consulting with the community members about whether they wanted to convert into a co-operative.

Government Lobbying and Initial Negotiations

Although there was a general sense that the community supported the idea of tenant self-management, it was crucial to have government support for the Alexandra Park initiative. Minister of Municipal Affairs and Housing Evelyn Gigantes announced in the Ontario legislature that the community had the ministry's support in principle to begin exploring the tenant self-management option.

> There are many levels of involvement by tenants that are possible within Ontario Housing Corp communities. They range from advisory committees to committees which would actually be given a budget and allowed to make all the decisions for the operation of the community, right through to some suggestions we've had that, in fact, the ownership of the community could change, for example, in the formation of a co-op group.
>
> As I understand it, the Alexandra Park proposal is in the middle range in which tenants would be looking for control of their own budget and decision-making of their own budget. I understand also they have received approval in principle from Metro Toronto Housing Corp [the housing authority] to do that, in which case they have all the clearance they need to go right ahead, work with the Metro Toronto Housing Corp and go ahead and move to the kind of self-management they're talking about. (Gigantes, 1993)

Although the support in principle was in place, there remained uncertainty as to whether the housing authority would work with the community to proceed with the conversion process. Thus, attaining political support involved lobbying for the creation and implementation of a plan for a formal conversion process.

Lobbying efforts were initiated by Sonny Atkinson in a 1994 letter to Minister Gigantes that framed the conversion as a "demonstration project to test the co-op self-management idea" (Atkinson, 1994a). In the letter he requested a meeting with the minister in order to explain the conversion idea and to acknowledge that the community would not be able to take management control without the residents' undergoing extensive educational activities. According to Mark Goldblatt, Sonny Atkinson felt that obtaining the minister's support would add to the momentum for the education process to proceed as well as ensure that the initiative would be taken seriously by the housing authority (personal communication, 14 November 1999). In a separate letter sent to the chair of the housing authority's board of directors, Pat O'Neil, he invited her to begin discussions of the proposed idea, which invitation she accepted (O'Neil, 1994).

Members of the Alexandra Park Residents' Association board met with Evelyn Gigantes on 7 April 1994, at which time approval was reiterated and it was indicated that follow-up would be initiated through the housing authority. The first formal meeting of members of the APRA board and the housing authority occurred on 4 May, and the parameters of the conversion process were agreed upon. This group in effect became known as the working group that was planning towards conversion of the property. According to the minutes of the meeting, a sense of frustration was expressed by the residents over whether the housing authority was planning to work in good faith. Pat O'Neil assured those present that the housing authority was "as anxious to get on with the process as the residents were" (Alexandra Park Residents' Association, 1994a).

Several key issues were identified at the 4 May meeting, including the cost of running and upgrading the project, an assessment of the property, and the way to inform the residents about the option of converting into a housing co-operative. It was deemed that these and other issues would have to be addressed if the conversion was to proceed after the referendum vote. One outcome of this meeting was the formation of a co-operative conversion committee intended to function as a working group of stakeholders. The working group comprised six residents, three community supports, and two representatives of the housing authority. Their role was to review the issues stated above as well as foresee and resolve others that would emerge (Alexandra Park Residents' Association, 1994a).

The next meeting of the working group was held on 19 May. The minutes of the meeting reveal a genuine desire to work as a group in order to see the conversion happen. Ms O'Neil stated: "It was important for both parties to do the terms of reference together, that way no one comes with a pre-decided agenda and no one is upset. It is important to think things through ... [In] the past, several groups have talked about co-op conversion but only Alexandra Park has come forward with a formal and serious proposal. That is why ... [the housing authority] is willing to work on the project with Alexandra Park" (Co-operative Conversion Committee, 1994).

At the meeting several questions were posed by the working group members of the Alexandra Park Residents' Association to the housing authority. The meeting was attended by the co-operative conversion committee with five additional representatives of the housing authority, including the chair of its board of directors, O'Neil (Co-operative Conversion Committee, 1994). Three main issues were discussed: funding of the conversion, the timetable for transferring management, and approval of the Alexandra Park housing project as a pilot project for co-op self-management (Co-operative Conversion Committee, 1994).

During the 19 May meeting the issue of funding the conversion took a significant amount of time. Ms O'Neil informed the group that Minister Gigantes would not support the cost of the conversion, which was estimated at $400,000. The argument was that it was not reasonable to put forward an amount for the entire conversion process since the residents had not had an opportunity to determine whether or not they supported the conversion. In the end, the housing authority's support for the initial consultation process included a smaller figure to reflect the fact that the process was in its early stages. The final sum of $40,000 was proposed by a resident representative and accepted by Ms O'Neil as a realistic amount that could be brought to the ministry for approval. The funds were intended for an education program, which would include hiring an outreach worker and creating written materials for the residents.

The second main issue discussed at the meeting was the necessity of establishing a timetable to move towards the eventual transfer of management responsibilities. The residents expressed the hope that the process would involve one year of negotiations with the housing authority and with the Ministry of Housing. However, Pat O'Neil stated that the timetable suggested by the residents and the housing authority should be flexible in terms of dates since this was a new process for all stakeholders (Co-operative Conversion Committee, 1994).

The third issue was whether the housing authority could provide formal approval for the residents to move ahead with the conversion process. Approval would take the form of designating Alexandra Park as a co-op self-management pilot project. It was not clear what being a pilot project entailed in the longer term. One member present summed up a general concern when he said, "I am not sure what that means," to which the response was, "Designating it as a pilot project implies that it is not being done anywhere else." Approval of the pilot project would be sought at the next board meeting of the housing authority on 21 June 1994.

At the 21 June meeting "a letter was tabled outlining a proposal from the Alexandra Park Residents' Association and requesting funding for outreach purposes" (Metropolitan Toronto Housing Authority, 1994). According to the minutes, the final motions that initiated the conversion process by approving the requested funding read: "[Be it] resolved that staff should work with the Alexandra Park Residents' Association to determine how the funding is to be used. [Be it] resolved further that an agreement between [Metro Toronto Housing Authority] and the Alexandra Park Residents' Association be established, incorporating the funding of $40,000 and the disposition of the funding, to avoid miscommunication and misunderstanding."

Although the amount of $40,000 was approved on 21 June, it would take four months of back-and-forth negotiations before the Alexandra Park Residents' Association actually received the funds to start the consultation process. The delay meant that, in anticipation of the referendum, the community had to rely on resident volunteers and the goodwill of supporters to build momentum in favour of the conversion. The housing authority provided the first draft of an agreement on funding the consultation process on 1 September 1994 (Ministry of the Attorney General, 1994).

The Alexandra Park Residents' Association had concerns with the draft agreement because it removed key aspects of the consultation process, such as hiring a consultant, and included excessive reporting to the interim chair of the housing authority (Atkinson, 1994b). After another two months of exchanges, a final agreement was reached, and the consultation process was initiated. Approval of the $40,000 was the result of successful lobbying by the residents and Mark Goldblatt. The implicit government support for the conversion provided the impetus for moving ahead to develop an education plan for the community consultation process. A date of 22 April 1995 was set for a referendum (Alexandra Park Residents' Association, 1994b), which gave the process a definite time frame.

Community Outreach: Consultation Process and Education Plan

An important part of the agreement between the government and the residents' association was to strategically develop an outreach strategy aimed at providing key information to educate the residents about co-operative living, which included its advantages and disadvantages. An equally vital function was to provide the residents with sufficient details in plain language so that they could make an informed decision in the upcoming referendum (Co-operative Housing Federation of Toronto, October 1994). However, the focus was on the advantages, which became a source of frustration for those residents who had serious concerns about resident self-management.

The outreach strategy involved a series of community development activities that focused on education and training and on encouraging resident participation. An education committee of fifteen people was formed, of which twelve were residents and three were community supporters (Goldblatt, 1994b). The final education plan had the following purpose: "To give all adults living in the 410 units of the Alexandra Park public housing project a detailed explanation of non-profit co-op housing and to provide residents with opportunities to have their questions answered and their concerns and opinions heard about the co-op conversion idea. [The intention was] to reach out to all 410 households and make the information available to all non-English speaking residents. Additionally, the plan was to involve the residents in the planning and implementation of the outreach" (Co-operative Housing Federation of Toronto, 1994).

A co-op consultant and an outreach worker were hired to implement the education plan. According to the plan, the consultant would be the primary resource person for the co-op education project and would be responsible for ensuring the accuracy of the information being disseminated. Mark Goldblatt was hired as the consultant; however, one challenge was that he did not live in Toronto, which meant limited access to his expertise. One of his first actions was to seek out and hire an outreach worker who would inform the residents about co-operative living. According to Goldblatt, "we needed to hire someone but we couldn't touch the existing funds used for community programming because that would compromise the community's ability to sustain existing initiatives, so we had to rely on the $40,000" (personal communication, 14 November 1999). The job description of the outreach worker involved the following responsibilities: "Provide written and verbal information on what is a non-profit housing co-operative and how Alexandra Park would be run differently if it was converted to a non-profit housing co-op. To communicate with residents one on one, in small group meetings (some of which would be in an ethnic language with interpreters) and large group general meetings of the residents" (Goldblatt, 1994a).

Undertaking the outreach effort was complicated and required a variety of resources, including funding and volunteers, both of which the community had been successful in obtaining in the past. Fortunately the promised $40,000 was received by the Alexandra Park Residents' Association in October 1994 (Wright, 1994b), and, using the funds, the association worked closely with Mark Goldblatt to hire Nick Saul to initiate outreach efforts within the community (Alexandra Park Residents' Association, 1994a). Resident volunteers and local support service agencies, such Ryerson Community School and Scadding Court Community Centre, assisted in different community organizing activities. The key message being presented to the residents was that for the first time they were being asked to help determine the future of their community.

Three tasks comprised the overall efforts to organize the community: individual resident outreach, small group information sessions, and community information meetings. Nick Saul developed the outreach plan to educate the residents about the individual and collective benefits of co-operatives, including co-operative philosophy, co-operative governance, and the difference between the policies and practices of co-operatives and those of public housing. Outreach worker Nick Saul stated: "The outreach strategy had to inform residents about the philosophy of co-operatives, as well as about how a co-operative governance structure operates and how co-operatives differ from public housing management. The strategy also had to deal with issues that were important to the residents, such as security of tenure" (personal communication, 10 November 1999).

The first outreach strategy involved residents engaging each other, with Nick Saul providing the required guidance, and he used a variety

of methods including door-to-door canvassing and face-to-face meetings. Tensions were high, and many residents stated that they felt unable
to express their concerns in public meetings for fear of reprisals by their
neighbours. Residents were worried about what the co-operative would
mean in practice. Specific issues included

- fear that the rent would increase,
- fear that their neighbours would be making significant community
  decisions,
- concern that they would have to pay for utilities,
- concern that the board would have access to confidential information,
- concern that they would be required to participate in clean-ups or
  maintenance, and
- concern that they would be forced to move out of the community if
  they did not support the conversion.

The second outreach strategy involved information sessions for small
groups of different residents, with the explicit intentions of informing them
of co-operative living and listening to their concerns about the process.
The sessions targeted the following groups from within the community:
residents who shared a common language other than English,[1] residents
who had not been contacted individually, and residents who had indicated that they wanted more information. An explanation of the governance process and the benefits of belonging to a co-operative was part of
these sessions. Most of the written material was in plain language – non-
technical and jargon free – which helped the residents to understand better the implications of converting into a housing co-operative.

The third outreach strategy consisted of organizing formal meetings
of the entire community with the goal of building mutual understanding of the change process. At these community meetings the Alexandra
Park Residents' Association board was questioned about the process
of conversion. Unfortunately it was difficult for many residents to participate in formal meetings because they were not totally conversant
with the APRA's procedures. Implementation of the strategies took
approximately six months, from November 1994 to April 1995, and
occurred simultaneously in order to build on the questions asked and
the interest shown at each outreach activity. The next section provides
further details of the individual strategies.

During the implementation period, volunteers and local support
service agencies provided assistance with the community organizing

activities. There was great excitement because, as Susan, a resident, stated, "for the first time we were being asked what we wanted to see happen in the community" (personal communication, 19 April 2003). Individual residents expressed various concerns about the notion of community control, ranging from outright support to anger over changes that residents did not perceive as possibly benefiting them. One resident expressed her concerns and support to Nick, as written in his filed notes: "How are we going to make people responsible? Peer pressure? A sense of ownership will mean more respect for space" (Nick Saul, personal communication, 13 September 1994).

Residents felt comfortable enough to express their concerns when they were approached individually; as noted above, many residents stated that they felt unable to express their concerns in public meetings for fear of reprisals by their neighbours. The recurring issues were addressed in a monthly newsletter called *The Alexandra Park Co-operative Times*. It was published in the five main languages spoken at Alexandra Park and had a section for questions and answers. For example, the fear around possible rent increases was addressed in the following statement: "Everyone's rent will continue to be subsidized on the same basis as in the past. This is guaranteed. If, for example, your income goes down because you become unemployed, then your rent will go down" (Alexandra Park Residents' Association, 1995).

In essence, nothing would change with respect to the rents, which left many residents wondering why they should support a change in the first place. This sentiment was shared across many groups in the community, which resulted in a heightened sense of confusion and suspicion among the residents that there was some other agenda driving the conversion process. Owing to the shared nature of the questions and comments expressed by many residents, it was felt that the community was prepared to share its concerns in community-wide information sessions and general meetings.

One of the key functions of the small group information sessions was to inform residents and to listen to their concerns. While there was a clear effort made to hold as many sessions as possible in the first language of the residents (for example, Vietnamese, Chinese, Portuguese, and Somali), non-English residents were also able to attend the English sessions with a family member or friend who could translate.

The previous two strategies targeted individuals and individual language groups, but a more formal gathering was deemed appropriate. In order to achieve the goal of building mutual understanding, several community information meetings were held at which the board of the Alexandra Park Residents' Association was questioned about the process of converting the community into a co-operative.

Residents began to comprehend that if they did not agree with the decisions or actions of the Alexandra Park Residents' Association's board of directors, they could question them. Unfortunately, owing to a lack of understanding of the way in which the APRA operated and of the meaning of living in a co-operative, many residents did not participate; this issue would be a source of the hostilities that would emerge several years later, after the co-op had formed.

Referendum Day

After the organizing efforts were over, the Alexandra Park Residents' Association held a referendum on 22 April 1995 on the question "Do you support Alexandra Park becoming a housing co-op?" I recall that there was a combination of excitement and confusion that day. According to Barbara, "I am not sure what we were voting for because we had what we needed. The problem was the bad people and not the landlord" (personal communication, 19 April 2003). In the end, Barbara and others with similar reservations supported the conversion because they felt "a change was needed." However, some opponents to the conversion chose to remain as tenants of what would become the Co-operative. For example, one long-time resident and former member of the Alexandra Park Residents' Association board was vocal in her opposition to the conversion because she felt that they were not being told the truth about what it meant to live as a co-operative. Repeated attempts on my part to interview this person failed because of her displeasure at the outcome of the referendum. Despite efforts from members of the Co-operative and CHFT, she consistently refused to become a member of the Co-operative for reasons of principle rather than clear evidence of any detrimental impact from the conversion

The referendum was organized by Nick Saul and a group of volunteers. The volunteers consisted of ten outsiders, thirty insiders, eleven poll clerks, and five scrutinizers from the housing authority and local support agencies (Nick Saul, personal communication, 22 April 1995). The volunteers were involved in getting residents out to vote as well as greeting people at the polling stations.

The results of the referendum demonstrated strong support for conversion, with 65 per cent of the eligible households voting and 72 per cent of the voters in favour of becoming a co-operative. This outcome gave the leadership a strong mandate to become a housing co-operative. For many, the result was not surprising; Sonny Atkinson stated that "we knew there was support but it was good to get that in writing" (Alexandra Park Residents' Association board minutes, 19 May 1995). Tom Clement said, "It was a better turnout than what you would get at a federal election" (Tom Clement, personal communication, 20 September 2002). Figure 3 shows those involved in the organizing the community referendum.

Significance of the Key Event to the Conversion Process

The result of the referendum gave the Alexandra Park Residents' Association a strong mandate to negotiate with Metropolitan Toronto Housing Authority to transform the structure of the project into that of a housing co-operative. It is important to note that the original intent of the housing and community supporters of the conversion process was to remove Alexandra Park from the public housing portfolio. As will be shown later, significant compromises had to be made by the co-operative housing sector and the residents in order to see the conversion completed. A key compromise was that the new entity would represent a form of co-operative arrangement that would still maintain a connection to the existing public housing system; Alexandra Park would not become a typical housing co-operative that operated autonomously. While the reason given by the housing authority was that the residents would be relying on some form of government assistance or housing subsidy, the insistence on this compromise represented a lack of faith in the ability of public housing residents to work autonomously.

A number of residents perceived that they would have a greater sense of security of tenure, but it was business as usual within the community. For instance, families were still being evicted or forced to move out of the community if they were over-housed (Eduardo Sousa, personal communication, 16 May 1997). The minutes of the 12 June 1997 meeting of the Alexandra Park Residents' Association board state that government lobbying needed to continue for the protection of existing residents during the conversion process. However, a provincial election was about to be called, and the result was a change in government. There was genuine concern that the conversion idea would never proceed to completion given this change.

In 1995 the political climate in Ontario shifted dramatically, and a Conservative government that was openly hostile to the social housing

Figure 3. Residents and Supporters after the 1995 Referendum. Sonny Atkinson is the sixth person from the left, with Nick Saul to his right. The others, organizers and politicians, include former mayor Barbara Hall in the middle. Image courtesy of Atkinson Housing Co-operative.

system was elected. It immediately cancelled all new non-profit and co-operative housing contracts. The new government's much publicized intentions to "get out of the housing business" (Quarter, 2000) had a significant impact on the Alexandra Park conversion process, including damage to resident morale and the slowdown of initiatives already underway. Many participants viewed the political changes as one of the major factors behind the delays.

The residents' association and the Co-operative Housing Federation of Toronto continued to pursue the conversion and to gain approval from a government that, on the surface, seemed unsympathetic; however, it was still prepared to listen. A letter of 19 December 1995 from the Minister of Municipal Affairs and Housing, Al Leach, to Sonny Atkinson stated that he required a business plan and a budget before approval of the conversion could be given (Atkinson Housing Co-operative, 1996). The letter clearly stated that no financial assistance for development costs would be provided but that staff would be available to assist the community by providing information and directing them to other resources as required (letter from Minister of Housing Al Leach to Sonny Atkinson, 19 December 1995). With the letter in hand, it was clear that the community itself would have to raise the funds, something that did not deter it or the co-operative sector from proceeding (Mark Goldblatt, personal communication, 19 November 1999).

As such, the Co-operative Housing Federation of Toronto and the Alexandra Park Residents' Association decided to go ahead with the conversion process, raising the necessary funds along the way. In seeking to develop and gain approval of a proposal to manage Alexandra Park as a co-operative, the federation and the APRA worked on a plan that had nine elements (Atkinson Housing Co-operative, 1996):

1. The Co-op will follow the basic organization of other non-profit housing co-operatives in Ontario with member meetings, committees, a board of directors, and paid management for day-to-day administration and maintenance.
2. The Co-op will offer co-op membership to every resident over sixteen years of age. Current residents who do not choose to become members will become tenants of the Co-op. Their relationship with the Co-op will be defined by the Tenant Protection Act.
3. The Co-op's units will be targeted to low-income households receiving rent-geared-to-income (RGI) assistance with the exception of "ceiling rents." Ceiling rents will apply when the rent a

household must pay is the same as or more than the market rent for a similar unit in the surrounding neighbourhood.

4. All vacancies in the Co-op will be filled by referrals from the public housing waiting list.

5. The Co-op proposes to lease the land and buildings for forty-nine years at two dollars per year. The lease will set out the operating relationship between the government and the Co-operative including basic standards in areas such as building maintenance. The lease will provide for the property to revert to government management if the Co-op fails to correct a major fault.

6. Before the conversion the Co-op will secure a financial commitment from the government to bring the property up to current standards over the first three to five years of the Co-op's operation.

7. The Co-op will negotiate an operating budget with the public housing authority at the start of each budget year.

8. The Co-op will have its own security plan that will include trained on-call staff who will be on duty when the office is closed.

9. The Co-op will provide continuing education and training for directors and committee members.

Approval in principle was granted by the Ministry of Municipal Affairs and Housing after receipt of the business plan in September 1996 (Atkinson Housing Co-operative, 1996). However, the minister did not commit any funds to support the conversion process.

The next step in the process was to decide on a name for the new co-operative. Both the Alexandra Park Residents' Association and the broader resident population felt that the new entity should not keep the name Alexandra Park, for two reasons: first, there was a federally funded housing co-operative in the area with that name, and, second, they needed to distance themselves from the original landlord. The community decided to have a contest in the summer of 1997 with the dual propose of raising momentum for the conversion and finding a new name. They settled on naming the co-operative after Sonny Atkinson, the long-time president of the Alexandra Park Residents' Association and the leader who had spearheaded the conversion. In December 1997 the community was incorporated under the Co-operative Corporations Act as Atkinson Housing Co-operative.

Following incorporation, the Alexandra Park Residents' Association functioned as the board of Atkinson Housing Co-operative (AHC) until the first election, in November 1999. The new Co-operative board and the Co-operative Housing Federation of Toronto began the next phase of the conversion process, which was to proceed in two parallel ways: one focusing on community development and the other working with the housing authority to create the legal agreements for the conversion. However, progress with the housing authority was minimal, owing largely to the political uncertainty about what to make of the Atkinson Housing Co-operative in light of anticipated changes to the social housing system in Ontario. As a result of this delay, representatives of the housing authority asked for further proof that the residents were still interested in proceeding, causing some of the key participants to feel that this requirement resulted in yet another unnecessary slowdown in the conversion process.

At a press conference at the Alexandra Park Community Centre on 5 June 1998, Minister Al Leach formally announced that the government had approved the conversion plan (Sarick, 1998). However, since it had been three years since the referendum, the board of the residents' association was forced to make sure that the co-op still had the support of the residents. The approach was to provide more education and then vote for or against the co-operative option. In 1998 the Atkinson Housing Co-operative's board, the Co-operative Housing Federation of Toronto, and the Ministry of Municipal Affairs and Housing established the parameters for a second community vote, which was held during the last two weeks of November and the first week of December.

The goal of the second vote, loosely referred to as a referendum, was to engage as many residents as possible and to have them vote. Unlike the first referendum, this vote was not anonymous (which was a concern for some residents) as the outcome was intended to reinforce the community's desire for a change – not to determine whether the conversion should proceed. For residents and community organizers involved in the conversion process, the condition of having a second referendum was unreasonable and demonstrated a surprising lack of faith on the part of the housing authority in how the conversion had proceeded to date. For that reason the community organizers decided just to circulate a petition to individual households, instead of having a vote that would resemble the full-fledged campaign that had occurred in 1996. The petition asked the residents whether or not they supported the conversion option.

The petition was translated into nineteen different languages (Co-operative Housing Federation of Toronto, 2002). Representatives of the co-operative sector and resident volunteers (including the author) went to each household, where a member was given the opportunity to complete a ballot. An independent agent tallied and verified the final count of the petition. Two scrutineers were present at the counting of the ballots, a representative of the Ministry of Municipal Affairs and Housing and a member of Ryerson Community School.

The outcome showed an actual increase in the level of resident support for the conversion. A total of 268 votes (65 per cent of total households) was received. Of these, 213 households (79 per cent) voted in favour of the co-operative conversion, and 52 (21 per cent) voted against, with three spoiled ballots. According to the Co-operative Housing Federation of Toronto (2002), of the 268 households that voted, 122 (45.5 per cent) voted in a language other than English, including Vietnamese, Spanish, Chinese, Somali, and Portuguese. The 79 per cent was a significant achievement for the community, and it provided the necessary fuel to see the conversion process proceed.

Following the second vote, in February 1999 a new working group of key stakeholders was established to develop the legal agreement for the conversion and to create a framework for the process to transfer management responsibility to the residents. The stakeholder working group included government representatives, co-operative sector resource persons, and several resident representatives. The group met for over two years, but with inconsistent representation by the residents and poorly organized meetings, resulting in very little advancement in the conversion process. Its meetings actually introduced more obstacles than impetus to moving the conversion along. Discussions tended to revolve more around how prepared the community was to manage rather than around creating the legal framework. Resident representatives had to prove to their government counterparts that they were able to manage the community, and the group appeared to be negotiating more than working together. In private discussions a government representative expressed difficulty in understanding the differences between the co-operative model and a tenant-management corporation (TMC) (referred to in chapter 3), since the latter would give the residents some decision-making authority while the government retained overall control (Koebel and Cavell, 1995). It is important to note that the tenant-management corporation was the preferred option for the government because the government would continue to have a close association with the community (Cyrus Vakili-Zad, personal communication, 15 November 2001). Consequently, it was difficult to determine how committed the housing authority was to completing the conversion.

An additional challenge emerging at this time was the existence of the two entities, the Alexandra Park Residents' Association and the Atkinson

Housing Co-operative board, both of which had legitimate and legal standing to represent the community. This challenge was highlighted as a potential area for conflict in early correspondence between a co-operative sector lawyer, Bruce Lewis, and Sonny Atkinson (Lewis, 1996). Since 1969 the Alexandra Park Residents' Association had been recognized as the representative body of the residents, and the hope was that the residents who were on the board of the association would also serve as the Atkinson Housing Co-operative board prior to election of the first board of the Co-operative proper. In essence, the Alexandra Park Residents' Association continued to be responsible for the traditional duties as well as the negotiation of an agreement with the housing authority. The added responsibility represented a fundamental change for a resident board that was usually concerned with matters of the community centre.

Once the Co-operative had been incorporated, the areas of responsibility of the APRA and the Co-operative's board were at times unclear because these entities comprised the same people. In 1996 it was decided that they would continue as two separate legal entities, each serving a different purpose, and both supporting the conversion process. As the Alexandra Park Residents' Association had a charitable number, it would be used for fund-raising for the co-operative conversion as well as for programming at the community centre; the AHC board would be responsible for the conversion process and would eventually oversee the Co-operative's operations. This strategy effectively reduced the presence of the Alexandra Park Residents' Association within the community; however, the implicit understanding was that a board of residents who were members of the Co-operative would eventually manage the community centre.

As the conversion proceeded and the issues became increasingly complex, there started to be more confusion among the residents as well as the board members. At this point the Atkinson Housing Co-operative board began to make greater use of committees to do the legwork and inform the board of their recommendations. However, there was great uncertainty with respect to managing the community centre. From the perspective of the residents, the changes created frustration, particularly for those who chose not to be members of the Co-operative but who cared strongly about the centre. Some residents erroneously believed that by choosing to be tenants of the Co-operative, they would not be able to access the community centre; this belief helped to fuel opposition to the conversion process. The confusion would later lead to serious divisions within the community, between the residents who were in favour of the Co-operative and those who were not.

In conjunction with the working group the Co-operative Housing Federation of Toronto and the AHC board initiated a member recruitment drive in 1998. According to the Co-operative Housing Federation of Toronto, the goal was to have 80 per cent of the total households become members, which would have been consistent with the results of the second vote. The federation hired Don Young as the membership coordinator. He was charged with signing up residents as members of the Co-operative and also teaching residents about co-operative living and what the conversion would mean for them. Those residents who resisted becoming members became tenants of the Co-operative (Atkinson Housing Co-operative, 1996).

Event 6: Passing of a Leader and Change Agent – The Death of Sonny Atkinson, 1997

The presence of strong and committed resident leadership was a key feature of Alexandra Park and would become the foundation for the conversion into the Atkinson Housing Co-operative. Sonny Atkinson became synonymous with the community's efforts for control and autonomy, his charisma and passion contributing to various successes that the community enjoyed from the late 1980s onward. Although Atkinson's vision of converting Alexandra Park into a co-operative was eventually realized, sadly he passed away from cancer in 1996 and was not able to participate in the latter stages of the conversion.

Sonny Atkinson's death constitutes a key event because of the impact he had had on the community's development when he was alive. He articulated a vision for the community that included security of tenure and the residents' being treated with dignity. His passing had a profound effect on the community's capacity to proceed with the conversion because of the absence of comparable resident leadership to carry forward his vision. In this sixth case I describe Sonny Atkinson and the impact of his death on the community's efforts to become a co-operative. Unfortunately I was not able to speak with Sonny about the conversion because my role as a researcher began after his death. However, I did know him in my capacity as a resident and as a member of the board. The information described in this case is primarily based on interviews with residents and government officials, with some documentation and participant observation, and is enhanced by my own interactions with Sonny Atkinson.

Background of the Key Event

Sonny Atkinson was born in 1928 in rural Nova Scotia. He moved to Toronto in 1956 and worked as a labourer until his retirement in 1974 at the age of forty-six after an injury (Barnes, 1997). Atkinson was one of the "originals," the second person to move into the Alexandra Park housing project in 1968. He took on different leadership roles in the APRA, including becoming its first president from 1969 until 1971 (Barnes, 1997). His lack of formal education seldom influenced his ability to advocate effectively for the community because supporters would assist him in writing letters and implementing his vision (Faye, personal communication, 19 April 2003).

Atkinson often stated that his purpose was to improve an already strong community and provide a voice for people who often could not speak for themselves (letter to the community from Sonny Atkinson, 8 October 1993). According to a former director of the community centre, Regini Sharma, he "worked 14 to 18 hours a day and was involved in all aspects of running the Community Centre" (Barnes, 1997). Those tasks ranged from managing the affairs of the centre to developing programs that would benefit the residents.

One of Atkinson's priorities was to make sure that the youth had access to opportunities to improve themselves so that living in public housing would not have a negative impact on their future. He believed that the APRA needed to encourage broader youth involvement. According to the March 1989 minutes of the Alexandra Park Residents' Association, Atkinson proposed that one seat on the executive be reserved for a youth member. According to Barbara, one reason for his concern about youth was that two of his children were involved in criminal activities, one being the leader of a notorious gang of bank robbers referred to as the "Dirty Tricks Gang." These first-hand experiences made him want to work with the youth to keep them from leading a criminal life (Faye, personal communication, 14 April 2002).

Sonny Atkinson became the president of the Alexandra Park Residents' Association again in 1991 (Alexandra Park Residents' Association meeting minutes, 25 November 1991). While some presidents only focused on matters internal to the community, Atkinson spent a considerable amount of time building external relationships. For instance, he became the chair of the Residents' Advisory Council of the housing authority in 1994 (Residents' Advisory Council minutes, April 1994) and would regularly give newspaper interviews to discuss his dissatisfaction with management practices (for example see Gadd, 1995). According to Bob Ellis, a former program director of St Christopher House, Atkinson was different from previous presidents in one crucial way: "The leadership was often more isolationist in their approach to programming and advocacy. Having worked with different presidents of the Residents' Association during the 1970s, I felt their focus was understandable, but there were other forces at work that were having a greater impact on the community. Sonny understood the need to go outside the community and get angry. He saw the need to lobby government and he was very good at it" (personal communication, 15 April 2004).

The unique relationships that Atkinson created were seminal to the conversion in that he created a coterie of supporters external to the community. According to Tom Clement, the executive director of the Co-operative Housing Federation of Toronto, it was an early connection with Atkinson, prior to the conversion, that made support of what the residents were trying to do all the more important: "I first met Sonny in 1977 when I was working in Regent Park. I knew who he was because I had heard about him from different individuals, but after meeting him I also got to know the Alexandra Park community better. I used to walk through the project on a daily basis, but it wasn't until I first met Sonny that I got a better understanding of the community." The Co-operative's consultant, Mark Goldblatt, expressed similar sentiments about his interactions with Sonny Atkinson: "I was very impressed with Sonny's ability to bring people together. I found him to be abrasive at times, but he represented the interests of his community, so it is understandable that he came across that way. I had heard of Sonny on other occasions so I thought he was a good person to meet with the idea of changing public housing into co-operatives" (personal communication, 19 November 1999). In an interview the local municipal councillor, Olivia Chow, referred to Atkinson as a "good symbol" that was a crucial "building block" for the conversion process to proceed (Olivia Chow, personal communication, 9 November 2001).

Sonny Atkinson's strength as a leader was his ability to develop, articulate, and act on his vision for improving the community. This vision became the basis for initiating the conversion process, but, more important, Atkinson was able to convince residents and government officials that what he had in mind was the best way forward for Alexandra Park as well as for public housing generally. He believed that under the housing authority's management the community would not improve. In a 2 November 1995 article in the *Globe and Mail*, Sonny

Atkinson stated: "We'd be cutting out the middleman ... I got sick of the hassle and headache. With the [housing authority] the more I fight the less I get ... We've got plumbers here, and roofers and electricians. We've got people who worked in maintenance who got laid off. They need work and self-respect. If you ask people what kind of work they do, and they say, 'I'm on welfare,' that's not good for them. This [co-operative conversion proposal] gives them a title and an earned allowance" (Gadd, 1995, A8).

Atkinson's vision consisted of ways to address poverty and social exclusion. It became his mission to see this vision become a reality through conversion into a housing co-operative. His plan of residents controlling the community decision making can be summarized in four points:

1. Provide employment opportunities for residents
2. Improve management
3. Provide a safe community
4. Improve the quality of life for residents

His leadership style focused on building bridges, and many residents and non-residents held him in high esteem. Other residents found Atkinson to be abrasive and confrontational and expressed their displeasure in interviews, as did Goreete, for example: "He was a man who was paranoid. He constantly expected people to be out to get him. He controlled everything associated with the community centre" (personal communication, 9 June 1999). Residents have also challenged the positive image created about Atkinson because they opposed his approach of advocating for an increased police presence and his support of a zero-tolerance policy for families of drug dealers (Wright, 1994a). Consequently, antagonism with some residents resulted: "People treat him as if he was a god. He wasn't. He was as bad as his kids and he ran the community centre like his own personal bank. He wasn't very nice and was mean to people who disagreed with him. I remember that one day my son was suspected of drugs and he wanted to evict all of us. Now, I am not saying whether my son was guilty or not, but he wanted me to be kicked out, which was not right" (Vera, personal conversation, 10 July 2004). However, most people appreciated Atkinson's good qualities, including his ability to engage and mobilize people and particularly his desire to improve the quality of community life. According to housing advocate and former mayor John Sewell, "Sonny was interesting. Yeah, difficult. Difficult guy, but interesting" (personal communication, 21 January 2002).

On 30 December 1996, Sonny Atkinson died at age sixty-eight from a year-long bout with cancer (Barnes, 1997). With his death, the community lost its primary advocate for the conversion to a co-operative, to the point that it almost jeopardized the conversion process. Cyrus Valkili-Zad, the housing authority's project manager, stated: "I strongly believe that if CHFT was not there when Sonny passed away, this process may have gone in a different direction or tenants may have lost interest. And the mobilization effort that CHFT put in place, I think, I strongly believe, that saved the whole process" (personal communication, 27 November 2001).

It is not insignificant that the housing co-operative that emerged from Alexandra Park was named after Sonny Atkinson. In spite of reservations that people had about his style of leadership, nobody questioned that Sonny Atkinson was the driving force behind the creation of the Co-operative and that without his energy and vision the conversion would not have reached first base. The Atkinson Housing Co-operative board minutes of 12 March 2001 formally recognized Sonny Atkinson's contribution, and by then his legacy was well established.

Significance of the Key Event to the Conversion Process

Since the inception of the Alexandra Park Residents' Association there have been four different presidents. As such, from 1969 to 1997 there was continuity in the leadership and an institutional memory within the association. There were no elections between 1991 and the Atkinson board elections in 1999; Sonny Atkinson was the last elected president of the Alexandra Park Residents' Association. His death marked the end of an era of strong, knowledgeable leadership within the community. The conversion process proceeded apace, and Sonny's absence was softened by third-party organizations – particularly the Co-operative Housing Federation of Toronto, which took an increased role and in effect became in loco parentis. Without this external support following Sonny Atkinson's death, it is possible that the conversion, which was becoming increasingly complex, would not have proceeded.

There was no shortage of people wanting to become the president of both the Alexandra Park Residents' Association and the AHC board of directors. However, the community seemed to lack individuals who were experienced, committed, and connected to the conversion in a way that was comparable to Sonny Atkinson's dedication. After his death there were four different presidents, and each had lived in the community for less than ten years; two of these individuals have since moved out of the community. Subsequent leaders had different approaches to working with the community, but they did not have the same connection or history with it as had Sonny. Don Young, the former membership coordinator hired by the Co-operative Housing Federation of Toronto, stated: "Well, you know, Sonny is legendary. I mean, anybody who is spending 16, 17 hours a day working here, you know, there's going to be some sort of a vacuum when that person is no longer around to do that. I mean, the people who followed were serious but they weren't spending 16 or 17 hours a day at it" (personal communication, 16 November 2001).

The frequent changes in leadership resulted in a loss of institutional memory and the vision that was required to complete the conversion process. As a result, there was an increased reliance on third parties and less collaboration among the residents. A challenge that the third parties had to face was re-establishing and sustaining the social capital in the form of trust of the new leadership, and each new leader had to learn about the process in a short span of time. These challenges demonstrated a lack of capacity within the community, a lack that had been hidden behind Sonny Atkinson's charisma.

One explanation for the impact of Sonny Atkinson's death was that he had consolidated power and ideas within his office, which made it very difficult for others to learn from him or to see his vision through. According to Pat Fletcher, a former community development worker hired by the Co-operative Housing Federation of Toronto to assist in the second community vote, the change in leadership provided the community with a unique opportunity to encourage new leaders to emerge: "I think Sonny was a character, and it would be impossible for anybody to fill his boots ... It would have been difficult for anybody to follow in those footsteps, and maybe it wasn't even right. You know, there's only one Sonny. I think it was a tough position to follow. But it also definitely needed change from then on, and I think the personalities were very different. I think sharing that load was important at the top, and it needed something new and different. But I think yes, it [his death] was bound to have created somewhat of a vacuum because he kept such a strong hold, you know" (personal communication, 21 November 2001).

Following Sonny Atkinson's death, the new leadership made efforts to improve their knowledge base because they believed in the community. According to Terry Skelton, the housing authority's acting director for Community and Tenant Services, his death was a huge loss, but following upon it there was a new and different dynamic occurring in the community.

> There was a big down when Sonny Atkinson passed away because he had such a huge vision, and it was wonderful that his vision lived on. He had spread that wide and far enough that people had it, and they just needed to kind of regroup and move on. And I think that that's a constant effort in communities such as ours. And that's a strong community. That's a strong community, but it still needs constant sharing of information, inviting of participation, making it easy for people to participate, helping them to grow intellectually, you know, all those kinds of things. And the more people you have involved, the lighter the load, so to speak – by the better chance for people to gain skills they need to take on the roles, small roles, big roles, whatever, as the program moves forward. But I think, what I've seen is a strong group of people that regrouped. (Terry Skelton, personal communication, 16 November 2001)

Both Pat Fletcher and Terry Skelton foresaw the potential of leadership within the community, a leadership that was younger and innovative; however, the regrouping following Sonny Atkinson's death did not proceed as smoothly as one would have hoped. The conversion process was complicated, so the new leaders reverted to the one common denominator that was tangible for the community – the operation of the community centre. This preoccupation with the community centre would initiate a type of discourse within the community that caused divisions and very nearly derailed the conversion process.

Completing the Conversion Process

In November 1999 the Co-operative's board of directors became the legal entity responsible for developing an operating agreement with the housing authority as well as taking on APRA's responsibility for managing the community centre. At times, the different responsibilities caused numerous conflicts among the board of directors. As will be shown, these conflicts had an impact on APRA's ability to sustain momentum for the length of time required to complete the co-operative conversion. For these reasons it became more urgent that there be a stable board that would be able to dedicate the time needed for the directors to learn their responsibilities and have the opportunity to demonstrate their capacity to eventually oversee the Co-operative. During this time the board established an organizational structure that was intended to be transparent and accountable to the members. One of the key decisions was to establish a committee structure in order to open up opportunities for members and some non-members to participate in the conversion process. Nevertheless, some tenants expressed concerns about not being able to participate in decision making, because there was a perception that their views were not considered significant enough to warrant attention.

As in most co-operatives, committees provide advice to the board of directors and also serve as a pool of volunteers for necessary activities. It was clear that the committees were charged with advising the board on issues and making recommendations. With assistance from the Co-operative Housing Federation of Toronto shortly after the 1999 elections, the board established two types of committees – standing and special. In 2000 there were six standing committees, each of which had a clear job description:

1. Rehab/Maintenance and Finance Committee
2. Parking and Security Committee
3. Welcoming and Member Education Committee
4. Landscape Committee
5. Alexandra Park Community Centre Committee
6. Newsletter Committee

Throughout the conversion process four special committees were established:

1. Co-operative Conversion Committee
2. Hiring Committee
3. Transfer Review Committee
4. Constitutional Committee

An individual liaison from each committee was appointed by the board to ensure that information was being transmitted. The liaison was responsible for bringing forward the recommendations of the committee and, where necessary, would request that a motion or letter be written regarding some issue. In all instances, the Co-operative Housing Federation of Toronto was instrumental in working with each of the committees and board liaisons in order to deal with the necessary matters in an organized fashion.

Despite this formal structure, one that was designed to facilitate communication, at times conflicts took over entire board meetings. The board tended to get bogged down in detailed decisions that should have been left to committees. For example, a conflict arose because the cutting of the bushes in front of the community centre was approved by the Parking and Security Committee, but such a decision was actually the responsibility of the Landscape Committee. The conflict subsequently dissipated, but it became clear that the committees had to communicate not only with the AHC board but also with each other.

Some members expressed disappointment with the level of participation in committees, but, in general, the committees were very successful in working within their individual mandate. Several indicators of success included an increase in community consultation; more residents voicing concerns in a constructive manner; a decrease in the use of valuable board time to discuss the details of particular issues; and increased awareness of the role of the committees in the community.

Creating the Community By-laws

Atkinson Housing Co-operative is different than most housing co-operatives in that all tenants and members pay on a rent-geared-to-income basis, and the housing authority continues to have significant input in the budget approval process. This posed a challenge in the conversion process. Nevertheless, as with other housing co-operatives, the members have increased control over their community through the creation and implementation of by-laws that set out the conditions for living in the community. The first by-law to be established was the organizational by-law that outlined the rules for membership, election procedures, and evictions, among others. Mark Goldblatt, and later the Co-operative Housing Federation of Toronto, worked with the board of directors to establish this by-law.

The first full meeting of the Co-operative, held in November 1999, saw the membership approve the organizational by-law and the Co-operative become a functional entity. The next step was to develop an occupancy by-law, a document that is similar to a lease in that it outlines the standards by which members are to abide in order to reside in the Co-operative. The process of establishing the occupancy by-law was similar to that of the organizational by-law; that is, members were able to put forward changes prior to its approval. A proposed occupancy by-law was developed by the membership coordinator and the board of directors, and the document was presented for discussion and approval to the membership at a community meeting in April 2000.

The community meeting was attended by the Co-operative's lawyer, Bruce Lewis, who answered questions about the occupancy by-law and the implications of any proposed changes. One of the main changes involved the occupancy size of a household. This was a concern because the housing authority's policies stated that two children, regardless of their age, must share a bedroom as long as they are of the same sex, whereas in most co-operatives the occupancy standard is one person per room. The amendment to the occupancy size reflected the co-operative standard, and the revised by-law was subsequently adopted by the membership in the fall of 2000. This was the first occasion on which the community was able to witness first-hand how open and transparent co-operative decision making could be. Since that time, other by-laws have been developed by the community with the advice of the Co-operative Housing Federation of Toronto on areas that include conflict of interest; spending; maintenance improvement and parking; arrears; and subsidies. Approval of the new by-laws followed the same process as that of the occupancy by-law, which ensured continuity of practice and resident engagement.

The Final Operating Agreement

The conversion presented many challenges for all the stakeholders. For example, the housing corporation, Metropolitan Toronto Housing Corporation – previously referred to as the housing authority – wanted to be assured that the model would be cost-effective, while the Atkinson Housing Co-operative (AHC) was primarily concerned that the residents to have control over decision-making practices as with most housing co-operatives. An operating agreement between AHC and the housing corporation was considered a method to deal with the differences between the two models, since the property was not going to be sold to the residents and such an agreement was the best way to account for the stakeholders' interests. The AHC board worked with its legal counsel and the Co-operative Housing Federation of Toronto to develop an operating agreement, which was then submitted to the housing corporation. However, it took almost two years for the housing corporation to submit a counterproposal to the AHC board. Many felt that this was an unnecessary delay.

The final agreement outlined the expectations of the two parties by laying out the obligations that the Co-operative had with the housing corporation and vice versa. The document was created according to four principles that established the relationship between them.[2] The first principle was that the community must have an associated resource group (for example, the Co-operative Housing Federation of Toronto) to provide it with key support and capacity-building resources. The second principle states that the housing corporation has the right to establish the rent ceilings, or the rent cap. The third principle outlines the selection process by which new tenants would be chosen from the centralized waiting list of the housing authority; future residents of AHC would be required to become a member of the Co-operative. Some residents raised the requirement of mandatory membership for new residents as an area of concern during the process. The fourth and final principle relates to the establishment of a budget and the generation of revenue. A budget would be negotiated with the housing corporation on an annual basis. The revenue is generated from rents, rental subsidies, and the small fees associated with parking and laundry. The revenues and expenses are monitored by both the Co-operative and the housing corporation on a monthly basis.

Although the four principles established the legal framework for the conversion, as a result of the final document AHC is atypical in that it does not retain the key elements of autonomy enjoyed by other co-operatives; this means that AHC is more akin to a hybrid than the co-operative model per se (Sousa and Quarter, 2005). Important differences include the budget approval process, the sources of revenue, and the existence of a capital reserve fund, as described in the next two sections.

The Budget Approval Process and Sources of Revenue

The operating budget makes a distinction between operating and fixed expenses. Operating expenses (for example, staff and maintenance costs) are those that can be controlled by the Co-operative. Fixed expenses are those beyond the control of the Co-operative, such as realty taxes and utilities. The annual budget negotiation involves a discussion about what constitutes an operating and a fixed expense. While in most housing co-operatives the bulk of the revenue comes from two main sources, namely subsidy top-ups and rental income,[3] Atkinson has access to the same revenue sources that it had when it was a public housing project.

However, because of the 100 per cent rent-geared-to-income require-ment the Co-operative's ability to rely on rental income is limited and can vary from month to month. Furthermore, the Co-operative cannot establish the market rent levels needed to meet expenses, which is a common practice in housing co-operatives.

The revenue requirements for operating expenses are estimated based on the previous year's budget and provincially approved bench-marks. The Co-operative collects the monthly rents and receives subsi-dies at the end of the fiscal year. A "pass-through" process was adopted as the mechanism for addressing the way in which the fixed expenses would be paid: the housing corporation[4] provides the revenue for all of the fixed expenses, such as realty taxes, in addition to the subsidy for operating costs. Consequently, the housing corporation determines the Co-operative's overall operational revenue amount and has input into deciding what is a fixed expense. However, the Co-operative can ultimately dictate the amount that will be spent on a certain item, for example the services of a security company.

Establishing a Capital Reserve Fund

Housing co-operatives normally have a capital reserve fund, which is replenished annually from rents and other sources of revenue, in order to finance rehabilitation and maintenance. However, in Ontario (and likely other jurisdictions) individual public housing projects do not maintain a capital reserve fund; typically, capital replacements for public housing in Ontario have been funded on an annual basis through a modernization and improvement budget sustained by a housing authority. In public housing projects the capital priorities are managed for the entire system, with requests coming from property managers. The fact that there are no reserves and the stock is ageing is a problem for all public housing properties in Canada. In the case of Atkinson, the property is over forty years old, and an assessment conducted by residents and co-operative sector representatives prior to completion of the conversion found that a significant amount of repairs would be required for many years to come. In fact, a whole set of row houses required new roofs in 2005. At the time, members of the co-operative housing sector believed, almost prophetically, that without a capital reserve Atkinson would have to compete with other public housing projects for the same resources whenever capital renewal was required. As will be described in the afterword, in recognition of the deteriorating property the Co-operative and the housing corporation have been developing a plan to revitalize the property fully, which will include replacing all the townhouses.

Event 7: Election of the Alexandra Park Residents' Association's Board of Directors, 2001

The final two key events describe significant developments that occurred in the conversion process. During this period of time, education and training became integral to the community's work with the housing authority to negotiate an agreement for the eventual transfer of management authority to the residents. However, divisions and conflict started to emerge within the community and contributed to delays in the completion of the conversion process. A partial resolution of the divisions was a significant contributor to the final agreement between the housing authority and Atkinson Housing Co-operative.

A group of residents mobilized in July 2001 and called for the removal of the responsibility for managing the community centre from the Atkinson Housing Co-operative board. As a direct challenge to the board, a new Alexandra Park Residents' Association board was elected on 15 October 2001, with the sole responsibility of managing the community centre. From 1995, following the incorporation of Atkinson Housing Co-operative, through to 2001 the members of each board had been the same people. The election resulted in the two boards comprising different individuals and working independently of each other. An unexpected outcome of the election was that some residents began to question openly whether the new co-operative would be inclusive of all members and tenants. The election constitutes a key event because it revealed sharp divisions within the community and also demonstrated limitations in membership education and training strategies. In this event, I describe how the two different boards of directors were formed and how they operated within the community. In order to make it easier to see the differences between the two boards, I use the term *board* to refer to the combined Alexandra Park Residents' Association and Atkinson Housing Co-operative board; otherwise, I refer specifically to a particular board.

The first election of Atkinson Housing Co-operative's board of directors, in November 1999, was organized by the Co-operative Housing Federation of Toronto. In order to vote, members of the co-op had to demonstrate residency and membership. As a result of this vote, the APRA's former mandate of working on behalf of all residents was at risk of not being achievable since only members of the Co-operative were allowed to vote, which represented a portion of the community at the time. For some residents, the interests of the non-members were perceived as a lower priority, which upset those who had chosen not to become members of the Co-operative. This situation would later exacerbate the divisions emerging within the community and seriously undermine the conversion.

The Atkinson Housing Co-operative board originally had fourteen members, the same number as had the Alexandra Park Residents' Association board. This number was larger than that of most co-operative boards but was preferred under the organizational by-law approved by the membership. The term in office was set at two years, with seven directors being elected every year.[5] After the first year one of the main challenges was achieving a quorum at board meetings, the lack of which often delayed the business of the community. As a result, in 2000 the board recommended a decrease in its size from fourteen to eleven.

The plan for the conversion process was that a new Atkinson Housing Co-operative board would replace the Alexandra Park Residents' Association board as the sole representative body. An objective of the conversion plan was to integrate the responsibility for managing the community into the evolving co-operative structure. The fate of the community centre became a key issue for residents. Losing the Alexandra Park Residents' Association was equated by some residents to a lessening of accountability for decisions regarding the community centre's programming. There were also doubts as to whether making the Atkinson board the primary governing body in the community would lead to the greater overall accountability called for by the residents.

Concerns about the loss of the Alexandra Park Residents' Association were compounded by the domination of a single ethnocultural group – Muslims – on the Atkinson Housing Co-operative board of directors. Historically, the residents had not had to grapple with the ethnocultural differences within the community; the resentment towards the leaders who were Muslim was a new phenomenon. Based on informal conversations with various individuals, the concerns were particularly vocal following the 11 September 2001 attacks on the World Trade Center in New York. As a result of these ethnocultural divisions, the conversion process suffered and there were doubts about whether the conversion could be completed.

One outcome of reconstituting the Alexandra Park Residents' Association was the increased awareness of divisions among the residents.

The divisions reflected differences of not ethnic background but also religion and culture. Some residents started to confront each other in potentially destructive ways. According to one resident, "you could walk into a room and feel that people don't like you because of the colour of your skin or for what you're wearing" (Safire, personal communication, 20 November 2001). Over the years many residents had experienced intolerance from each other and from outside the community, but this was the first time that the intolerance and conflict had manifested in such a public way.

Prior to the completion of the conversion, Alexandra Park was very diverse in terms of citizenship and ethnicity; this diversity was one of its key features and a characteristic observed generally in public housing in Toronto. According to a survey conducted by the Metropolitan Toronto Housing Authority (1995), the distribution of the residents by age shows that there was a relatively high concentration of young children and youth, who made up 38 per cent of the population. Over half of the residents (51 per cent) were between nineteen and fifty-nine years of age, and only about 11 per cent were sixty years or older. A Metropolitan Toronto Housing Corporation survey (MTHC, 2001a) revealed a community that was home to families of different sizes. For instance, 332 families made up 81 per cent of the households, while seniors accounted for 10 per cent of the households, and singles and childless couples 9 per cent. While such a heterogeneous population is not uncommon within social housing communities, particularly in large public housing projects in Toronto (Murdie, 1992), such a reality does present many challenges to the building of a common message, the message of residents' gaining control over the decisions that directly affect their lives. It is my belief that the fact that the community was not homogeneous makes the story of this conversion process all the more compelling

While a number of tensions can be attributed to ethnocultural differences, these tensions were exacerbated by the elections to the Atkinson Housing Co-operative board. For example, a number of people felt that block voting (perceived to be based along ethnic and cultural lines) had occurred. Therefore, some residents simply decided that it was pointless to stand for election if they were not from a particular segment of the community, and they therefore withdrew from the community's political process. No one was prepared for these divisions, and the training and education provided by the Co-operative Housing Federation of Toronto did not anticipate such problems.

Background of the Key Event

The community centre has been a source of pride for the residents, both as the focal point of resident involvement and activism and as the one tangible area where residents can exercise significant control over decisions. Resident involvement in the centre demonstrated that a group of residents had the capacity to manage a community-based organization, and helped to legitimize the call for greater control in the management of the community itself (Tom Clement, personal communication, 20 September 2002).

The incorporation of the Atkinson Housing Co-operative resulted in the existence of two resident boards. At the time, both boards were led by Sonny Atkinson; this overlap was not questioned because the community trusted him, and the arrangement was functional until his death in 1997. However, the two boards created an extra layer of complexity for which the stakeholders were not prepared. Bruce Lewis, the Co-operative's lawyer, foresaw that there could be difficulties: "I am concerned that the Community Centre will have a separate board and be separately incorporated, but be appointed by the board of the co-op. It is not necessarily simple to do this. However, these are mainly legal technicalities, so we should discuss how that will be done. The main concern would be not to jeopardize the charitable status" (Lewis, 1996).

The issue raised by Lewis was resolved by maintaining the status quo whereby the Alexandra Park Residents' Association would be used for fund-raising purposes and managing the community centre, and the Atkinson Housing Co-operative board would pursue the conversion (Mark Goldblatt, personal communication, 9 November 2000). A key feature of this plan was that the two entities were to be made up of the same people. The actual working of these two entities was made possible by the division of each board meeting into two sections, one for issues facing the community centre and the other for issues dealing with the co-operative conversion. The maintenance of two entities for different purposes was consistent with the natural progression of events, but as the conversion process progressed, a key issue became the community centre's management.

What the lawyer deemed to be a legal technicality became a significant issue for the community, one that was not formally addressed in the education and training activities (Don Young, personal communication, 9 November 2002). The education and training did not focus exclusively on community centre managers making the transition to co-operative managers. Instead, the aim was to establish a new system of governance that involved more than overseeing a community centre (Mark Goldblatt, personal communication, 9 November 2000). However, there was great uncertainly about what would happen once the conversion had been completed, namely, whether the community would support the management of the community centre by the Co-operative's board. This was compounded by the belief that the community centre was being neglected in favour of the conversion process (Atkinson Housing Co-operative, 1999). By the spring of 2001 a group of residents had started to voice concerns that combination of the two boards would mean the end of APRA and an uncertain fate for the community centre (Annette, personal communication, 4 April 2001).

The residents' concerns were exacerbated because funding to the community centre had declined since 1997, and this had negatively impacted the availability of community programs (Alexandra Park Residents' Association, 1999). Some staff members had been laid off and others had quit (Alexandra Park Residents' Association, 1999). For example, the community centre director, who had been very involved in the 1995 referendum, resigned in 1997 because there was no stable funding available to support her position (Alexandra Park Residents' Association, 1999). As a result, the centre was without on-site supervision from 1997 to 1999 (Alexandra Park Residents' Association, 1999). During that period, volunteers (including the author) helped to supervise a few programs, but there was only one funded program and the person administering it was also in charge of operating the centre (Alexandra Park Residents' Association, 1999).

After two years of reduced programming, perceived inaction of the Alexandra Park Residents' Association, and the loss of the community centre funding (owing to loose accounting practices and absent supervision), two members of the board of directors sought to increase the association's presence in the community by improving the status of the community centre. In the summer of 1999 the board's president, Desmond Wilson, attempted to rebuild the community centre's prominence (Alexandra Park Residents' Association, 1999). The board addressed this problem by working with the City of Toronto to develop a strategic plan.

Desmond Wilson and I met with the City of Toronto's Community Services Grants Division on 8 September 1999 to negotiate a plan to reinstate withdrawn or held-back funds. City of Toronto staff highlighted several organizational problems as being barriers to improving the centre's funding base (Desmond Wilson, personal communication,

19 July 1999). The main obstacle facing the board was the absence of reliable financial systems within the community centre, a problem stated in a management letter from the auditors in 1998 (Alexandra Park Residents' Association, 1999). The meeting resulted in the community receiving $14,000 from the Community Services Grants Division to hire a community development worker who would create an organizational strategy for the community centre. An additional condition was that AHC work with a third-party trustee and with city officials to develop transparent financial accounting systems (Alexandra Park Residents' Association, 2000). Janet Fitzsimmons was hired in January 2000 to develop a strategic plan, and she was also given the broader responsibility of managing the community centre (Alexandra Park Residents' Association, 2000).

Following the first election of the board of directors for the Atkinson Housing Co-operative, a governing structure was now in place, one comprising individuals who could represent the legal entity during the conversion process. However, this structure did not include a formal group, such as an executive committee, to manage the community centre. Consequently, the new board of directors formally assumed many of the APRA's responsibilities, including the management of the community centre. These new tasks in combination with bringing the conversion to completion were daunting for an inexperienced group of residents, but there was hope that the community centre would be the hub for co-operative education in the same way that it had been a gathering place for residents, and would continue to hold a special place in the hearts of the community (Olivia Chow, personal communication, 24 October 2001). Thus, greater attention had to be given to managing the community centre. According to board minutes for the Alexandra Park Residents' Association (2000), a new approach was introduced under the agenda item "New Organization for Alexandra Park Residents' Association Board." The proposal called for a committee to assume managerial responsibility of the community centre: "The loss of funding and departure of the Centre's Executive Director meant a significant reduction in its activities. The Board for the Centre has been the same as the Board for the Co-op but has been pre-occupied with the formation of the Co-operative and has not had sufficient time to deal with the revitalization of the Centre. Jorge proposed the establishment of a separate Board, or special Committee for the Centre, which would report on its activities. The Committee would be composed of some Directors from the Co-op, plus volunteers from the community appointed by the Atkinson Board."

The new Community Centre Committee had two primary objectives: first, to reduce distractions for the Atkinson board of directors so that they could focus on matters related to the conversion; and, second, to maintain a connection between the board and the operations of the community centre. With these objectives, the board accepted a new model of staff supervision. The Community Centre Committee, reporting to every board meeting, was asked to review the APRA's constitution and "make recommendations for amending it to comply with this reorganization" (Alexandra Park Residents' Association, 2000).

The committee was very successful in managing the community centre, but it was never able to review the Alexandra Park Residents' Association's constitution because so much time was spent on the operations of the centre (Atkinson Housing Co-operative, 2000). The hope of formally integrating the task of managing the community centre into the co-operative structure was problematic because of the potential risk to the community centre's charitable status, the latter being an important tool to fund-raise for the community centre and for the co-operative conversion. A special committee that was struck by the Atkinson Housing Co-operative board on 23 March 2000 met with the Co-operative's lawyer to develop a strategy and discuss options for dealing with this issue. Again, the outcome was to maintain the status quo until a community meeting could be held to get a general direction with respect to the future of the Alexandra Park Residents' Association (Bruce Lewis, personal communication, 19 April 2000). That meeting was never held because of subsequent issues emerging within the community, issues that will be described below.

Over the following three months a committee structure emerged that seemed to be accomplishing the goal of focusing more board meeting time on the essential issues related to the conversion process. However, the board enthusiastically took on the role of overseeing the Community Centre Committee, and an unintended outcome was that the committee's reports dominated the board's meeting time, particularly in dealing with the relationship between the board and the community centre staff. In December 2000 the issue of board's micro-management forced the coordinator to resign her position, and she expressed concern that much of the work that had been accomplished was being damaged (personal conversation, 16 November 2000). Furthermore, the president, Desmond Wilson, was reducing his role in the community, which meant that the coordinator lost a key ally on the board.

The board accepted her resignation and hired a new coordinator in January 2001. Alina Chatterjee was responsible for improving fund-raising and increasing the number of programs, and she was very successful in meeting those goals (Atkinson Housing Co-operative, 2001a). For example, the Ontario Trillium Foundation approved a $300,000 grant over three years, essentially guaranteeing the operations of the community centre for that period. However, the funds were contingent on the establishment of responsible and transparent systems of accounting (Ontario Trillium Foundation, letter, April 2001), which meant changing the culture of micromanagement that had led to the resignation of the previous coordinator (Alina Chatterjee, personal communication, 18 September 2002).

Alina Chatterjee started to encounter incidents of micromanagement and questionable expenditures that were consistent with those experienced by previous coordinators. She asked Latchman Ramkhalawan, who was the president of the Alexandra Park Residents' Association following the departure of Desmond Wilson, to intervene (Chatterjee, 2001). A letter sent by Latchman Ramkhalawan to the board outlined three problem areas that needed to be improved in order for the community centre to function productively: directors' negative statements about the daily operations, a tendency to micromanage these operations, and direct interference in ongoing programs (Ramkhalawan, 2001a).

The board agreed that the problems were distracting the staff, and it supported Alina's strategies to improve the community centre (Atkinson Housing Co-operative, 2001b). The president sent a letter to the staff that clearly acknowledged strong support for their work and stated that there would be changes to the relationship with the board (Ramkhalawan, 2001b). These actions were intended to resolve the outstanding issues, with the hope that the focus could return to the conversion process. However, board members, including the president, continued to be too involved in the managing of the community centre.

At a meeting on 26 June 2001 a member of the board expressed concerns that the actions approved on 29 May were not being followed by President Ramkhalawan himself (Burnette, 2001). The meeting went in camera, under the pretence that the Alexandra Park Residents' Association board was now meeting to address these "internal issues." The outcome was the transfer of responsibilities for the community centre from the Atkinson Housing Co-operative board to a re-established the Alexandra Park Residents' Association executive (minutes of the AHC board, 26 June 2001). At this point the community again had two separate boards.

A key concern was that the very same people whom many residents saw as the source of the problems appointed themselves to the executive of Alexandra Park Residents' Association. For instance, the president of Atkinson Housing Co-operative appointed himself as the president and supervisor of the staff of the community centre. For a number of residents, this was unacceptable because of his micromanaging style and the allegations of fraud that had started to surface against him (Atkinson Housing Co-operative, 2001c).

The conflict surrounding the operation of the community centre climaxed on 23 July 2001 when thirty residents mobilized and called for changes to the management of the community centre. Interestingly, residents had seldom attended board meetings prior to that evening. The group called for an end to the micromanagement style of the board (Atkinson Housing Co-operative, 2001d). The issue that precipitated the mobilization was the 19 July resignation of a long-time staff member of the community centre because of an argument with the president of Atkinson Housing Co-operative (Atkinson Housing Co-operative, 2001d).

Residents also called for an improved system of accountability and representation by Atkinson Housing Co-operative's board. Further, they insisted on reconstituting the Alexandra Park Residents' Association as the sole governing body of the community centre. The association was reconstructed with a mandate to manage the community centre on behalf of the entire community, that is, both members and non-members. However, the residents were unsure of the way to commence the process of restarting the APRA.

The Co-operative Housing Federation of Toronto became involved in the process by working with representatives of the new, interim APRA board and with the AHC board in the form of a joint committee. The federation provided assistance through Don Young, the membership coordinator. The joint committee consulted with the community over a period of two months to create a new constitution for Alexandra Park Residents' Association. The first draft combined elements of its original constitution and the Co-operative's organizational by-laws, such as term limits for positions on the association board and specific executive responsibilities. The constitution was presented and approved at a community meeting on 19 September 2001. The draft outlined the association's aims and objectives as follows (Alexandra Park Residents' Association, 2001a):

1. Manage the Alexandra Park Community Centre
2. Further better community relations in the neighbourhood

3. Further a good sound relationship with the housing authority, Atkinson Housing Co-operative, or any successor
4. Provide social, recreational, and education activities for the community

Most important, the constitution pushed for a separation between the two governing bodies: "Anyone serving on the co-op board cannot serve on the Alexandra Park Residents' Association board at the same time but can volunteer on Alexandra Park Residents' Association committee; and anyone serving on the Alexandra Park Residents' Association board cannot serve on the co-op board at the same time but can volunteer on co-op committees" (Alexandra Park Residents' Association, 2001a).

Preventing any overlap between members of the Atkinson Housing Co-operative board and the Alexandra Park Residents' Association was a slap in the face to the former but was seen by residents as a legitimate response to ongoing concerns.

Election and Surfacing Divisions

The election for the new Alexandra Park Residents' Association board was held on 15 October 2001. I was asked to chair the meeting, an invitation that I promptly accepted. Twenty supporters and 162 voting members attended the meeting; the attendance was much larger than at any community meeting to date, including the community meeting in 1993. During the evening there were two different votes: the first for the full board, and the second for the executive committee. For the full board there were ten positions available and twenty-one candidates, and each had an opportunity to speak to the audience.

According to the returning officer, there were 162 registrations, 158 ballots cast, and 4 spoiled ballots (Alexandra Park Residents' Association, 2001b). By the end of the evening there was a new Alexandra Park Residents' Association board and executive committee, the composition of which was perceived as being much more diverse than that of the Atkinson Housing Co-operative board.

A problem, however, was that the new Alexandra Park Residents' Association board lacked the resources and training to proceed with the business of managing the community centre. The Co-operative Housing Federation of Toronto offered assistance in the form of training because it saw that the lack of experience facing the new board would have an impact on the conversion process (Tom Clement, personal communication, 20 September 2002). However, most of the support was declined as the board wanted to begin on its own terms and be separate from the co-operative conversion.

As an unfortunate outcome of the elections, the ethnic and cultural divisions within the community became much more apparent in people's actions. Some of these divisions reflected antagonism towards those of different racial backgrounds but were also compounded by religious and cultural differences. The divisions were often glossed over during the conversion process because it was an uncomfortable topic for some of the organizers, while others hoped they could be attended to once the conversion process had been completed.

The divisions also contributed to significant misattributions that were highly prejudicial. There was an ongoing perception that the Atkinson Housing Co-operative board had an over-representation of those who self-identified as Muslims or who were persons of colour. This was an accurate description of the members of the Co-operative's board; however, the belief that this group had a hidden agenda was never proven and, to be frank, was quite racist. The underlying assumption, directed at the Atkinson board, was that a single group wanted to take over the community centre and was making it impossible for anyone outside of that group to be involved. After repeated attempts to interview residents with questions regarding intolerance, it was clear that this topic left many people nervous. In a personal conversation with the author, the former community centre coordinator stated, "There was the idea that there was block voting, and being on the Atkinson Housing Co-operative board became a popularity contest rather than for people who would be qualified or committed to being involved" (Alina Chatterjee, personal communication, 3 August 2001).

It was suggested by various sources that these problems had been brewing for many years, but residents claim to have lacked an outlet through which to address concerns around the co-operative conversion and about the community centre in general. Another concern was that the board was never really accountable to the membership. According to one resident, "they did what they wanted with the community centre. What's to prevent the same from happening with the co-op?" (Shane Bartraw, personal communication, 15 February 2002). In order for the residents to trust the process once again, they needed to be convinced that checks and balances existed within the new co-operative structure. According to Don Young, "I think that perhaps we as community developers should have tackled the problem of the community centre earlier. I mean, it was a huge distraction for a long time and we should have dealt with it sooner than later, as far as I'm concerned" (personal communication, November 2001).

Efforts to resolve these issues were led by the Co-operative Housing Federation of Toronto, who proposed to the AHC board that the 2001 elections be postponed until January 2002 in order to begin to heal some rifts in the community and to regain momentum for the conversion process. An additional proposal was made to hire a conflict-resolution team to bring the community together through developing a common understanding of the problems and a strategy to heal the wounds. Starting in December 2001, the Atkinson Housing Co-operative board and the Alexandra Park Residents' Association board participated in a conflict-resolution process facilitated by St Stephen's Community House. The final report from the conflict-resolution team was very comprehensive and started with the following statement:

> Deep differences have emerged regarding the management of the Community Centre. Three different co-ordinators have been responsible for the programs. At one time, a committee was set up to provide management for the centre, and at another time, management was undertaken directly by the executive of the co-op board. By late summer residents had undertaken to reinstate a separate board for the management of the Community Centre. Elections were held in mid October, and the Alexandra Park Residents' Association elected at that time has now met several times.
>
> Controversy remains regarding the election process for the Alexandra Park Residents' Association board and continuing management issues regarding the Community Centre. This led to concerns about the effectiveness of the operation of both boards [sic] and the well-being of the community. (St. Stephen's Community House, 2002)

The conflict-resolution team identified five concerns. The first focused on accountability and fair process – namely, whether responsibilities were carried out according to the specific board roles outlined in the constitution and whether decisions made at regular board meetings were implemented accordingly. The resolution was made to strengthen the systems of financial accountability, ensure the inclusiveness of the election process, and provide further board training. The second concern related to respect of each other as members of the same community. According to the report, "people have experienced being discouraged from speaking due to criticism or to facial expressions found by people visiting the centre and discouraged to participate in activities."

The third concern related to the management of the community centre. Some of the main points emphasized the need for further board training and the completion of a needs assessment. The fourth concern, divisions within the community, got at the heart of the problem:

A common concern among those we interviewed is division within the community between Muslim and non-Muslims. There are also concerns about division on the basis of white/people of colour, on the basis of length of [residency] in the community, and on membership/resident status (whether co-op member or not).

There is a widely held perception that not all residents are equally comfortable in accessing the programs and services of the Community Centre. Board members expressed the desire that through outreach programs and community-building events, the different communities would be able to work together and participate together in events and programs of the Community Centre.

The fifth concern related to communication between the two boards. It was suggested that openness could be enhanced through joint meetings of the two boards and by the community centre staff reporting to the Alexandra Park Residents' Association board. The recommendations of the report focused on the Co-operative's board holding joint meetings with the APRA board to resolve outstanding issues. The report was reviewed by the different parties who had participated in the process, including the Co-operative Housing Federation of Toronto and the Toronto Community Housing Corporation.

The conflict-resolution team held several meetings with both boards and with concerned residents from December 2002 to February 2003 (St. Stephen's Community House, 2002). Its final report was reviewed by the different parties who had participated in the process and was not available for public viewing because there was no process in place for recognizing and acting on the recommendations. Following the conflict-resolution process, the Co-operative Housing Federation of Toronto adapted its education programs to reflect better the need for sensitivity towards the community's diverse population. Particular emphasis was placed on reaching out to the major ethnic and language groups. Today, the divisions that nearly tore apart the community have diminished to some extent. Some residents at the centre of the conflict have passed away, while others have moved on to other communities, and others have remained in the community, focusing their attention on other matters.

In spring 2002 the Co-operative Housing Federation of Toronto and the AHC board undertook an intensive membership drive and further community development activities, with the following three goals: educating the community about co-operative living, raising awareness of the ongoing conversion process, and maintaining momentum for the conversion to proceed (Co-operative Housing Federation of Toronto, 2002). The community development plan targeted six major language groups that had been identified during the second referendum, namely, English, Vietnamese, Spanish, Chinese (including Cantonese and Mandarin), Portuguese, and Somali. Meetings were held with each group and included an interpreter; in addition, newsletters were printed in these six languages and distributed to each household (Co-operative Housing Federation of Toronto, 2002). The efforts to involve the different language groups and to diversify the way in which information was disseminated produced a noticeable increase in membership levels and a general interest in co-operative board elections.

Significance of the Key Event to the Conversion Process

The community culture of Alexandra Park has always been grounded in the community centre. The final report of the conflict-resolution process focused primarily on matters related to the community centre. However, it served as a warning to the Atkinson Housing Co-operative board and to other stakeholders that similar problems could emerge once the residents took control of the property (Albert Koke, personal communication, 5 March 2002).

After the elections to the Atkinson Housing Co-operative board of directors had been held in January 2002, the new board met on March 11. The final report of the conflict-resolution team from St Stephen's Community House was presented, and according to the minutes from the meeting, "there had been clarification of concerns but deep divisions still exist in the community. These divisions still have to be bridged with improved communications and outreach" (Atkinson Housing Co-operative, 2002a).

Some members of the Atkinson board felt that the actions of the Alexandra Park Residents' Association had been retaliatory. It was clear that many unresolved issues remained to be dealt with in joint meetings with the board of the Alexandra Park Residents' Association. For example, the Atkinson Housing Co-operative board was asked by the APRA board not to have board meetings in the community centre, which meant that the presence of the AHC board was not as visible within the community (Atkinson Housing Co-operative, 2002a).

At the same meeting in which the new executive officers of the Atkinson board were elected, Latchman Ramkhalawan was selected as president for another term. According to the minutes of the meeting, "he hopes the board will work as a team and wanted directors to know that he will be there for them." Tom Clement of the Co-operative Housing Federation of Toronto also announced that the Toronto Community Housing Corporation had provided the board with a proposed operating agreement. These words provided a sense of hope for the new Co-operative board and a reason to focus on the conversion process. However, at a special meeting of the board on 18 March 2002, Latchman Ramkhalawan abruptly resigned and Nazeer Ahmed was named the new president.[6]

Throughout the events that led to the re-establishment of the Alexandra Park Residents' Association the housing corporation was noticeably silent. According to the minutes of the 3 April meeting of the Atkinson board, it was clear that the housing corporation was very aware of the problems and was prepared to delay or even cancel the conversion process. According to the property manager, Albert Koke, it "wanted to wait and see how the community resolved them" (Albert Koke, personal communication, 5 March 2002). Representatives from the Toronto Community Housing Corporation openly questioned whether the community had the capacity to become a co-operative in light of the findings of the conflict-resolution team. The corporation's conversion project manager, Cyrus Vakili-Zad, made the following comments:

> We are quite concerned about the St. Stephen's report. We must present the proposal to [all levels of government], and their confidence has been shaken. In particular, they are concerned about the following issues: First, whether the board represents the community; second, the low level of participation among members and residents; and, third, the level of expertise on the board required to manage the property.
>
> This is a pilot project, and the first three years are crucial. Representation on the board from the diverse elements in the community and greater participation of members in the operations of the co-op are very important. If participation doesn't increase, the co-op may not go ahead. In addition, more skills and expertise are needed on the board to manage the community. The housing corporation is partially responsible for the first three years and wants to do everything possible to help this project succeed. (Atkinson Housing Co-operative, 2002b)

Vakili-Zad added that the Atkinson Housing Co-operative board must meet three requirements if it wanted to go ahead with the conversion process:

1. Hold full board elections in the fall and work between now and then on increasing the level of member participation;
2. Introduce language into the co-op's by-law that will permit non-resident experts to sit on the co-op board; and
3. Help deal with current divisive issues in the community, in particular financial discrepancies at the Community Centre. (Atkinson Housing Co-operative, 2002b)

These statements came as a surprise to the board but not the Co-operative Housing Federation of Toronto. Tom Clement commented:

> We are trying to do something that has never been done before. If we don't do it right, here and now, no one will get a chance again. But the co-op has had many successes – two positive referendums, approval of the major by-laws, proposed operating agreement, three board elections, 70% of households signed up for membership. This is a big hurdle but we can handle it. The board has to comply with [Toronto Community Housing Corporation's] requests if it wants government support and approval. It must also deal with the discontent ... The board has to reach out with a door-to-door campaign with translators, similar to the referendum in 1998, a campaign to significantly increase participation amongst the 70% already signed up and to recruit more members. (Atkinson Housing Co-operative, 2002b)

Ian Fitchenbaum, the director of administration for the housing corporation, agreed with many of the points raised but "emphasized that the board has to take the St. Stephen's report seriously. Member and non-member involvement, the lack of expertise and centre finances all have to be addressed" (Atkinson Housing Co-operative, 2002b). These statements provided a wake-up call for all stakeholders that immediate intervention was required. The AHC board and the Co-operative Housing Federation of Toronto acted promptly on the requirements stipulated by Toronto Community Housing Corporation.

The requirement of locating and appointing non-resident members to the AHC board of directors was achieved in July 2002. A community development strategy was worked out with the goal of improving the turnout for the new elections to be held in the fall. The purpose of the strategy was to help the Co-operative board regain community trust and rebuild the relationships that had been strained during the periods of conflict. In other words, the efforts were intended to build positive forms of both bridging and bonding social capital in order for the conversion to be completed and for the management to be turned over to the Co-operative. It was hoped that the endeavours would have the effect of increasing the number of members participating in the Co-operative's activities. In the spring of 2002 the Co-operative Housing Federation of Toronto and the Atkinson board implemented a plan with the following objectives:

- Educating the community about co-operative living
- Raising awareness of the ongoing conversion process
- Maintaining momentum for the conversion to occur

Interestingly, the community development plan mirrored several of the strategies that had contributed to the successful outcome of the referendums referred to earlier in this chapter as well as the efforts at conflict resolution. For example, individual meetings were held with members of the predominant language groups, and newsletters were printed in the major languages and distributed to each household. Efforts to include the different language groups resulted in a noticeable increase in membership levels and a general interest in the Co-operative board elections held in September 2002 (Atkinson Housing Co-operative, 2002c). Following the elections, the housing corporation later expressed renewed support for the conversion process, and the date for the transition of authority was finally announced as 1 April 2003.

In spite of the divisions that emerged within the community, the conversion proceeded towards completion. Removing the community centre from the Atkinson board's responsibilities was a constructive step, but it is unfortunate that it had to occur because of such difficult conditions. While implementing a new governance structure is never easy in any context, the residents met the challenge with support from the Co-operative Housing Federation of Toronto. In spite of many improvements, however, the problems persisted, and owing to a lack of trust, the two boards did not collaborate. The final steps to the eventual completion of the conversion will be explored in the next key event.

Event 8: Transfer of Management Authority, 2003

The novelty and uncertainty involved in the conversion process meant that it was difficult to plan the types of tasks that residents were reasonably able or prepared to undertake. Accordingly, support from resource groups was crucial for sustaining momentum within the community. The education and training activities were intended to prepare the residents for negotiating the legal agreements as well as for living as a co-operative community. However, repeated delays caused the additional challenge of always having to convince the housing corporation that members of the Atkinson Housing Co-operative would be able to take control of the property and build a healthier community.

As the conflicts and divisions started to negatively impact whether or not the conversion would occur, the Co-operative Housing Federation of Toronto became more directive and involved in all facets of the conversion process. The transfer of management authority constituted a key event since it was the end of a ten-year journey to transform the community into a co-operative. Moreover, the official opening of Atkinson Housing Co-operative represented a new beginning for the community. In this key event, I describe how third-party groups were crucial during the final steps that led to the opening on 1 April 2003. The information in this case is based on a review of meeting minutes, on interviews, and on participant observation of key meetings.

Background of the Key Event

An important responsibility of the Atkinson board of directors was active participation in the negotiations with Metropolitan Toronto Housing Corporation. A source of concern was that the board did not appear to understand what was being negotiated. Representatives of the housing corporation and the provincial government were involved in the discussions (Atkinson Housing Co-operative, 2001a). Delays emerged because of such unanticipated situations as retirements, career advancements, new community leadership, Sonny Atkinson's death, and the cultural and ethnic conflicts. These contributed to a loss of institutional memory because many of the significant participants who had been involved in the conversion process decided to completely disengage, resulting in an ongoing need to educate new directors about the same conversion-process issues as well as their responsibilities as board members.

The conversion process had started in 1992, when Sonny Atkinson sought alternative management arrangements for his community, and was completed in April 2003. The length of time was frustrating for both the community and the co-operative sector. According to research by Lapointe and Sousa (2003), there were a number of reasons for the delays:

1. The lack of a plan or blueprint in place to guide the conversion process
2. The impact of the devolution of social housing to municipalities
3. Changes to the provincial government, which meant that the Co-operative had to seek renewed approval in 1995
4. Government uncertainty over whether the community was prepared for self-management
5. A lack of institutional memory on the part of the government, causing many of the steps to be repeated
6. Slow government response time to proposals tabled by the Co-operative board
7. Changing leadership within the community
8. Emerging community conflict
9. The lack of funding that would have ensured the undertaking of the required community development work

It is difficult to point to any one group of participants or to a particular circumstance as being the main reason for the delays (see Lapointe and Sousa, 2003). The more likely case was a combination of stakeholder and circumstantial considerations.

The length of time it took to complete the conversion caused uncertainty and frustration within the community, to the extent that support waxed and waned. Another serious consequence was the draining of resources – resident, volunteer, and financial – and the turnover of tenants. The community started preparing itself for a significant change to occur in 1992; however, preparation for the transfer of management would not begin until 1996. Volunteers who had been motivated to see the conversion happen became disinterested in participating because they were unable to experience the benefits of living in a co-operative as quickly as they would have preferred.

The question of whether or not the community was ready was difficult to answer. There were no milestones or benchmarks to let the residents know if the process was on track. Uncertainty remained over whether the conversion would be formally supported by the housing corporation.

Without formal approval, there was no real sense that it would be completed. Seeking approval from the board of directors of Metropolitan Toronto Housing Corporation became a goal. The Atkinson board, Tom Clement of the Co-operative Housing Federation of Toronto, and representatives of the housing corporation convened a working group in early 2001 to develop a proposal to present to the housing corporation's board of directors in the summer. A key feature of the proposal was to establish a capital reserve fund for future repairs to the property.

The working group presented the proposal at the 15 August meeting of the board of directors for Metropolitan Toronto Housing Corporation. Presentations were made by Tom Clement, Cyrus Valkili-Zad (the housing corporation's project manager), and an Atkinson board member. They focused on the conversion process, the status of the negotiations, and the community development work to educate and train the residents on managing a community.

Tom Jakobek, a director of the Metropolitan Toronto Housing Corporation, outlined three broad questions with respect to the conversion proposal. The first question related to the establishment of a capital reserve fund. He expressed concern that there would be an inherent inequity across the social housing system should the proposal for a capital reserve fund be approved and that allocating maintenance funds to a co-operative from existing public housing funds would not be appropriate. Since public housing projects operated on a system-wide basis and maintenance was handled on a priority basis, providing guaranteed funds to one project would be not only uncommon but also unfair. The second question regarded who would determine the rent ceilings at the co-operative. The third question concerned whether the existing tenant-selection process would have to change in light of the conversion.

Members of the working group responded to each question. The rationale given for the capital reserve fund was that much work was required on the property as it was approaching a critical stage in its life cycle. Metropolitan Toronto Housing Corporation would still establish rent ceilings, and new tenants would come from the existing centralized waiting list (Cyrus Valkili-Zad, personal communication, 15 August 2001). Valkili-Zad responded that all of those questions would be elaborated in the final operating agreement that was to be developed. Three recommendations were made by the staff of the housing corporation:

1. That its board of directors approve in principle the conversion of
   the Alexandra Park public housing project into a resident-managed,

non-profit housing co-operative, and authorize staff to take the necessary actions to effect the approval;

2. That staff administer the operating agreement and introduce adjustments or revisions to the model as required to protect [Metropolitan Toronto Housing Corporation's] interests and ensure the proper delivery of management services to the residents; and

3. That staff evaluate the effectiveness of the co-operative management model as an alternative method of managing public housing before implementing similar projects in the future. (Metropolitan Toronto Housing Corporation, 2001b)

The housing corporation's board of directors unanimously approved the recommendations. The decision to support the conversion was a tremendous victory for the Alexandra Park community after its pursuit of the conversion process for so many years. The next step was to seek provincial ministry approval since the Province owned the property. In addition, new provincial legislation that devolved responsibility for social housing onto municipalities had to be considered in the final agreement. Three key documents had to be created: a budget, an operating agreement, and a lease. In order to build on this momentum, the Atkinson Housing Co-operative submitted a proposed operating agreement in the fall of 2001.

In the community the residents were unaware of the significant decision that had occurred on their behalf. Stronger opposition to becoming a co-operative surfaced during the fall, and by the end of 2001 and for most of 2002 the conflicts and divisions described in the seventh key event effectively delayed the conversion process. It is difficult to isolate the reason that the divisions were not as visible earlier in the process, but their impact on the conversion process was very significant.

Members of the community were losing faith in their belief that a new co-operative community could emerge. Moreover, members of the board of directors and representatives of the housing corporation were questioning the ability of the residents to manage the property because of the perception that theirs was a divided community. Furthermore, members of the Co-operative expressed concerns that the existing leaders did not possess a real understanding of the process. When asked whether the board understood what the conversion was about, Kate Black, a former member of the Atkinson Housing Co-operative board, stated:

I do, but I can't speak for the rest of the board. You know? But I think there is about two, three of them, maybe four of them that do not understand what's going on. We have a treasurer that has never seen the books, that has never seen the account, don't know if she's coming or going. Got a secretary don't know where she's coming or going. But I can't judge them for that, just that they have to learn. And to be, right now, to be on the Board of Directors, you have to know what you're doing. Especially coming down to this time of the conversion, because we're acting as a co-op right now, but we're not a co-op, we're not self-managing. The thing is, what gets me, we're a co-op but we're not. Some of the board members say, "Well, if we're not a co-op, we don't have to follow the rules." But we're still a co-op, we still have to follow the rules. That's my babble right there and right now, with the board members we have, plus myself, I feel right now that my voice is going to be just plain ignored, because maybe I know too much and I over – maybe like not overstep but maybe over – I challenge them too much. (Kate Black, personal communication, 24 February 2002)

Kate Black's statement illustrates a concern that individual members of the Atkinson board were not unified in their understanding of the co-operative conversion. Unease was surfacing with respect to whether or not the type of education was appropriate for the community. In the same interview Kate Black commented: "Well, there's not enough proper information. Okay? They go on the key information, saying that the rent would be the same, calculated the same way and everything like that. Sure, fine. But it's the other information that the person needs. Like to be able to run a co-op properly, you have to know all the rules and regulations, you have to follow the by-laws, and you have to follow the Act. If you don't do that, it's never going to work. And we have a board that do not follow rules and regulations. They just take control all of the property" (personal communication, 24 February 2002).

The representatives of Toronto Community Housing Corporation were also concerned about the education and training of the members. They were uncertain whether or not the residents were accessing available resources, including the education activities. When I asked Lou Canton, director of private management for the housing corporation whether he felt that the residents had accessed the education and training opportunities available, he responded:

I would say no. I think a lot of residents have made an unbelievable effort to try to grasp and get an understanding of what the issues are. And some of them have a very good knowledge. But I don't know if they have a full scope understanding. And this is not to take anything away from anybody.

But all I'm saying is that the business is a complicated business, and, you know, unless you get into it for a while and have a good understanding, obviously you're not going to be as qualified and as experienced as someone else. But that's not to say that you cannot participate and you won't be able to make decisions, management decisions. Because they could ask for the information, and based on the information they could make their own decisions. (Personal communication, 22 February 2002)

It was apparent from these statements that an assessment and a subsequent intervention were needed. A major difficulty was that no one expected the preoccupation with the community centre to be so entrenched in the minds of the directors. There was concern that the conversion might not be completed despite the expressed desire of those involved in the process to have it happen. Various residents and resource persons wanted to give up on the process, but the potentially good outcome of successfully converting into a co-operative outweighed dropping the conversion altogether. There was a desperate need to maintain the momentum, so greater help from outsiders was required. It was at this point that the Co-operative Housing Federation of Toronto and Toronto Community Housing Corporation switched from being advisers to developing strategies for their direct involvement as change agents in most decisions.

While the divisions within the community were surfacing in the summer of 2002, a number of factors helped to move the conversion process along. One factor was that the momentum to maintain the conversion was sustained by the Co-operative Housing Federation of Toronto. It was committed to seeing the new co-operative operate, "which is what we promised Sonny many years before" (Mark Goldblatt, personal communication, 21 July 2002). A second factor was that the changes to provincial housing legislation were actually beneficial for the conversion because the community's efforts were consistent with the government's agenda of reducing its role in the management of social housing. Furthermore, the legislative changes accelerated the process because negotiations had to occur with one level of government rather than two. A third factor was that the housing corporation's project team started to involve key decision makers who wanted the conversion completed.

In the fall of 2002 Toronto Community Housing Corporation finally submitted a draft operating agreement to the Atkinson board of directors. The AHC directors now had a document that could help them envision the way in which the new co-operative would operate. A working group composed of three Co-operative board members, Tom Clement of the Co-operative Housing Federation of Toronto, and the Co-operative's lawyer, Bruce Lewis, reviewed the agreement during the remainder of the year. According to the minutes of 13 January 2003, the AHC directors met with their lawyer, who presented them with a letter that contained one hundred points "to cover the issues great and small" (Atkinson Housing Co-operative, 2003a).

A significant issue highlighted by Bruce Lewis was the "right to terminate the agreement without cause with a 60-day notice" (Atkinson Housing Co-operative, 2003a). This statement was interpreted to mean that the agreement was for sixty days. According to the president, Nazeer Ahmed, this stipulation really represented "a lack of faith that they have in us" (personal communication, 20 February 2003). It was felt that this issue was serious enough to warrant rejection of the agreement unless it was dealt with (Atkinson Housing Co-operative, 2003a). The draft agreement was turned over to Bruce Lewis, and the AHC board was able to focus on making decisions that would allow the co-operative to operate once control had been transferred.

The first decision was to hire a company to manage the property. Four board members and Tom Clement were appointed to interview prospective companies and to report to the board with a recommendation. The process involved site visits by the companies and site visits by the committee to properties managed by the companies being considered. According to the minutes of 13 January 2003, the members supported hiring Community First Developments, Inc. They commented that the company's presentation was impressive and demonstrated efforts to build a greater understanding of the Atkinson community. Moreover, Community First Developments, Inc., was currently managing two other co-operative properties that were in "serious difficulties when Community First took over and they had been completely turned around" (Atkinson Housing Co-operative, 2003a). The board approved the hiring of Community First on 13 January, which represented the first major decision made by the new co-operative. At this meeting a second motion was approved by the board, albeit with some reluctance: "[BE IT RESOLVED] THAT the board authorize signing officers to sign a contract for three years after the co-op's lawyer and CHFT review the contract" (Atkinson Housing Co-operative, 2003a)

Including the Co-operative Housing Federation of Toronto in the second motion was an indication that the board had come to rely on its expertise. Members of the AHC board who attended the meeting were visibly uncomfortable with including involvement of the Co-operative Housing Federation of Toronto, but they were resigned to continue receiving guidance because it was necessary in order to see the conversion completed.

The issues regarding the operating agreement continued to occupy the board's subsequent meetings. According to the minutes of the 13 February meeting of the AHC board, most of the points raised by Bruce Lewis had been addressed by the housing corporation. The date of 1 April was still a very realistic goal for signing the contract, and the term of the agreement was for a fixed ten-year period, with a review after three years (Atkinson Housing Co-operative, 2003f). In addition, third-party involvement in the governance of the new co-operative was required.

At this meeting there was a discussion concerning the role and power of the non-resident directors. A review of the minutes from December 2002 to March 2003 reveals that the non-resident directors provided valuable support and were not overly directive but supportive. For instance, the advisers would ask questions such as, "Is this what you guys want?" or they would remind the board of the way in which its decisions would impact the community (Atkinson Housing Co-operative, 2003a). However, the requirement to have non-resident directors as part of the organizational structure appeared to constrain the board's ability to make some key decisions. According to Nazeer Ahmed, two of the three non-resident directors had to be at a meeting in order for there to be a quorum, effectively limiting the role of the resident directors to the co-operative business that could be completed should the non-resident directors be unable to attend a meeting (personal communication, 20 February 2003). For instance, at a meeting to approve new members, Don Young of the Co-operative Housing Federation of Toronto asked for board approval, but that could not be given because of the lack of a quorum on account of the non-resident directors not being present (Atkinson Housing Co-operative, 2003b).

An additional issue expressed by the directors was the state of disrepair of some of the units, which would ultimately be the co-operative's responsibility to rectify. The lawyer commented that it was "his impression that the operating agreement will continue to be renegotiated throughout its term," which would include financial responsibility for capital improvements (Atkinson Housing Co-operative, 2003c). The board of directors of the co-operative continued to express concerns that the maintenance issue was not being addressed satisfactorily before the transfer of authority and that once the authority had been turned over, the co-operative would be liable for the many repairs – an issue similar to that faced in previous conversions of private properties into co-operatives. Two items were proposed that stressed the anxiety:

IT WAS AGREED THAT an article would be published in the conversion newsletter asking residents to request maintenance work be done by the ... [Toronto Community Housing Corporation] now prior to the conversion, instructing them to do it in writing, to keep a copy and, if they wished, give a copy to the co-op office.

IT WAS AGREED THAT a letter would be drafted by Don to [Toronto Community Housing Corporation] from the board saying that many complaints about maintenance are being received, that the board is concerned that maintenance work is being deferred and that it would like to have [Toronto Community Housing Corporation] complete all of the requests for maintenance by residents prior to conversion.

Unfortunately, those became action items as opposed to formal motions because at this point in the meeting the quorum had been lost; the non-resident directors had left (Atkinson Housing Co-operative, 2003c).

As the negotiation proceeded, Tom Clement stated that it would be necessary to have weekly information meetings in order to keep the board up to date (Atkinson Housing Co-operative, 2003c). A member of the board stated that there used to be combined meetings with the housing corporation, "but now directors don't know what is happening" (Atkinson Housing Co-operative, 2003c). It seemed that the member wanted to be involved in the finer details of the transition, which may not have been appropriate, and it also indicated that micromanaging might be an eventual problem. Tom Clement replied that there had not been secret meetings and that the staff of Community First Developments, Inc., was meeting with the housing corporation to finalize the transition details.

A second decision facing the Atkinson Housing Co-operative board of directors was the hiring of a security company. A committee of the board met with Community First Developments, Inc., on 7 March to create a job description and to search for possible companies. The property management staff advised the board on an appropriate company, and the board approved the hiring of Intelligarde International, Inc., as the co-op's security company. (Atkinson Housing Co-operative, 2003d).

For some individuals this decision seemed routine, but for me, as the author and a former resident, it meant that the dream by many residents of having a say in the security concerns was finally realized.

As the transfer date approached, it was crucial to highlight potential issues involving the transition because of the expected uncertainty and confusion that would result once the responsibilities had been turned over. The property management staff made the following arrangements regarding potential problems (Dione Nembhard, personal communication, 5 May 2003): a new general phone number was set up for members to call with regard to maintenance requests and questions; rents were to be paid to the co-op beginning on 1 April by cheque or money order; and maintenance staff hired by the co-operative would begin to be on site prior to 1 April.

There was a discussion about the office items that the housing corporation would leave behind after 1 April had passed, and those that the co-operative would need to purchase. A concern was that new expenditures would have a negative impact on their budget from the onset. Bruce Lewis commented that "according to the agreement, everything needed was supposed to stay." Unfortunately, on the day of transfer the office was empty, save for a few desks and computers with erased hard drives" (Dione Nembhard, personal communication, 5 May 2003).

The 12 March meeting of the Atkinson board was a turning point for the directors. There was a sense that the significant issues that had emerged over the past months had been dealt with collaboratively by the Co-operative Housing Federation of Toronto, the property management staff, and the Atkinson board of directors. However, as with other important meetings, the board again faced a loss of quorum because the non-resident directors had to leave. It seemed that whenever progress was being made, another challenge would come up. In response to the loss of quorum, Tom Clement stated that he "would work on a proposal to change the quorum for board meetings to get rid of the necessity for two non-resident advisor directors to attend all the time. In the meantime, [he] will attempt to find a fourth person to serve in this capacity and thereby make the existing system more workable" (Atkinson Housing Co-operative, 2003e).

By the end of March 2003 the pieces were in place for the conversion process to finally end at the 1 April deadline. What was noticeable throughout January to the end of March 2003, when the bulk of the legal agreements were being developed, was an absence of regular Co-operative members being involved and asking questions about the process. Moreover, there were no such members attending the board meetings, which is an indication that participation was an ongoing challenge.

The transfer of management authority officially occurred on 1 April 2003. The arrival of the day was anticlimactic after all of the challenges and obstacles faced by the community throughout the conversion process. The energy from the resident mobilization against the AHC board in the previous year had demonstrated that the community was still vibrant, but their absence on this significant day was quite striking. There was no press coverage associated with the opening of Canada's first public housing co-operative. I personally contacted the major newspapers and community newspapers to tell them that the conversion had been completed, yet no mention of the conversion process ever appeared in the daily newspapers. Frankly, there was no way of knowing the significance of the day unless one witnessed the "chaos in the office" (Dione Nembhard, personal communication, 5 May 2003). Repeated efforts to see whether the housing corporation had made a public announcement about the opening of the Atkinson Housing Co-operative resulted in the realization that it had taken a low-key approach.

According to various sources, there was a conscious desire to keep the opening day low-key given the divisions that still remained within the community. According to Tom Clement, the poor weather and anticipated office chaos were additional factors that influenced the decision to keep the day as inconspicuous as possible (personal conversation, 5 May 2003). I was surprised in view of the wonderful tendency of the co-operative housing sector to champion and celebrate significant achievements, and the Atkinson Housing Co-operative certainly represented a major achievement akin to the creation of government programs in the early 1970s.

A celebration was held on Canada Day, three months after the official transfer of power. Dignitaries in attendance included the local municipal councillor and Derek Ballantyne, the chief executive officer of the Toronto Community Housing Corporation. The purpose of the day was to open up the co-operative to the wider community, but the significance was diluted because the event shared the day with the national holiday.

Significance of the Key Event to the Conversion Process

The co-operative officially took control of the property on 1 April 2003. That the date is commonly known as a day of pranks was not lost on any of the stakeholders. In this last case I have described the final steps involved in a conversion process that had started ten years prior to this date, a process that created Canada's first public housing co-operative. After ten years one would have expected the community to have been ready, but the consequences of the process that surfaced during the final stages revealed important lessons for future conversions. Those who were involved in the conversion process accepted that it would take at least another ten years for members of the co-operative to realize many of the benefits of having gone through a very challenging journey. As will be shown in the afterword, the co-operative has been in operation for ten years now, and many members feel they have yet to see the advantages of supporting co-operative living. However, as I will describe later, the members are comparing the co-operative arrangement with management by a government housing authority, which is an error in scope and understanding.

The conversion process was initiated out of the spirit of collaboration between Sonny Atkinson on behalf of the Alexandra Park Residents' Association and advocates supporting co-operative housing. Over time, Sonny Atkinson's vision was implemented in very practical terms. During the final steps that led to the transfer of management authority, the board worked constructively and collaboratively, largely owing to the more direct approach taken by the Co-operative Housing Federation of Toronto and the Toronto Community Housing Corporation as well as to the desire of the community to heal its wounds.

The community faced a number of challenges prior to the completion of the conversion that could have derailed the entire initiative. However, exclusive focus on the conversion allowed the process to be accomplished, which in turn gave the residents an opportunity address the "injuries." The spirit of co-operation that pushed the conversion to fulfilment would also contribute to the community's efforts to heal the wounds. According to the president, Nazeer Ahmed, "we do not need any more problems. We need to move forward" (personal communication, 1 July 2003). However, the reality of having two boards on the property continues to have a significant impact on the community's development.

Since the completion of the conversion process in 2003 there have been a number of improvements that reflect the original intent of Sonny Atkinson and other leaders. First, the maintenance requests have been answered at a much more efficient pace than when they were the responsibility of the housing corporation (Dione Nembhard, personal communication, 5 May 2003), implying that maintenance response time improved immediately. Second, there was a broader belief that a representative board had been elected. In fact, co-operative members stopped looking for cultural differences as the basis for division, and many of those expressing opposition accepted that the selection process was based on the commitment of the candidates to the community and on the experience they would bring to the board. However, there was recognition that the divisions needed to be dealt with more openly, and support came from the non-profit sector to assist in addressing them.

A race relations task force of members of the Atkinson Housing Co-operative and other stakeholders was convened to deal exclusively with the racial divisions that emerged during the conversion (Alina Chatterjee, personal communication, 20 June 2003). However, elements of the original Alexandra Park Residents' Association culture remains, which have found it difficult to accept the new housing co-operative. For instance, the group that should take the lead in encouraging youth to be involved in the community's development, in the areas of programming or governance, is a highly contested topic. The few examples of youth members on the board of directors have resigned because of their perceived inexperience as well as the paternalism expressed by the older members. Most of all, the youth do not feel as connected to the board, because of their potential for upward mobility as well as their engagement in disputes that reflect a legacy of poor relationships. However, the youth have expressed a desire to leave the past behind for the sake of the community, which has been a positive development.

Regardless of the ongoing challenges, Canada now has the first example of converting public housing into a co-operative, which is a significant step in integrating a marginalized population into society. For the community, the road to healing continues, but at the very least they have determined the road that has been best for them as they have come to make decisions first and foremost in the interests of the co-operative.

Summary

In this chapter I have described the journey that the Atkinson community and the other stakeholders took to complete a conversion process that created Canada's first public housing co-operative. The Atkinson Housing Co-operative is atypical in that the final model blends key characteristics of a co-operative and public housing. Based on many conversations with individuals involved in the process, I have come to believe that there was a general desire and effort to look beyond the traditional notions of what constitutes a co-operative, otherwise the conversion would never have been completed.

Establishing Atkinson Housing Co-operative was a difficult process for all those involved. It was apparent that, at different times, the conversion represented transformative opportunities for both the residents and the housing corporation, although the latter would not support this assertion given the divisions that emerged towards the end of the conversion process, divisions that resulted in a delay to the completion of the final agreement. In 2003 the Atkinson Housing Co-operative was at a critical point in its history in terms of seeing greater member engagement that would result in the benefits found in other housing co-operatives. I believe that it is too early to determine the overall success of the new model in spite of it being close to ten years since the completion of the conversion, because official transfer of management involved a focus on management knowledge and not enough on community building.

Two concerns that manifested at the end of the conversion process remain unresolved. The first is related to the perception that some members had obtained more power than others because of their participation in the conversion and on the co-op's board of directors. A second concern is whether the board would be responsive to the needs of all residents, including non-members, or would it behave like the very landlord that had precipitated the calls for community-based control. Despite the absence of a prototype for the conversion and despite the different obstacles encountered throughout the process, the members had still been able to become a housing co-operative. The actions taken by the residents of Alexandra Park to overcome the stigma associated with public housing had been aimed at gaining control over the fate of their community by becoming a housing co-operative, the first Canadian public housing project to do so. The underlying factors associated with the community and with the process that enabled the creation of the Atkinson Housing Co-operative will be explored further in the final two chapters.

5 Theoretical Analysis of the Alexandra Park Conversion Process

The goal of the conversion into the Atkinson Housing Co-operative was to empower the disenfranchised residents living in Alexandra Park public housing. The members *were* empowered to become involved in the governance as well as the daily operations of the housing co-operative because of their stake in the success of the community. Housing co-operatives depend on the goodwill of the members to volunteer in their community and on the links between co-operatives that lead to support and education as a means to building stronger co-operatives and a stronger co-operative movement. Unlike the residents of housing co-operatives, those of public housing projects lack a meaningful connection to their project because they do not have control over the fate of their community (see for example Cooper and Rodman, 1992). As will be demonstrated, the goal of the Alexandra Park conversion was to adopt and integrate the key factors that have made the co-operative model successful. In this chapter, the eight key events are interpreted using the seven elements that were derived from a synthesis of research on co-operative formation and community development processes, identified in chapter 2. The seven elements are as follows:

- Community assets: the role of volunteers, technical assistance, and access to funding
- Forms of social capital: development of co-operative social processes based on trust and norms of reciprocity
- Styles of community leadership: transactional and transformative styles and the role of change agents
- Community consciousness: attachment to community, and the expression of a movement perspective

- Role of government: expansion of the role of landlords to include gatekeeping and a stakeholder partnership
- Cultural change: a shift in the approach and perspectives taken by stakeholders, resulting in improved communication patterns
- Resource mobilization: the emergence of focused activism for a common goal

Determining the presence or absence of these elements is integral to understanding how it was possible for a public housing project to convert into a tenant-managed co-operative. The analysis in this chapter forms the basis of a community development framework that can be applied to other low-income communities that want to convert into some form of tenant-managed arrangement. I will describe the actual framework in the next chapter.

From its inception the Alexandra Park housing project appeared to be an uncharacteristic property within the public housing system in that there was a residents' association focused upon improving the quality of community life. The conversion to a housing co-operative, also one of a kind, followed from the tradition described earlier in this book. In the following sections I use each element to interpret the key events as the means to explain the underlying factors that contributed to the completion of the conversion process.

Community Assets

The phrase *community assets* refers to individuals, physical structures, and businesses that operate to improve the quality of community life. These assets are formed from resources available within and in close proximity to a geographical community. In the context of the Alexandra Park conversion, accessing and using different resources effectively was a major contributor to the creation of a sense of pride and the building of greater confidence among the residents, all of which helped to support co-operative living. These resources functioned as tools for transformative learning and community building that established a culture of self-reliance, a self-reliance that ultimately aided the conversion process. Three resources are identified here as having had a significant impact on the conversion process: the role of volunteers, technical assistance, and access to funding. Note that these resources were found either internally or externally to the community, but all served to support the conversion process.

Role of Volunteers

Volunteering always had a significant function within the Alexandra Park housing project. Ellis and Noyes' definition of *a volunteer* as a person who acts "in recognition of a need, with an attitude of social responsibility and without concern for monetary profit, going beyond one's basic obligations" (1990, 4), describes the type of role that volunteers have had in the community. Throughout its development volunteers have included residents and external supporters, both of whom were motivated by the belief that the community could be improved by collective efforts.

The community from its inception has always comprised strong-willed and capable people. Advocating for improvements to the management practices led to the formation of the Alexandra Park Residents' Association, which served as a conduit for coordinating volunteer activities. The committees and community programming organized through the residents' association helped to build a reputation for initiatives aimed at improving the community, for example, construction of the community centre. A unique feature of the centre was its management by public housing residents, a feature that to this day is still uncommon. This accomplishment projected a positive image to groups outside of the community, including the housing corporation. The resident volunteers gained managerial experience that became the basis of the co-operative's governance structure. They demonstrated an ability to identify needs within the community and to engage in constructive activities intended to satisfy those needs. Many activities and initiatives could not have happened without the knowledge of the community volunteers as a basis. Volunteer participation was integral to deciding upon and implementing the different community-based programs, which gave legitimacy to initiating the conversion process.

Through their activities the volunteers developed a variety of skills that were both instrumental and critical, which had the effect of increasing their knowledge about the needs of the community as well understanding the nature of political action. The residents needed to be able to communicate and interact effectively with government bureaucracy, the media, and police, and also to approach conflict resolution in a constructive manner. Some examples of the skills included written and oral communication; the abilities needed for management and governance; diplomacy both within and without the community; and media relations. In addition, the residents needed to learn complex tasks, such as creating and reading budgets and having meetings that followed rules of order, and to communicate effectively their understanding of these tasks. These skills were integral to the conversion and the ability of the community to manage a multimillion-dollar property.

The knowledge possessed and generated by the residents can be described as a form of indigenous knowledge, which is the local knowledge unique to a given culture or society (Warren, 1991). According to Warren (1991), this knowledge is the basis of local decision making in such areas as agriculture, health care, and education. In the context of the Atkinson conversion, such indigenous knowledge influenced the way in which the conversion process proceeded because it informed the strategies for organizing the community for the 1995 referendum, for instance, by developing an environment where the residents felt they could express various concerns without fear of repercussion.

A critical aspect of indigenous knowledge is that it contains the hidden discourse present within the community, that is, knowledge of customary and unwritten rules and practices as well as potential sources of conflicts. Hidden discourse allowed volunteers to successfully advocate for the co-operative alternative because they were aware of and could best understand why advocacy was required. For example, residents expressed the concern that their neighbours would have access to their confidential information once the conversion was completed. Resident volunteers were able to communicate this concern to the Co-operative Housing Federation of Toronto, which, in turn, had to include information on how a co-operative board of directors cannot readily access personal information. Thus, the issue around the perception of confidential information being accessible to neighbours became resolvable because volunteers were able to both identify and understand the motivations underlying this concern.

As the conversion process progressed, new volunteers who did not have the same understanding of the community's hidden discourse became involved. This disjuncture became a source of division because there was a perception that earlier volunteer efforts were unappreciated. According to different interviewees, the new volunteers seemed to forget the work and efforts that had occurred from 1969 to 1995. Individuals felt that their efforts were minimized, as shown in the confusion following the replacement of the Alexandra Park Residents' Association with the Atkinson board of directors. The new group of volunteers seemed to develop a sense of entitlement to special privileges that reflected their status in the community as co-op board members. This feeling had the effect of alienating many long-time residents and reminded them of their treatment by the housing corporation. The intergenerational tensions were exacerbated in the final stage of the conversion and became fused with interracial concerns, leading to apathy, division, and eventually conflict, all of which caused delays in the conversion process.

An interesting aspect of the conversion was the participation and commitment of external volunteers, that is, individuals who once lived in the community, had friends there, or were inspired by Sonny Atkinson's commitment to wrest control from Metropolitan Toronto Housing Corporation. The unwavering support from external volunteers provided operational assistance and expertise throughout the conversion process, for example, by writing letters, translating, and door-to-door canvassing. However, the external volunteers were always reminded that they did not reside in the community, which in essence created a conflict between their specialized knowledge and the residents' indigenous knowledge when it came to understanding the community's needs and creating ways to address them.

Technical Assistance

Technical assistance refers to the expertise, guidance, and advice that can contribute to the development of a community initiative. Examples include educational materials and training intended to assist in building community capacity. From 1969 onwards technical assistance came in a variety of forms, primarily as educational resources, which were available to those residents involved in the community-building activities. Early in the community's development, the assistance was focused on what was immediately useful to managing the community centre and to implementing community-based programs.

Different types of materials were developed to assist the Alexandra Park Residents' Association, for example a personnel manual and a board handbook, both of which were created in the late 1980s. Those documents provided crucial information about running meetings and being managers. In one document, for example, a diagram of the organizational structure showed the lines of accountability within the residents' association. However, the early technical assistance was mainly for individuals actively involved in the association's operations.

Once the conversion process had been initiated, there was a change in the type of technical assistance required because the community's focus shifted from managing a community centre to becoming members of a co-operative. In essence, the educational material became oriented less to the community centre and more to the broader community, for example, in relation to becoming a co-operative. The technical assistance addressed complex problems in communication, materials were translated into five different languages, and information was made accessible in plain language.

While the approach taken to convert Alexandra Park into the Atkinson Housing Co-operative was based on previous conversions, this conversion was unique, and previous knowledge was not always a good fit for the Alexandra Park community. In other words, applying a co-operative model to a public housing context required adjustments to the way in which the model was presented. Educational materials created by the co-operative sector assumed that the audience had some knowledge of governance and community well-being. Also, there were unique features to the Atkinson conversion, such as the existence of a prior residents' association and a community centre, which available educational materials did not address. Even though the intent of the materials was to facilitate the conversion process, many residents were unable to appreciate how this new knowledge was to be applied.

Also, the educational materials used were difficult to understand by those not involved in the residents' association. For example, providing information on how to be a director or committee member was important, but residents who were not involved in governance could not relate to these concepts. There was a sense that co-operative living was too top-down and disconnected from the grassroots needs of the membership; in other words, there was a perception that the outcome would be similar to living in public housing except that a small group of residents would be the new landlords. Shifting the residents' thinking, from their being public housing residents to being co-operative members, required training opportunities that built on the community's strengths and accomplishments.

The Co-operative Housing Federation of Toronto provided the residents with opportunities to participate in workshops, but this was intimidating for many of them because the workshops were held off site and at inconvenient times and relied on individuals' having formal education. Although there were on-site workshops, and Don Young provided informal training sessions, many residents did not take advantage of those opportunities.

The problems that beset the technical assistance program can be explained by the fact that it was difficult to know in advance what an appropriate strategy would be to convert public housing into a co-operative. Although some residents took advantage of the training and educational materials and later became board members, the impact of the program was unclear. Over time, residents questioned the efficacy of the training, but they did not articulate what could be done to improve the assistance from the Co-operative Housing Federation of Toronto.

Access to Funding

The Alexandra Park Residents' Association was very successful in raising and managing funds, thanks to the specialized skills of the volunteers and staff. The community's ability to raise funds was further enhanced by accessing the community centre's charitable status. The residents applied for money from different foundations and government agencies, and the funds ensured that there was community-based programming, on-site staff, and employment opportunities for residents.

Accessing funding for the conversion was a challenge because the housing corporation stated that it would not provide money for this purpose beyond the funds for the community education leading up to the first referendum. Since the community was already used to fundraising, doing so for the conversion was not seen as an insurmountable challenge. However, the slow pace of the conversion meant that costs were higher than initially expected.

According to Tom Clement, the executive director of the Co-operative Housing Federation of Toronto, the cost of the conversion was approximately $300,000, including consultant advice, legal costs, and educational resources. The latter came in the form of printing, translation of printed materials, hiring translators for meetings and community outreach, and other meeting expenses. The Co-operative Housing Federation of Toronto managed to mobilize financial and in-kind support from sources friendly to the co-operative sector, including the Atkinson Foundation, the Co-operative Housing Federation of Canada, the Co-operative Housing Federation of Toronto, the Co-operators Insurance Company, and Metro Credit Union (now Alterna). The residents did not seem to realize the magnitude of the funding required because it was being raised by other sources.

The use of the community centre's charitable number was a source of confusion because some donors expected that those funds would be spent on the community centre even though they were being targeted for the conversion. Some costs were hidden because volunteers provided services and the Co-operative Housing Federation of Toronto did not receive full payment for training and educational programming. According to one long-time co-operative housing sector leader, "counting on fund-raising to conduct a conversion is unrealistic. I don't think the fund-raising capacity is there to do this" (Tom Clement, personal communication, 11 February 1999). As a result, there was increased reliance on volunteers from within the community and from the co-operative sector.

Forms of Social Capital

The presence of social capital in the Alexandra Park housing project and throughout the conversion into the Atkinson Housing Co-operative demonstrates how integral it was in engaging the residents with each other, mostly in constructive ways. While in most public housing projects the residents are often isolated from one another, the creation of the residents' association helped to change that reality. Many benefits of social capital are derived from membership in a group. This common membership creates a kind of bond or relationship whereby individuals can gain access to resources to improve their lives as they promote community values. A common element that brought the residents together was the need to overcome the stigma of living in a public housing project and of receiving a low income. Thus, the residents' association became the face of the community's desire to be seen as capable.

Within the community, trust – a central component of social capital – was a key feature of the implementation of the many successful initiatives that created a foundation for building a sense of community. There was both awareness of problems and the recognition that they were being dealt with through different measures aimed at instilling a sense of pride among the residents. Trust was also found in the decision-making process that existed within the residents' association. The norms established through the work of the association were based on a belief that concerns could be raised and dealt with co-operatively. As shown in the second key event, building and managing the community centre created a context that emphasized trusting relationships and fostered a belief that the community was able to manage and control an important community asset.

From the residents' perspective, all action revolved around the community centre, as it was the basis for free expression and the location of what I am referring to as social capital formation. Events held at the community centre enabled the residents to witness the effectiveness of coming together for a common purpose. At these events, norms were established to which the residents were expected to adhere and which helped establish ties within the community that contributed to its resilience in overcoming obstacles and to its many successes; these included norms related to not participating in illegal activities. There was a strong belief in working co-operatively in committees and as a board of directors.

Another way that social capital functioned within the Alexandra Park community and later as part of the conversion process was in the extent to which the residents were prepared to volunteer their time and participate in different community-oriented activities. For example, the block representative program established a culture of residents protecting each other, which resulted in a social practice that contributed to people feeling safer and more secure. However, the management agreement that institutionalized this social practice created the suspicion that individuals were only involved because it was a job that contributed to their income, rather than an expression of a commitment to a safe and secure environment.

In the late 1980s and early 1990s, drug dealing and prostitution started to affect trust among the residents because there was the perception that some residents were the actual perpetrators of the crimes. These issues challenged the social capital that had been created, and a siege mentality emerged because residents were not always sure whether or not their neighbour was contributing to the social problems, for instance as a drug dealer. People were afraid, so they stayed indoors, which reduced the possibility of organizing any collective action. However, the residents' association did successfully mobilize the community against drugs and prostitution, a reflection of the social capital built up over the years.

Social capital also promotes forms of social control because of norms intended to bring people together into a common understanding. Norms such as the unacceptability of participating in illegal activity were reinforced through programs offered at the community centre and monitored during the foot patrols. The event that helped to revive trust and co-operative action was the community security march of 1992. With this march the residents saw first hand that they could protect each other and that the outcome would be favourable for the community.

Promoting the solidarity of the group relied on the existing stock of social capital, which contributed to the success of the community march. Through its social capital the community initiated a discussion of why its needs were not being met and how the residents themselves could work co-operatively to improve the entire community. The community march was a way of demonstrating to each other that in the face of problems there is not only strength in numbers but also interest in working together to promote and plan for a positive vision of the future. Furthermore, the political support reinforced the notion that the residents could manage as well as advocate.

Social capital can build the social infrastructure of a community, but it can also create conditions that allow the emergence of subgroups whose interests can potentially conflict with the needs of the whole. The presence of these small groups became very apparent when divisions arose as the conversion was being completed. The co-operative leadership was challenged, and there was a general sense that the trust that had been established was being eroded.

The erosion of trust at the collective level created strong ties within subgroups based upon ethnocultural and religious differences. Ethnic niches started to emerge in which it seemed that people could rely on each other, but only if they belonged. This attitude carried over to the election of the co-operative's board of directors, and subgroups vied for control rather than electing directors according to their ability. This perception did not instil confidence among many residents that the community's general needs were being met. There was little effort made on the part of the factions in power to quell these fears; in Putnam's (2000) terms, there was a lack of bridging capital, which made it difficult to involve others in implementing solutions to the social problems because trust and reciprocity were not apparent.

The resulting confusion meant that the residents reverted to what they knew best – allowing the Alexandra Park Residents' Association to have a prominent role within the community. The original divisions, which had to do with how the community was being managed, were transferred to the conversion process. The divisions became based on those who supported the co-operative versus those who did not. As stated by St Stephen's Community House during the conflict-resolution process, the residents had to be able to trust each other if they wanted to live co-operatively. This position was shared by the housing corporation, which was prepared to cancel the conversion if there was not demonstrable proof that the board of directors of the Atkinson Housing Co-operative could overcome these challenges.

The presence of social networks with attachments external to the community (for example, the Co-operative Housing Federation of Toronto) provided a mediating mechanism for dealing with the conflicts. As an outsider, the Co-operative Housing Federation of Toronto was viewed with suspicion early in the process. The federation had a successful record of developing housing co-operatives, which demonstrated its technical expertise, but it was Tom Clement's relationship with Sonny Atkinson and his familiarity with the community that helped the residents to trust this organization' leadership in the conversion process.

Styles of Community Leadership

Strong and committed community leadership was intrinsic to the conversion process and a strength of the Alexandra Park housing project. Throughout the key events described in chapters 3 and 4, the stable leadership played a pivotal role in supporting the conversion process. In particular, two leadership styles, transactional and transformative, were exhibited by different individuals and contributed in varying ways to the building and maintaining of a strong community through the periods of growth. The two leadership styles that facilitated the residents' mobilization were supported by an evolving vision of a future co-operative community. In this section I describe the ways in which each style contributed to the conversion process.

Transactional leadership seeks to motivate followers by appealing to their self-interest (Burns, 1978). According to Bass (1990), transactional leaders view the leader-follower relationship as a form of reciprocity. This style of leadership encourages goal-oriented behaviour and works best when there is a clear direction and expectation of what is required of different actors. In Alexandra Park the transactional form of leadership was the predominant style exhibited during the formative years. In the early stages of the community's growth it was important for the residents' association to operate under this type of leadership because the focus was on programs and advocacy, not necessarily on building a new community.

The Alexandra Park Residents' Association was organized through its constitution such that participants knew their roles and the residents knew what to expect from the association. The leader worked with supporters to reinforce each role and to achieve the different objectives of the association. The APRA's presidents of applied this style of leadership in order to develop and promote community-based programs.

A change in leadership style resulted when the residents expressed frustration with the maintenance and security in the 1980s and rallied against the drug dealers; this created the media perception that vigilantes were rampant in the community. Sherman Middleton, the president of the Alexandra Park Residents' Association at that time, supported the actions taken by the residents, but his leadership style was transactional and focused on addressing the immediate problem. Sonny Atkinson's style was more transformative, and he used this opportunity to link the crime in the community with the housing corporation's inadequacies. In response, in the late 1980s, he introduced a vision of a self-managed community, but before the community could begin to grapple with it, issues of greater preoccupation – the drug problems and poor maintenance response time – had to be addressed.

Sonny Atkinson's vision involved transforming the way in which the residents saw their role in the community, by understanding the negative impact of the housing agency's policies. His vision of an empowered community through tenant self-management resonated across the community during a pivotal time. The message emphasized the achievement of autonomy so that the residents would have opportunities to gain income, develop local solutions to the problems, and implement local policies that reflected the community's interests. Atkinson expressed these sentiments in the following statement: "It [the housing corporation] just hasn't done anything to help us. We know where the problems are and we want more control over our rights to kick these bad cowboys out" (Shephard, 1995).

The establishment of links with diverse groups was made possible by Sonny Atkinson's involvement in external committees, such as the Resident Advisory Council in 1993. His legitimacy, both internally and externally, was grounded in the trust Atkinson had attained because of his proven track record of success based on an unwavering commitment for his community. He found that his vision was consistent with the work of other people and groups at the time (for example, Mark Goldblatt and the Co-operative Housing Federation of Toronto), which explains how he was able to garner such strong support within the community for an idea that was perceived by the housing corporation as not feasible.

The key events illustrate how the transformative leadership style led the community through two important transitional points: the security march and the referendum. These were crucial events in the steps to becoming a co-operative, and the community supported them in part because of Atkinson's charismatic presentation of the tenant self-management vision. And, of course, Atkinson's death was a blow because of his stature inside and outside the community. Not every-one was gracious about Sonny Atkinson, and some found his confron-tational approach alienating. However, he managed to mobilize and build support, which became a legacy of community action that was best appreciated after he had passed away in 1997.

Atkinson's status and charisma were also very intimidating, and following his death individual residents were reluctant to take on a leadership role because of his legacy. Representatives from the hous-ing corporation believed that there was strong leadership within the community, but they did not realize that Atkinson's death would lead to a loss of institutional memory and to increased mistrust among the residents as well as by government towards the residents. The fact that there were four different presidents from 1997 to 2003 reflected the community's inability to develop new leaders. The problem of leader-ship continuity was significant, but the residents did not appreciate the extent to which Atkinson's vision had been developed for over twenty-five years from his involvement in the community and working with others in different capacities.

Following the second referendum, the absence of a transformative leader had a significant impact on the conversion process. Since there was no unifying figure to lead the community through the process by which residents became members as well as managers, there was an urgent need to identify and prepare individuals to become leaders in the community. The individuals who followed Sonny Atkinson had a trans-actional style, with a focus on solving immediate problems rather than holding to and communicating a long-term vision. The focus was on instrumental tasks associated with the conversion into a co-operative, but the dependency on outside resources increased. Also, individuals came forward whose motivation seemed to be grounded in self-interest, in that they were trying to build status within the community. Some-times a new leader would want to make an immediate impact, but he or she would not have the skills to unify or represent the residents; as a result the leader often lost sight of the reason for the conversion. While Atkinson was able to keep the conversion process moving forward, he was also able to maintain the community centre. However, subsequent leaders were unable to successfully balance the two responsibilities and instead focused on one at the expense of the other.

Support for the conversion was strong outside of the community but was dwindling within the community after Sonny Atkinson's death. The loss of funding for the community centre was hurting morale among the residents and staff, which explains the re-emergence of the Alexandra Park Residents' Association and its competition with the Atkinson Housing Co-operative's board. Reconstituting APRA can be interpreted as reverting to the way things were before, as a best approach. At times, it seemed as though the community wanted a pause in the conversion to resolve some of the outstanding conflicts that existed among the residents as well as with the housing corporation's bureaucracy. An intervention was required that would maintain the momentum of the conversion process by supporting the current leadership and providing reassurances to the residents and the housing corporation that discontent was an inevitable part of community change.

A shift of the momentum occurred in the increasing reliance on external leaders to act as change agents, with the expectation that they would be more active in moving the community forward to completion of the conversion. Initially, the Co-operative Housing Federation of Toronto served as a change agent whose primary purpose was to promote the conversion. While it maintained this role throughout the process, with the weak leadership following Sonny Atkinson's death it had to either vary its role or take on the multiple roles of change agents, quasi-leaders of the co-operative, and intermediaries between the housing corporation and the co-operative. These roles were challenging and confusing, but the Co-operative Housing Federation of Toronto became the de facto leader of the conversion. To this day it continues to be very involved with the community and maintains a leadership role for external purposes. There have been varying degrees of success in developing a new generation of leaders in the Atkinson Housing Co-operative.

Community Consciousness

The fourth element that explains the conversion process is community consciousness. In the context of public housing, the various activities and social processes found in the community demonstrated a strong capacity to address problems with local solutions. This capacity was indicative of a consciousness that motivated the residents to be active participants in creating a sense of community. Pursuing greater control involved the realization that the community included residents who could not afford to rent in the private market and residents who wanted to remain in the community because of the convenient location and the sense of belonging. Ultimately, the residents knew that becoming a co-operative would not lead to economic benefits, such as decreases in their housing charges, but there was broad agreement that the conversion would lead to a safer community with a collective sense of ownership as well as improved responses to maintenance concerns and repairs.

Wilkinson and Quarter (1996) characterize community consciousness as consisting of two components: members feeling an attachment to their community and members exhibiting a movement perspective aimed at supporting all co-operative communities. The presence of these components in the unfolding of the key events helps to explain how the profound connection that the residents had to their community was an important element in the conversion.

Community Attachments

A group of residents developed a strong connection to the community shortly after the housing project opened in 1968. They formed the Alexandra Park Residents' Association in order to promote the interests of the new community and to avoid the many problems found in other public housing projects, with the focus of their work being quality-of-life issues. The formation of the Alexandra Park Residents' Association represented the first example of the community's commitment to transform self-interest into the interest of the group through various initiatives and programs. The subsequent building of the community centre gave the residents' association a central locale within the community and formalized its role. Over time, strong bonds emerged and residents participated and expressed their sense of belonging to the community. The result became the organizing of social and political events that were intended to create and maintain a safe and vibrant community. Another indication of the strong attachment that the residents felt towards the community was the willingness to volunteer their time.

The assault on the mother and son in 1990 became a catalyst for the residents to re-emerge as protectors of their community. For many residents, like Sonny Atkinson, an objective became the creation of an image of a community actively working together in the face of growing security and maintenance problems. The subsequent community march was a demonstration against the housing corporation, but it also became a show of the strength of attachment and of community solidarity.

The conversion proposal converged with the attachment felt by the residents as this was the only solution that would allow them to address the security and maintenance problems that they faced. In fact, all key individuals involved in the conversion process had some connection to the community regardless of whether or not they had lived there. The shared characteristic was the community's desire for improvements. The attachments that the residents had to the community involved personal relationships as well as a commitment to the well-being of the whole community. These attachments helped to sustain the conversion during some very difficult times. Even when divisions and conflicts emerged, there was a sense that people had to return to the table for the good of the community, thereby requiring self-interest to be set aside in favour of completing the conversion.

Movement Perspective

The second component of community consciousness involves incorporating a movement perspective into the actions undertaken by a group of people. The Atkinson Housing Co-operative was formed with the help of the co-operative movement, which provided a perspective to the conversion based on a tradition of empowering oppressed people through local control and a common identity (Mark Goldblatt, personal communication, 15 July 1997). For the Alexandra Park conversion to proceed, the community's collective identity had to be reflected in various mobilizing efforts aimed at protecting the members of the community from the housing corporation's constraining policies and disrespectful practices. The residents knew that, in addition to their shared experience, they were part of a community because of the awareness that collectively they could make a difference, and this knowledge formed a basis for their movement. The co-operative housing sector, through the Co-operative Housing Federation of Toronto, knew it needed to build on the strengths existing within the Alexandra Park housing project.

Another factor associated with the movement perspective that the Co-operative Housing Federation of Toronto included in its activities was the consideration of the community's critical consciousness (Wilkinson and Quarter, 1996) as an asset. This critical consciousness was found in three main areas. First, the hidden discourse within the community consisted of identifying problems and being able to integrate that knowledge into the technical assistance that informed the management of the community centre and later the conversion process; the residents became quite adept at recognizing problems and developing solutions. Second, there was an understanding of the impact of the housing corporation's neglect on the residents' ability to live in a safe and secure environment. A third indicator involved either having the ability or developing the ability to initiate some change through individual or collective action. Developing programs to help the residents or to pursue an issue for the benefit of the greater community good underlined the actions of the Alexandra Park Residents' Association. This critical consciousness caused outside groups, such as the Co-operative Housing Federation of Toronto, to actively support the community's goal of becoming a co-operative.

The movement perspective supported the conversion in a variety of ways. First, the conversion built on the community's critical consciousness, which legitimized community resistance to the housing corporation; the necessity of gaining control to improve their community was seen as the only solution. Second, the social benefit was the underlying purpose of becoming a co-operative since there would be no direct economic benefit – but there would be security of tenure; in addition, individuals realized that personal gain and improved self-worth could be attained through collective action. Third, the building of a governing structure meant that social and accountable power at the community level was an attainable goal, given the presence of the Alexandra Park Residents' Association.

In spite of strong support, the movement perspective did not extend beyond the Atkinson Housing Co-operative community, which contrasts with what Wilkinson and Quarter (1996) found in their study of the community economic development activities of the Evangeline community of Prince Edward Island. Sonny Atkinson recognized the implications of the conversion for public housing generally, but new leaders did not adopt that knowledge. The Co-operative Housing Federation of Toronto had framed the movement perspective in the terms that the co-operative model would improve the quality of life for the residents as it had in many other communities across the county. The Metropolitan Toronto Housing Corporation recognized the implications of this conversion for the broader social housing system, and for this reason the Alexandra Park conversion was described as a pilot project. However, there was scant recognition that what the residents were doing would have repercussions across the public housing system, both locally and internationally.

Role of Government

The role of government in public housing properties is primarily that of landlord and of supervisor of the agency that manages the properties. Residents are not normally involved in making and implementing key decisions made by the housing corporation. In 1993 the Metropolitan Toronto Housing Authority's role in the Alexandra Park property changed in that the corporation had to address the new issue of conversion into a housing co-operative that was under consideration. As the conversion process continued, its role expanded to include forms of gatekeeping and partnership and, as will be illustrated, was quite ambivalent at times.

Nature of Changing Function

The Alexandra Park community was unique within the public housing system as, even before the conversion process had started, there was an established working relationship between the community and the housing corporation, with elements of a partnership. For instance, as described in the first two key events, the management agreement that formalized the community created a block representative program, and the creation of the community centre showed that there was potential for the Metropolitan Toronto Housing Authority and the community to work in a constructive and co-operative manner. These instances demonstrated government agency support as well as confidence in the community's ability to manage vital aspects of the property.

As social problems began to emerge in the community, the power differential started to strain the constructive relationship. It started to deteriorate as housing agency policies and practices conflicted with the Alexandra Park Residents' Association's ability to address the social problems. Particular areas of conflict included safety and security, security of tenure, and maintenance response time. The residents believed that the inaction was deliberate, and explicit dissatisfaction with the housing agency's management approach became more vocal. It became clear that inclusion of the residents in meaningful participation was at the Metropolitan Toronto Housing Authority's discretion, and this produced resentment among the residents. Therefore, the relationship between these two stakeholders, which at times was collaborative, could also become adversarial, with residents feeling disempowered and unable to improve their community.

Clarifying the government agency's role was an important step in the conversion process in that the government agency had to manage the community while appearing to support the conversion proposal. There were often conflicting actions around whether the housing corporation perceived itself to be working with the community as a landlord or as a partner. For instance, the residents expected improved security of tenure after the positive referendum results, but they still had to transfer out of the community if they were over-housed (Eduardo Sousa, personal communication, 5 September 1998). The residents realized that they were vulnerable to the different policies and practices implemented by the government agency. Some resident volunteers believed that their housing was at risk if they confronted the agency, thereby causing some to reconsider their involvement. Fortunately, a moratorium on transfers was negotiated between the Metropolitan Toronto Housing Authority and the Atkinson Housing Co-operative board of directors in 2000.

The community meeting in 1993 was the key event in demonstrating community support for converting into a co-operative, and it also led to a change in the government agency's role. The government agency supported the conversion in principle by working with the Alexandra Park Residents' Association and the co-operative resource person to establish the parameters of the 1995 referendum. Moreover, it did provide clear direction on the steps required to complete the process. However, the Metropolitan Toronto Housing Authority was still the landlord, and it was not completely forthcoming with information throughout the conversion process. While the reasons for the lack of co-operation were never made explicit, it too was dealing with uncharted territory, and one could speculate that the government agency was concerned about public criticism of the turnover of a public asset to a group of public housing residents.

The community development work associated with the outreach was not a priority for the Metropolitan Toronto Housing Authority, but it did fund the community education component prior to the referendum, and this was important for the effectiveness of the referendum. However, the funding took five months to arrive, which was perceived by the community as an indication of the bureaucratic inertia that could potentially occur throughout the conversion process. The Alexandra Park Residents' Association and the Co-operative Housing Federation of Toronto expressed concern that, in spite of good intentions, the agency was behaving inconsistently and its expectations were unclear.

After the successful referendum in 1995 it was hoped that the conversion would proceed expeditiously, but this did not occur. Rather, the role of the government agency started to change to that of gatekeepers of the process, whereby the agency controlled the availability of information. In essence, the Metropolitan Toronto Housing Authority was able to control the conversion process by virtue of its ability to determine what information would be made available and what was deemed appropriate. The government also controlled the length of time that it would take to provide responses to the proposals of Atkinson board, which contributed to escalating legal costs and diminished institutional memory.

The Metropolitan Toronto Housing Authority, and later Toronto Community Housing Corporation, encouraged the residents to pursue the conversion but did not provide them with resources, direction, or funding to allow a quick completion of the conversion. According to the agency representatives, as this was a new process they did not always know the appropriate support and guidance to give. Consequently, they also relied on the expertise of the Co-operative Housing Federation of Toronto, which in addition to its other roles in the conversion process served an intermediary role between the residents and the housing corporation.

The working group formed after the 1995 referendum created some stability within the community leadership because the Co-operative Housing Federation of Toronto was involved. Establishing this group was a crucial step to convincing the government agency to have a greater role in the conversion by working more actively with the residents. This new role for the agency caused unanticipated challenges, such as those around determining whether the community had the capacity to manage the property as landlords, and promoting co-operative values. Consequently, the working group turned into negotiators as the residents had to demonstrate convincingly that they were ready to take on the role of managers. It can be argued that the government agency did not really know what to expect from the residents in terms of the final agreement. One housing corporation representative involved in negotiating the agreement stated: "I think people really were not sure of what this was going to look like. Like, I honestly believe that people were so entrenched in co-op, okay, and what that meant, that they were not prepared to see beyond that. They were expecting – I know for a fact that some of my colleagues were expecting, could not see themselves through this because they didn't see a co-op evolving in the true sense. It's still not; it's not a co-op really" (Lou Canton, personal communication, 22 February 2002).

The actions of the government representatives throughout the conversion process reinforced the asymmetrical power relationship between the residents and the government administrators. While the latter seemed to encourage the conversion, their role as gatekeeper constrained the process, as new obstacles were introduced at different stages in the conversion. For instance, the government representatives would not share crucial information (in the form of a list of residents) on the grounds of confidentiality, and they insisted on a second referendum. As a result, negotiations were very difficult; at one moment the residents were being asked to assume managerial responsibilities, and at another they were reminded that they were residents who could not handle information appropriately.

The slow pace of the conversion process caused considerable frustration within both the community and the Co-operative Housing Federation of Toronto. In spite of reassurances from government representatives, the predominant view within the community was that the Metropolitan Toronto Housing Authority continued to undermine the process. The representatives stated that caution was required because this conversion was unprecedented. Their involvement, they argued, represented a significant departure from the culture that had informed planning strategies and tenant relations since the 1940s.

It was apparent that the government agency administering public housing did not have complete control over its own decision making. Changes in social housing legislation affected the length of time of the conversion process and also had an impact on determining the role that the housing corporation was able to take. The legislative changes made the municipalities major players in social housing and, in effect, meant that three levels of government were involved in the conversion process in some capacity at different points in time. The federal government owned the property initially, and the provincial government managed it through the Ontario Housing Corporation. However, all public housing properties were subsequently downloaded to the provinces beginning in 1993 (Prince, 1998). Following legislative changes that were introduced in 1999 by the Province of Ontario and implemented in 2000, the municipal government became a primary stakeholder in the Atkinson conversion. These changes created uncertainty for the government department that was responsible for public housing and therefore slowed its response to the Atkinson conversion.

Although the Atkinson Housing Co-operative board of directors and the Co-operative Housing Federation of Toronto were involved in discussions with the Metropolitan Toronto Housing Authority, the delays caused uncertainly and frustration within the community that helped to fuel the divisions. The residents who were opposed to the conversion used the delays to argue that the effort that was going into the conversion of the property into a co-operative was better spent elsewhere. One long-time resident summed it up best: "I don't know if I am coming or going with this thing. It is better to have the devil you know" (Betta, personal communication, November 1999). Another consequence of the delays was the draining of resources, both of volunteers and of the limited funds provided by the Co-operative Housing Federation of Toronto. Volunteers lost interest in the conversion and, in some cases, moved out of the community. The Co-operative Housing Federation, which had backed the conversion financially since 1996, found it difficult to sustain its commitment to do so as the process was prolonged. In spite of the challenges all partners maintained their commitment to seeing the conversion process through to completion. The Atkinson Housing Co-operative worked with the federation and the Metropolitan Toronto Housing Corporation to develop proposals that were eventually presented jointly to the housing corporation's board of directors on 15 August 2001. The board's approval opened the door for finalizing the legal basis of the conversion. As a result, the municipal and provincial governments contributed to accelerating the pace of the conversion process in early 2002. Indications included timely responses to the proposals introduced by the Atkinson Housing Co-operative board of directors as well as explicit support for the conversion process, both financially and bureaucratically. However, as the housing corporation became more directive and transparent with its expectations, the community was forced to make significant concessions.

Arguably, the final agreement reflected a general lack of faith on the part of Metropolitan Toronto Housing Corporation in the community's ability to manage the property. For instance, the requirement to have external representatives sit on the co-operative's board of directors suggests that the housing corporation did not believe the community was prepared to completely take on management responsibilities. Their addition to the board was also a response to the residents' concerns that had been expressed when the divisions emerged; in other words, the membership desired external support. Tom Clement stated that these elements were intended to alleviate the concerns voiced by the different stakeholders involved in the conversion process (including the residents).

Figure 4. Governance Structure of a Typical Housing Co-operative. The members are intended to be the ultimate decision makers in the co-operative. The property management is hired by the board and is therefore directly linked to the board of directors.

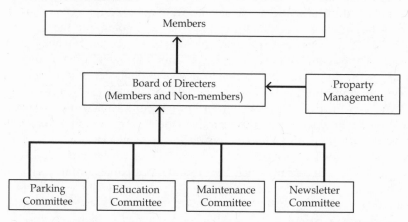

The conflicts and divisions that emerged towards the end of the conversion process probably influenced Toronto Community Housing Corporation. Similarly, the corporation's insistence on the involvement of a third-party resource group and on additional reporting requirements (for example, annual budget approval) also suggested concern about whether the co-operative could manage its own affairs. The final agreement ensured that Atkinson Housing Co-operative was going to be different from other housing co-operatives, particularly in the greater role that an outside group would have in the decision-making process of an autonomous organization. Figure 4 shows a typical housing co-operative's governance structure.

By comparison, in Atkinson Housing Co-operative, the Co-operative Housing Federation of Toronto, and non-members are part of the governance structure (see figure 5).

The Co-operative Housing Federation of Toronto seemed to have some reservations about the community's capacity to manage itself and therefore supported the government's assertion that more education and training were needed before the community was able to take over management responsibilities. However, I want to be clear that the Co-operative Housing Federation of Toronto recommended the final agreement with reluctance because of the unusual restrictions.

Figure 5. Governance Structure of Atkinson Housing Co-operative. While the structure is similar to that of other housing co-operatives, there are two additional stakeholders involved in the decision-making process. The direction of the dashed line represents their connection to the co-operative, which is an outcome of the final operating agreement.

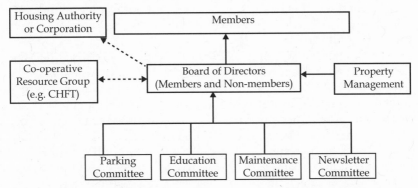

In analysing the role that the different levels of government played throughout the conversion process, it is possible to see changes, in that there was a shift from being a typical landlord and gatekeeper of housing policy towards becoming a partner in the conversion process. However, at the time that the conversion was finalized, the partnership was not equal, and arguably the government was a senior partner that maintained an in loco parentis role within the community. However, since the government became a primary stakeholder, the Atkinson Housing Co-operative started to resemble a multi-stakeholder form of co-operative, a form that was emerging in the different economic sectors in which co-operatives had a significant presence (for example, see Co-operatives Secretariat, 2009).

Cultural Change

Although aspects of a culture of dependency were present in Alexandra Park, the community's tradition of resident activism, which emerged shortly after the community opened in 1968, has challenged the commonly help perception that public housing residents are passive and incapable of being independent of the state on matters intended to improve the community. This tradition created a foundation for the development of a sense of community pride and a commitment to community building that eventually led the residents to embrace the co-operative housing model and to pursue the conversion. Although it would be too simplistic to argue that the culture of dependency that pervades public housing did not exist in Alexandra Park, evidence from the key events indicates that from the beginning this community differed, and dependency was intermixed with a form of self-reliance that grew over the years and helped lead to and sustain the conversion process once it was underway.

Even though the Metropolitan Toronto Housing Authority had the final say in all matters relating to this community as Alexandra Park (and to an extent continues to have such a say in financial matters and capital repairs), the conversion process pressured it to redefine its relationship to a public housing project by accepting a management model that extended greater latitude to the co-operative than is normally found in public housing. On the one hand, without this pressure it is unlikely that the housing corporation would have become a partner in the conversion, unless there was openness to redefining the existing relationship. On the other hand, without a tradition of seeking greater self-reliance through activism and community development – which is atypical across public housing communities – it is unlikely that the Atkinson board, with the help of the Co-operative Housing Federation of Toronto, would have been able to convince the housing corporation that a new management model could be successfully attempted and implemented in a public housing project.

Therefore, even though the key events are distinct, there is a common thread that connects them: the actions and characteristics of a culture that has been part of this community since the late 1960s and has thrived because of the various successes and constructed opportunities. Although creation of the Alexandra Park Residents' Association should not be seen as the sole predictor of the community's efforts to convert into a co-operative, the first key event helped to establish the community's culture of pursuing greater self-reliance. The formation of the Alexandra Park Residents' Association assisted in demonstrating the community's capacity to be organized and purposeful. The association's successes led to the forging of the management agreement that fostered a period of meaningful collaboration between the residents and the housing corporation. In addition, building and managing the community centre demonstrated capacity within the community to responsibly deliver and manage services. In Alexandra Park there was a strong belief in the value of working with the housing corporation to improve the community, a belief that was strengthened by the residents' experiences of the association and the community centre.

Arguably, there were setbacks in the 1980s, such as the increased crime that generated fear and some feelings of helplessness, but unlike many other public housing projects, Alexandra Park mobilized itself, and the community security march in 1990 helped to solidify the community's resolve to improve its conditions – with or without the housing corporation's support. The community's initiative captured public attention, and the mayor and municipal councillors joined in the residents' calls for improved security. For instance, the demand to tear down the walls (a haven for drug dealers) was a local solution that required political support in order to convince the housing corporation to support the initiative. It took almost two years for the walls to be torn down, but the community persevered in the face of Metropolitan Toronto Housing Authority's apparent inertia. The garnering of political support during the community security march helped the residents to come to believe in their capabilities and capacity to tackle other issues such as the conversion.

During the early years of the conversion process (1993 to 1995) several of the key events laid the basis for sustainable cultural change. At this time the community's desire to gain control over the management functions of the property was not viewed as credible by the provincial government. The government representatives required additional convincing because it was unheard of for residents to be capable of undertaking such responsibilities. Once the Alexandra Park Residents' Association had started working with Mark Goldblatt, the co-operative consultant, the conversion proposal began to receive explicit support from the Ministry of Municipal Affairs and Housing. This support essentially forced the Metropolitan Toronto Housing Authority to consider the conversion proposal worthy of pursuit.

The community meeting of 1993 was consistent with the culture of self-reliance emerging within the community, in that the residents were presented with the option of becoming a co-operative. The voice of the community and its representative organizations was articulate and passionate and could not be silenced by the housing authority's initial reluctance to work with them in achieving this goal of self-reliance.

The referendum in 1995 was further indication of the community's advancing culture of self-reliance. A substantial minority in the community did not support the referendum and worried about losing their government benefits, an indication that the culture of dependency that pervaded public housing was still part of Alexandra Park, even

Figure 6. Communication Patterns between the Stakeholders. The solid lines represent the direction of communication associated with the negotiation process.

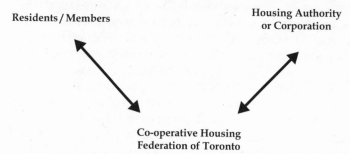

on the cusp of the conversion to the Atkinson Housing Co-operative. However, the majority of the residents wanted greater self-reliance and expressed themselves as such in the 1995 referendum and again in 1998 when the government demanded more evidence.

During the challenging conversion years, divisions arose within the community, and the Co-operative Housing Federation of Toronto helped to sustain the changing culture by acting both as a support to the Atkinson Housing Co-operative's board of directors and as an intermediary between the residents and the housing corporation. Figure 6 depicts the communication patterns between the key stakeholders in the conversion process.

Toronto Community Housing Corporation expressed concern over the poor communication between it and the residents. The disconnect had the effect of making it difficult for either side to express and communicate its position with respect to the conversion process. What the housing corporation's representatives failed to realize was that the asymmetrical power relationship between the housing corporation and the residents established a cultural divide that was reinforced by years of suspicion and mistrust. While the emergence of the co-operative reflected a culture of self-reliance that was greater than that of public housing projects in general, the support of the Co-operative Housing Federation still was needed. Without this important support, it is unlikely that the conversion would have been completed, thereby illustrating the limitations of cultural change at Atkinson and the power of the barriers that constrained the residents.

During the negotiation process the patterns of communication between the key stakeholders changed (see figure 7), reflecting greater capacity among the Atkinson Housing Co-operative directors and a perception

Figure 7. Flow of Communication among Stakeholders Involved in Finalizing the Conversion Process. When divisions and other concerns started to delay the conversion process, Atkinson Housing Co-operative needed to communicate directly with Toronto Community Housing Corporation. However, throughout the final negotiations the Co-operative Housing Federation of Toronto had to act as an intermediary, as indicated by the dashed lines.

by the housing corporation that the co-operative could sustain increased self-reliance.

Nevertheless, in the final agreement Toronto Community Housing Corporation was unwilling to extend the same degree of autonomy to the Atkinson Housing Co-operative as is found in other housing co-operatives, thereby reflecting some lack of confidence in the co-operative's ability to manage its own affairs. Regardless of how much power the Atkinson Housing Co-operative now has, the evidence suggests that there was a significant cultural change in this community from the norms for public housing, that this greater self-reliance was apparent from the early years of Alexandra Park, and that it increased as a result of various successes over the years. The culture of self-reliance had its limitations, as was apparent in the conversion process when Sonny Atkinson's death created a leadership vacuum in the community. However, Atkinson Housing Co-operative is a dynamic community, and with the increased experience of self-management, the cultural change has developed further towards becoming an key agent in the revitalization of the neighbourhood, a point to which I return in the afterword.

Resource Mobilization

Throughout the community's development the use of mobilizing as a strategy helped to establish the Alexandra Park Residents' Association (and later the co-operative's board) as the representative voice of a community of committed people willing to work out problems together. The association provided the opportunity for residents to share concerns and develop local solutions to various problems, such as the issue of tearing down the barrier walls, which became a priority because the residents collectively saw the need to decrease the number of spaces used for illegal activity. The resource mobilization approach (McCarthy and Zald, 1977) assisted in raising awareness within the community of the problems and in strengthening the existing social capital as the means to deal with them.

The community security march in 1990 serves as a prime example of the application of the resource mobilization approach. This event represented the community's response to ongoing frustrations with the security problems, from a perceived lack of action to a lack of interest in protecting them. Mobilizing the residents for this cause was an invaluable experience for the community, as people who were normally afraid to be involved joined in the collective action. The fear of retribution, which had been a barrier to organizing the residents, was replaced with a message of hope that something meaningful could come from the action.

In addition to raising awareness, the community security march helped to raise the profile of the community. Resource mobilization was crucial to convincing the housing corporation and other external groups that change was required with respect to maintenance of the community and treatment of the residents. In essence, through mobilizing itself around these important issues, the community developed a public profile that furthered its ability to receive support and resources from the co-operative sector, politicians, and sympathetic representatives of the housing corporation. Moreover, the very visible political support that led to the barrier walls' being torn down motivated the residents to build on this success in order to improve the community in a sustainable way – which was the hoped-for outcome of organizing the community meeting in 1993.

The 1995 referendum represents another instance of the community using the resource mobilization approach to build its profile, both internally and externally. The security march and the community meeting had created a passion that carried over into the referendum. The residents made an informed choice to become a co-operative and, in effect, to determine the future direction of their community.

Resident resources as well as support from external sources contributed to demonstrating an emerging capacity to manage the property while fostering a greater sense of community. Individual residents realized that they were not alone in their sense of living in fear, and in general they became more informed about how the struggles they were all facing were partly the community's responsibility, but, more important, that the dangers were also a reflection of the asymmetrical relationship they had with the housing corporation. The residents became politically aware – referred to as *conscientization* (Freire, 1972) and further explored in the next chapter – and they began to recognize that their issues with the housing corporation could be addressed through collective action, one expression of which was the formation of Atkinson Housing Co-operative.

Leadership was critical to mobilizing the community, and following Sonny Atkinson's death the leadership vacuum created uncertainty and confusion among the residents, as there was a search for some direction in order to maintain the momentum. This leadership vacuum became critical later as divisions developed that threatened the conversion process. Again, the residents mobilized themselves, as was now their tradition, but this time the target became the very leadership of the co-operative's board. A group of residents rallied to reconstitute the Alexandra Park Residents' Association because many felt that the Atkinson Housing Co-operative's board was unresponsive to their needs, particularly with regard to management of the community centre. The residents' association was reconstituted and assumed responsibility for managing the centre.

Throughout its history the community has used mobilization strategies to address concerns that threatened its success and safety. The key events illustrate many examples of these strategies, with mobilization being oriented towards addressing issues, internal crises, and unreasonable external expectations. Resource mobilization was confined to addressing issues of local concern rather than those of a more general nature, but nevertheless, it was an important part of the community dynamic that eventually led to the conversion of a public housing project into a co-operative.

6 Extending the Conversion Experiment

In this book I have documented, analysed, and interpreted a community's journey towards becoming Canada's first public housing co-operative. The seven elements derived from the key events have helped to demonstrate the importance that the events had on defining the direction taken by the community, a direction that resulted in the eventual formation of the Atkinson Housing Co-operative. While chapter 5 identified and analysed the critical elements that explain the conversion process, in this chapter I will synthesize the seven elements and the lessons learned from the key events into a development model that I refer to as the *framework for community-based control*. The purpose of formulating the model is to encourage and assist other low-income communities in their pursuit of a conversion process, one that would take into account the Atkinson Housing Co-operative's experience. The intent is not to suggest replicating that experience but rather to prevent a situation in which a community tries to reinvent the wheel.

I have selected the term *community-based control* rather than simply *community control* because the intention is to aid others in constructing a process whereby the decisions and practices reflect the needs of the community. In this case, community development is a tool to strengthen the assets discovered within local contexts in order to promote principles of self-reliance and resiliency. I conclude this chapter with a discussion of the policy implications of the Alexandra Park conversion, as well as provide the reader with a series of lessons learned from the conversion that can inform future conversion processes. Part of this discussion will demonstrate how the framework for community-based control could serve as a valuable tool.

Framework for Community-Based Control

The stakeholders involved in the Atkinson Housing Co-operative accomplished the conversion without a systematic plan or guide. They relied on the community's assets and external expertise to develop a process that was somewhat ad hoc, yet reflected the Alexandra Park community's desire and ability to manage a housing property co-operatively. As demonstrated in chapter 5, the seven elements used to explain the conversion process were integral to the community's desire to become a co-operative. Although they are described as discrete, their compartmentalization is analytical in that each element had particular functions at different points in the conversion process. The framework for community-based control, shown in figure 8, is presented as five components to be associated with the transformation of a community in a planned manner: namely, community assets, building capacity, demonstrating capacity, critical consciousness, and goal attainment.

The framework for community-based control adapts features of the community-based development models described in chapter 2. The

Figure 8. Framework for Community-Based Control. The figure depicts the framework as constructed from the Atkinson experience. The solid lines represent the clear direction of steps in the conversion process, but the dashed lines represent the iterative nature of the community development process that could and should occur as a community moves towards community-based control.

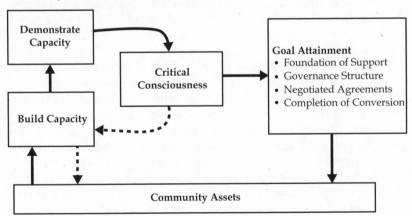

seven elements that explain how the conversion process was undertaken are the constituents that form each component of the framework for community-based control. An important feature of the framework is that it illustrates that community members have opportunities to learn new skills and apply them in meaningful ways in a planned manner that results in the attainment of postulated goals. Although the components are described below in serial order, it is not a staged process, and each of the components can be given more or less emphasis that reflects a point in the development of a community and its strengths.

Community Assets

The first component of the framework for community-based control is community assets, which are resources that function as the building blocks of community organizing (McKnight and Kretzmann, 1999). The presence of different community assets within the conversion to the Atkinson Housing Co-operative encouraged – indeed, empowered – the community to pursue the conversion process and convinced the housing corporation that the community contained the components essential to managing the property as a co-operative. The community's assets that proved to be crucial to initiating and completing the process are broadly identified in three areas: local resources, social capital, and leadership styles.

The resources identified in the interpretation of the key events are an important component of community assets. Throughout the conversion process volunteers and technical assistance were two critical examples of internal and external resources. First, the resident volunteers developed various activities that enhanced the strength and identity of the community. Through volunteer actions the residents had opportunities to meaningfully participate in activities that would improve the living conditions for the community as a whole and that would also be personally fulfilling. There were two main outlets for resident volunteering: the residents' association and the community centre.

The Alexandra Park Residents' Association was founded on the premise that working co-operatively can lead to opportunities for accessing resources for learning and for improving one's life. The early mission of the association was to ensure that past mistakes of other public housing projects would be avoided. Over time, the different initiatives and activities implemented through the stock of volunteers helped to foster an attachment on the part of the residents to the community, especially to the community centre. As a result the volunteers acquired important skills and knowledge that founded a culture of co-operation and reflected a capacity to understand what was required in building a sense of community.

The residents' association worked to sustain programs at the community centre, another community asset that was critical to demonstrating growth and development. The ability of the resident volunteers to raise funds, another community resource, was only possible because of the initiative taken by the residents' association, an initiative that contributed to the attainment of charitable status for the community centre. A significant outcome of managing the community centre was the ability of the volunteers to develop skills in order to achieve (albeit with varying levels of success) important objectives that were not normally associated with residents in public housing projects – for example, raising annual funds for community-based programming, providing financial reports to funders, and explaining the social impacts of the different programs to members of the community as well as to government representatives and to funders.

The resources provided by external organizations (for example, the Co-operative Housing Federation of Toronto and government agencies) and local politicians came in the form of technical assistance, such as education and community-organizing strategies for the referendums. These resources complemented the community's assets and were important for the conversion because they helped to build local capacity for management. The education and training resources provided to the residents resulted in a cognitive shift that crystallized the way in which the responsibilities involved in managing the community centre were transferable. However, as noted in the key events, this process did not always go smoothly, because, for many residents, the co-operative conversion introduced new ideas that they were not always ready to implement.

The second element of community assets is social capital. As the glue that binds a community, social capital was evident in the form of relationships among the residents that developed levels of trust within the community. The programs offered at the community centre helped residents to engage with each other in positive ways and, therefore, became a source of social capital that could be transferred to the conversion in terms of enhancing both the breadth and the experience, as well as the level, of resident participation. Volunteer participation in the different activities offered through the residents' association helped form and sustain the social capital.

The residents' association helped to build bonded social capital by providing the volunteers and residents in general with group membership status that fostered a greater sense of community. Group membership contributed to the residents' understanding that the problems within the community were not isolated to individual households and that the housing corporation was neglecting the needs of the community. For instance, in the case of security, the block representative program of the 1970s was successful because it involved residents who were aware of the problems, and the rest of the residents trusted that, should problems arise, their block representatives would be of assistance. Tellingly, the block representative programs ceased once they were no longer seen as being volunteer-based. As one interviewee stated, "once it became a job, it became a competition for who would get which shift."

Another feature of social capital evident in the community was the creation of and adherence to norms such as co-operation and the protection of each other. Participation in activities was a norm for the community, as was the expectation that contributions would be reciprocated by others giving of their time and energy. The community had a long-standing tradition of informal co-operation that seems to have been transferred to the conversion process.

The final element, which reflects the important role that community assets have in community-based control, was the local leaders themselves. In general, the leaders exhibited qualities through their interactions within the community that revealed a particular type of leadership style, that is, either transactional or transformative (see chapter 4). Each style had an important role in the community's development into a co-operative. Through important vehicles like the residents' association and the community centre, leaders emerged who were interested in seeing the residents thrive in a safe and constructive environment. Transactional leaders to helped mobilize resources and manage the community centre, whereas transformative leaders became the public face of the efforts of the community to convert itself into a co-operative. Both styles served to address the threats to community safety and to support the building of capacity to achieve community-based control. While different forms of leaders are important for any community, they do serve different purposes and may not always serve the best interests of a community. Each style clearly had an impact on the conversion process, but the fundamental challenge to maintaining momentum was that each person who came forward did so under particular circumstances rather than as a result of a deliberate attempt to identify an individual with a particular style that would support the forward movement of the conversion process. In actual practice, whoever wanted and was able to be involved as a leader was encouraged to do so regardless of ability.

As an example that demonstrates the integral role of leadership forms in the conversion process, the housing authority (and later the housing corporation) expressed significant reservations about whether the community had the required capacity to become a housing co-operative. Government representatives had the power to decide if the conversion to a co-operative would be completed. Many delays resulted because the residents needed to provide assurances that the concerns were either baseless or being addressed. Yet this was a catch-22: The housing corporation officials wanted to see that the residents could demonstrate the capacity to manage and to work co-operatively in decision making and implementation; however, unless the conversion were completed, the residents could not actually demonstrate this capacity. As a result, the negotiated agreement was developed under very tense and stressful conditions. Eventually the housing corporation did not know for certain whether the residents could function as members of a co-operative, but its support was influenced by the ongoing commitment of external support (or leaders) to help strengthen local community assets. This guarantee came in the form of the Co-operative Housing Federation of Toronto's providing volunteers and technical assistance for the purpose of building leadership capacity.

Building Capacity

The second component of the framework is building capacity. In community development processes the primary consideration must be that social change is sustainable, which is accomplished through the creation and implementation of different capacity-building strategies for the community's assets. Building capacity in a community setting involves the development of skills and knowledge that decrease dependency and increase self-reliance by engendering empowerment. The stakeholders of the Alexandra Park conversion wanted to make sure that the community was prepared for different responsibilities by, for example, having knowledge of complex financial practices such as budgeting and planning and being able to work as both landlords and neighbours. They also wanted to know that the residents were ready to handle problems with accountability and transparency. In essence, if the management of the community was to be transferred to the co-operative, then the members needed to develop the requisite skills by building capacity. These strategies built upon existing community assets with the intention of applying and transferring new skills to different problems (Minkler and Wallerstein, 1999). Capacity building is derived from the interaction of four elements: internal or external resources, social capital, leadership styles, and the role of government.

Communities normally have more capacity than is first thought; assessing it is often accomplished by the use of an inventory or a needs assessment (Minkler and Wallerstein, 1999). At Atkinson an assessment was not conducted, because the stakeholders did not think that it was necessary. Initial capacity was evident in the community's resources, including the volunteers and technical assistance. The residents were fortunate to have had opportunities through the experience of managing the community centre to develop skills and knowledge that created an understanding of how to conceptualize and address the different needs of the community members. The board of directors of the residents' association, the Co-operative Housing Federation of Toronto, and the initial government representatives believed, or perhaps hoped, that the skills derived from these opportunities could be transferred into the co-operative. However, the capacity to manage a small-scale organization is vastly different than that of managing a co-operative, which involves decisions on a much broader array of issues such as maintenance and security costs.

Strategies associated with building capacity in the Alexandra Park conversion used local resources such as technical assistance in identifying best business and governance practices, the purposeful use of volunteers, community organizing, and targeted fund-raising. These strategies focused on enhancing individual and organizational capacity. For individuals, the skills were largely instrumental: arranging meetings, using rules of order, understanding governance, managing human resources, locating sources of information, and communicating constructively. Transferring these skills became the basis for building capacity in other areas – for instance, conducting community meetings with simultaneous translation and involving residents in negotiation meetings with the housing corporation.

A primary source for building capacity was the Co-operative Housing Federation of Toronto, which was adept at working with groups that were seeking to form new housing co-operatives. However, this resource lacked experience in working with public housing residents, and its approach had to be adapted to a unique environment without creating another form of dependency.

To build capacity there was reliance on the bridging social capital, created over time, which assisted volunteers in working with outside groups and individuals to promote the community's assets and acquire new resources. These external connections were also useful for developing new leaders, an important component of capacity building. For instance, when Sonny Atkinson worked with Mark Goldblatt to introduce the co-operative alternative, the intention was to strengthen the Alexandra Park Residents' Association as well as to transfer the skills and experiences into new initiatives that would reinforce the community's capacity. Thus, fostering partnerships and producing a base of external resources to undertake new and innovative tasks was a key component of developing capacity.

Social capital was also central to capacity building. The focus for the capacity-building strategies with respect to social capital was to build on the existing social processes promoting co-operative relationships and the reciprocal feature of resident participation, such that residents were more likely to be involved in activities when others demonstrated such commitment. The capacity-building strategies were intended to expand on previous actions and encourage future participation by showcasing previous examples, such as volunteering in the community centre and deciding to be on the board of directors of the Alexandra Park Residents' Association.

As a key aspect of social capital, trust was an important factor in sustaining resident involvement within the Alexandra Park housing project. The residents trusted that the leadership was acting to promote the interests of the community, and this faith in the leadership, in turn, provided the impetus for greater resident involvement. Through activities related to the community centre such as fund-raising, acquiring external support, and creating programs, participation became a norm that was essential for the community to operate as a co-operative.

Social capital was crucial for capacity building as the residents needed to trust that the activities involved in converting the property were purposeful. Moreover, they had to trust that those elected would support activities suggested by external organizations that served the interests of the broader community, especially in relation to the community centre. Reconstituting the residents' association in 2001 was a way of emphasizing that the leaders needed to be trusted. As a result, an overlapping governance structure was created that demonstrated the importance that the community placed on having an accountable residents' association to manage the community centre.

The third element that was part of the strategies to build capacity was leadership styles. Although there was no explicit strategy to develop new leaders, leadership potential was plentiful, and there were many examples of leaders to serve as role models. The capacity-building strategies with respect to leadership were intended to provide opportunities and resources for residents to learn new skills, such as interpersonal communication and public speaking, that would help bolster their confidence and encourage individuals to take on leading roles in tasks associated with the conversion process.

Throughout the conversion process, differing leadership styles were crucial. In Alexandra Park the leadership style tended to be transactional, that is, directed to the completion of specific tasks associated with running the community centre. However, the visionary style was integral to an analysis of the underlying problems in the community and for offering solutions to problems; for example, Sonny Atkinson decided to conduct the foot patrols in order to provide a visible presence of residents willing to protect each other against criminal activity, while he was also pursuing the tenant self-management alternative. Furthermore, Atkinson's ability to serve both as a visionary and as a leader for solving specific tasks was critical to the community's capacity building around such events as the community vote in 1993 and the referendum in 1995.

The leadership in the Alexandra Park housing project was able to consolidate the knowledge from capacity-building strategies and help the Alexandra Park Residents' Association to focus attention on seeking an alternative management arrangement. The priority of the capacity-building strategies for individuals involved in the residents' association or the Atkinson board of directors involved learning and developing a sophisticated analytical ability in areas of finance, politics, diplomacy, and public speaking. For instance, these leaders needed to present their recommendations with regard to the negotiations for the final operating agreement to the broader community in ways that demonstrated an understanding of the intricacies of budgeting and management and that allowed the members of the community to grasp their relevance. Fortunately in those instances the Co-operative Housing Federation of Toronto was present to ensure that the message was conveyed accurately and appropriately.

The conflicts and divisions that emerged revealed the limitations of the community's capacity to address member discontent and the limitation of the external resources available for anticipating those problems. Two examples highlight these limitations. First, following Sonny Atkinson's death, a leadership vacuum emerged in part because leadership training was not a formal part of the conversion process. A variety of new leaders were strongly encouraged to be involved, but they were often individuals whose interest was far narrower than what was needed to lead a community through a significant social change. The second example is that the community appeared to have an insufficient capacity to address internal conflict. Until the referendums had been completed, the community was regarded as homogeneous by the housing authority, with all residents supposedly having the same needs. When the conflicts emerged, divisions became apparent. Although divisions in a community setting are commonplace and to a degree can be viewed as a strength, in the latter stages of the conversion process they had a negative impact. In the absence of the capacity to resolve conflicts locally, the community relied on the Co-operative Housing Federation of Toronto.

Building capacity can be a lengthy process, especially for transforming a community. When expectations became clear, the community was able to consolidate its assets for a common goal. Furthermore, as shown in figure 8, the strategies associated with building capacity were intended to enhance and develop new community assets by introducing new resources or introducing innovative roles for volunteers, such as chairing committees and representing the community in different functions. However, it was important for the community to not only build capacity but also demonstrate it. In particular, the residents needed to demonstrate their capacity to manage to both the housing corporation and each other.

Demonstrating Capacity

The third component of the framework, demonstrating capacity, involves showcasing a community's ability to undertake different tasks, either by the implementation of clear objectives in an organized way or through collective action. The goal is to apply what was learned from the building activities and demonstrate what the residents are capable of doing. While the notion of demonstrating can seem both obvious and trivial, seeing one's efforts result in something that could benefit the entire community can have a profoundly positive psychological effect on an individual. For that reason the importance of this component should not be minimized; rather, it should be considered as a development lever supporting community-based control. This component is made up of two elements: the role of government as partners, which includes a housing authority like the Toronto Community Housing Corporation; and resource mobilization.

Working in partnership with government through the housing authority and later the housing corporation provided the residents with the opportunity to demonstrate their capacity for understanding and to negotiate the steps that would lead to a final operating agreement. For instance, the working group created after the 1995 and 1998 referendums gave the Alexandra Park Residents' Association an avenue for joining the housing corporation at the table and demonstrating to the community that the overwhelming support for the conversion process was meaningful. The working-group experience encouraged a partnership to form between the residents' association and the Metropolitan Toronto Housing Authority. As a result, the direction and capacity requirements became clearer for all stakeholders. However, representatives of the housing authority viewed the ongoing support of the co-operative consultant Mark Goldblatt and the Co-operative Housing Federation of Toronto as hindering community growth because of concerns that a culture of dependency might continue. When the community was able to demonstrate capacity, the housing corporation became more confident that the residents could be granted greater latitude to manage their community. Metropolitan Toronto Housing Authority's support for the co-operative, in turn, became a confidence builder for the members of the co-operative. Until that time, however, the constant scepticism expressed by the housing authority helped mobilize the residents and their association to learn new skills that would enable them to eventually manage the property. The community applied two strategies that demonstrated capacity for becoming a co-operative: organizational competence and collective action. In both cases, the role of volunteer participation was integral.

Organizational competence refers to operating an organization with accountability and transparency. The ongoing role of the Alexandra Park Residents' Association was a salient indicator of organizational competence. Examples include organizing community meetings, holding elections, targeting services to membership, and facilitating collective decision making. The intention of this strategy is to promote, in a planned manner, the ways in which a safe and secure community can develop for the membership and to show others that constructive community-based control can be achieved through resident control. The changing role of government was an important aspect of the community's ability to show capacity as it helped to determine the skills to be demonstrated and the ways the residents could participate in decision making, for example, by attending community meetings and joining committees.

As the conversion process proceeded, the limitations of the APRA's organizational competence were revealed. The composition of the APRA board of directors did not always reflect the broader community, and the AHC board of directors had difficulties in guiding the conversion process while maintaining the community centre. Consequently the housing corporation did not feel that there was the capacity to manage the property and, as a result, placed constraints on the Atkinson Housing Co-operative, such that the latter resembled a multistakeholder housing co-operative.

Collective action, the second strategy that demonstrates capacity, refers to activities involving a collective voice on what is needed to improve the community. The element of resource mobilization was very important for the community in convincing others that there were problems and that implementing local solutions was an option that had to be pursued. The residents' association was very successful at mobilizing the residents and other interested individuals to raise awareness of the problems within the community, which is a strategy to raise the profile of problems generally (Wandersman, Goodman, and Butterfoss, 1999). For instance, within Alexandra Park there was a heightened awareness (partly as a result of initiatives of the resident association leadership) of the consequences of living in fear of illegal activities and government neglect. Residents became aware that it was a real challenge to improve their community because the decision-making power was situated within the housing corporation.

The use of the resource-mobilization strategy in the form of collective action was applied as a reaction to the adverse effect of external forces on the community. Two excellent examples of collective action that relied on this approach were the community security march and the referendums. The first was a reaction to the neglect and to the illegal activity that caused the residents to live in fear. The assault on a mother and her son within the community became the catalyst that initiated the mobilization of the residents. This action also reflected many years of anger and frustration. The tangible outcome of tearing down the barrier walls illustrated the community's ability to use its assets to mobilize with results; however, the housing corporation was not convinced that there was the capacity to support transformation of the community. They required objective proof that the community supported the co-operative alternative, and this demonstration was critical to the conversion proceeding.

The second example of collective action in this community was the referendums (arguably two examples, since the procedure was carried out twice). For the housing corporation, the referendums served as the objective measure to determine whether there was support for conversion into a co-operative. The Alexandra Park Residents' Association relied on the referendums to showcase its ability to mobilize the community's assets. However, the parameters of the voting in both cases and the outcome had to be accepted by the housing authority. Furthermore, the second vote was done to essentially appease a government representative and not as part of a process towards self-reliance. The greater support that emerged from the second vote can be seen as a reaction to the government's efforts to quell the momentum to convert the project into a housing co-operative. While the referendums were a step towards self-reliance, new strategies of community building were required before competence in managing a co-operative could be demonstrated.

Once the conversion process had started, the primary responsibility of the residents' association expanded from managing the community centre – which involved handling budgets, advocacy, and community programming – to leading the conversion process, initially with the intention of having the Alexandra Park Residents' Association board transform into the co-operative's board. The transition to becoming co-operative managers introduced unanticipated challenges for the residents' association because the new responsibilities required additional skills and, especially, planning by the residents rather than reacting to external forces.

The key events that occurred throughout the community's development, including the conversion process, helped to build and demonstrate varying levels of capacity. However, as stated above, whether the required capacity and knowledge should be the same as those of other housing co-operatives or should be a bit different was unknown to all participants in the conversion process because a similar conversion within the public housing system had never been completed. The steps in the conversion process required the residents to repeatedly demonstrate the skills associated with managing and maintaining a co-operative, which involved understanding the needs of the future membership. As the process continued, the residents started asking questions regarding the by-laws and how the co-operative structure would lead to improvements in the community. In essence, they were exhibiting a form of critical consciousness.

Critical Consciousness

The fourth component in the framework for community-based control is critical consciousness, which is the outcome of a process of reflection on the strategies that demonstrate capacity. The development of critical consciousness relied on demonstrating capacity and two of the elements, cultural change and community consciousness. According to Shor (1993), critical consciousness comprises four qualities. The first is an awareness of where oppressive power structures are situated. The second is the development of an ability to analyse social contexts and understand the impact of those oppressive structures. The third quality is a process of desocialization that occurs in which individuals challenge myths and behaviours that cause oppression. The fourth quality is the ability to self-organize for the purpose of initiating activities towards transforming the traditions of authoritarian and undemocratic relations. This quality bridges critical consciousness and social action, but the focus is on developing essential abilities rather than immediately acting on the desire for social change. Shor's four qualities are relevant for the conversion into the Atkinson Housing Co-operative in that each quality occurred at different points in the process. Moreover, one goal of the conversion was to develop critical consciousness even though this was not an explicit objective initially.

In the context of public housing, the residents are an oppressed population, one that is disenfranchised, neglected, and under constant scrutiny. Resident consciousness involves an experience of powerlessness, which is indicative of naive consciousness (Freire, 1973). The residents normally define the cause of their problems as being beyond their control and rely on the housing corporation for solutions. In fact, residents are often afraid that their minimal security of tenure will be at risk if they participate in some form of collective action. Naive consciousness is also shown in the language used by residents when describing why they did not support the conversion process: for example, "I don't want to lose my housing if she [the property manager] finds out," or "I heard that the board of directors could walk into my home anytime and the [housing corporation] needs to give me 24 hours notice. I don't want anybody barging into my house whenever they feel like it, so I want to stay with the way things are."

The element of cultural change was most evident in the development of a critical consciousness among the residents. For Alexandra Park residents, the goal of the conversion process was to create a knowledgeable population that believed that the community itself could work cooperatively in establishing solutions to social problems. Using Shor's terminology, awareness of the negative impact of the existing power structures created an understanding among the residents that change could occur through local solutions. This awareness was based on the knowledge that the housing corporation's approach was not the solution, but part of the problem. The residents of Alexandra Park became aware of the consequences of the housing corporation's neglect and their naivety in believing that the housing corporation could solve their problems; thus, believing in themselves became a key part of building capacity. Associating problems, such as those of maintenance and security, with the housing corporation reflected the ability to problematize issues. From a political perspective, by their action the residents intended to bring power closer to themselves by transforming their role from being passive to advocating for a healthy community.

Cultural change was reflected in a transformation of what the residents believed they were capable of doing in spite of living in public housing. The residents had to believe it was possible to address their problems, and they could do so by understanding the deeper nature of the issues. Initiating the conversion process at the community meeting in 1993 and then confirming it through the referendum in 1995 are arguably examples of the community's ability to self-organize with the goal of transforming the way the community was maintained. Demonstrating capacity became a means of developing a new form of consciousness in public housing.

The shift from naive to critical thinking was indicative of a cultural change whereby the residents realized that the problems of their community were solvable and not outside their control once they had the power to make decisions. In other words, this change is reflected in the transformation of a culture of dependency into a culture of self-reliance. The key events reflect many examples of the residents coming together to solve problems, instances that helped to engender trusting relationships and establish norms of reciprocity. Moreover, as the conversion advanced, the simple act of participating in the process, it must be noted, was consciousness changing for the residents involved – and indeed, even for some who were sitting on the sidelines.

In the steps towards greater conscientization, the consideration of indigenous knowledge can lead to proper contextualization that could prompt a clearer and thoughtful understanding of local problems, which in turn should lead to some form of united action. A culture of self-reliance arose because of the integration of new knowledge into existing social practices; for example, solutions became focused on what the community *could* do and not what the housing corporation *should* do. The new knowledge was shared, and meaning was created, through experience that resulted in a greater appreciation of the democratic process. This knowledge and experience is the foundation of co-operative living. Schuguerensky (2004, 614) describes one powerful yet simple approach to learning democracy: "Although it may sound like a cliché, it is no less true that one of the best ways to learn democracy is by doing it, and one of the best ways to develop effective civic and political skills is by observing them in the real world and exercising them."

In effect, it is through participating in democratic processes that citizens develop not only a variety of civic virtues (like solidarity, tolerance, openness, responsibility, and respect) but also *political* capital – the capacity for self-governance and for influencing political decisions through democratic means. Two examples of learning democracy in key events were the support that the community showed to proceeding with the conversion process following the referendums, and the approval of the by-laws aimed at operationalizing the management of the co-operative. Democracy was evident in the implementation of decisions and through reliance on trust and reciprocity, trust that the decisions would be followed through by both the leadership and the membership. As a result, individuals become more adept at understanding the oppressive societal power structures that limited their ability to improve their community.

The second element of critical consciousness is community consciousness, involving both community attachment and a movement perspective. The residents were driven to improve their community because of a cohesion created by a strong attachment to their neighbourhood. They spent considerable time and energy improving their community, and the attachment created a sense of pride and a psychological sense of ownership. Moreover, this strong attachment fuelled the community's desire to resolve the problems of government management; residents shared the belief that improvements could only be sustainable if they were involved in both the decision making and the implementation.

The second component of community consciousness is the movement perspective. As described in chapter 5, the movement perspective was not evident among the residents. The residents of Alexandra Park and later the members of Atkinson Housing Co-operative did not view themselves as participating in a broad social movement; however, the conversion should be viewed as a local movement. Through the conversion process, the residents developed a different form of consciousness or, put simply, a confidence in their ability to govern their own community.

The movement perspective played a greater role within the external organizations and for their individual agents. Sonny Atkinson was certainly aware of the co-operative movement, and that helped to give legitimacy to his pursuit of the co-operative alternative. Consultant Mark Goldblatt originally pursued the idea of converting public housing projects into co-operatives as a means to improve the quality of life of the residents. A broader movement perspective provided by the Co-operative Housing Federation of Toronto was crucial to connecting the residents to a reality that what they were trying to achieve had been accomplished in other communities, but not before within public housing. The link to a broader movement gave external organizations the motivation to participate. Furthermore, the involvement of the external volunteers associated with the Co-operative Housing Federation of Toronto illustrated the solidarity that drives the co-operative movement, which reflects the sixth principle of a co-operative identity: Co-operation among Co-operatives (International Co-operative Alliance, 2013).

Goal Attainment

The fifth and final component of the framework of community-based control is goal attainment, a component that represents innovation and the application of new structures. At this stage, residents have attained the necessary skills and understanding that will enable them to meet the specific goals associated with managing a housing co-operative, for example taking on governance responsibilities or making decisions that reflect co-operative living. In the conversion process at Alexandra Park there were different goals set that contributed to the creation of a new co-operative. These goals were related to the resolution of the different objectives associated with the various steps involved in the conversion process. The framework for community-based control accounts for four different goals: foundation of support, governance structure, negotiated agreements, and the completion of the conversion (see figure 8).

The first goal refers to building a foundation of support between the membership and external organizations that provides the basis for member involvement in the new entity. Furthermore, the support provides a legitimate basis for pursuing control of the different facets involved in managing the property. The second goal is to establish a governance structure that includes members in future decision making and works with a given housing corporation towards negotiating the legal agreements (which is the third goal) that form the parameters for eventual community control of the property. The fourth goal is the completion of the conversion process, accomplished by the transfer of management authority to the new co-operative. This transfer can only occur when the previous goals have been achieved.

Each of the four goals is the result of the previous components, together resulting in productive outcomes. For example, the Alexandra Park Residents' Association was transformed into the Atkinson Housing Co-operative board when certain structures were in place, such as the by-laws decided by the membership and the agreements signed between the co-operative and the housing corporation. Implementing a new governance structure was possible because of the critical consciousness possessed by the community, specifically the change in beliefs and the attachment to the community. The stakeholders had the belief and trust that a member-elected board of directors could work with the members to promote a vision of community control. However, unanticipated resistance led to a questioning of whether a critical consciousness was present.

In the Atkinson experience the conflicts and divisions that emerged had the effect of slowing the organizational change and caused the community members to revert to a comfort zone that relied on the Alexandra Park Residents' Association as the sole governing body. One of the benefits was that members of the community had be engaged in a self-reflexive process that resulted in a dialogue among the residents about the type of community they envisioned – for instance, whether transforming the Alexandra Park Residents' Association into a co-operative board of directors meant the end of the community centre, and what would be the consequences of block voting by ethnocultural groups. Thus, the community was not immediately able to achieve change, because organizational competency needed to be enhanced, which required further capacity building and demonstration. The outcome of change was not positive in the sense of successfully becoming a co-operative of the standard type, but rather in becoming a different kind of community that was inclusive in all aspects.

The transfer of management authority was achieved once these issues had been addressed, but the result was not the expected co-operative model that the stakeholders had envisioned at the beginning of the process. For the housing corporation, the multi-stakeholder or hybrid approach had allowed them to maintain some control, while for the Co-operative Housing Federation of Toronto, there was enough of a co-operative identity for it to support the final outcome. For the members of the Atkinson Housing Co-operative, the community change has resulted in a form of residents' control and the hope that the community's capacity will continue to develop towards full co-operative status. Movement towards becoming such a co-operative will rely on the enhancement of the community's assets, and this, in turn, will determine the future success of the Atkinson Housing Co-operative.

Lessons Learned from the Conversion

The unique experiment undertaken by the Alexandra Park residents has demonstrated that the tenants in a public housing project can convert it into a housing co-operative within the public housing sector. A number of lessons can be learned for future public housing communities or agencies wishing to explore conversion to a co-operative as a potential alternative to the direct government-management model. In this section I highlight five features of the experience.

Consider Alternative Models

In the case of Alexandra Park, a small group of residents decided that the co-operative route was appropriate after briefly considering tenant self-management. This meant that the community development and education practices needed to be more about explaining to people the benefits of co-operatives than about the social outcomes of co-operation or alternative management models. Residents never really had a chance to assess whether or not there were other ways of obtaining greater control outside of conversion into a co-operative.

For the housing authority and later the housing corporation, meaningful resident participation and community control were very foreign concepts. The decision to pursue the co-operative alternative created a concern for government representatives because there were no similar cases to refer to and they needed to rely on the Co-operative Housing Federation of Toronto to assist them in understanding the implications of such a change. In the opinion of one of the interviewees, it would have been much easier for Alexandra Park to pursue tenant self-management. The resulting multi-stakeholder model suggests that the community was not quite ready to become a co-operative.

A community needs assessment should be the first step in determining whether or not a public housing community should proceed towards a co-operative conversion or some other type of tenant involvement in decision making. The assessment should also address the potential costs and benefits of the conversion; for example, the conversion may result in residents learning new skills and increasing their employability. Also, there is the potential for lower maintenance costs because of local management control and reduced crime, with the associated community effect of the formation of social capital.

Inform Residents about Co-operative Management and Living

The initial discussions within the community led to the endorsement of converting into a housing co-operative, which was seen by many as a desirable and achievable option that should result in an improved community. However, even after the co-operative concept had been explained, many residents continued to have difficulty understanding the implications of conversion, for example, that the rents would not change and that community life might improve once the housing corporation was no longer involved in managing the community. Nevertheless, a majority did understand that they would have more control over their housing and its management and that living in a co-operative required member participation in decision making and also in maintaining their housing community. Although the Co-operative Housing Federation of Toronto devoted a great deal of time to explaining the meaning of co-operative management, based upon my interviews there appeared to be a significant level of misunderstanding and confusion. The members of the Atkinson Housing Co-operative board went through extensive training in regards to managing a co-operative, but it is unknown whether other residents have benefited from those opportunities.

As this was the first co-operative conversion of a public housing development in Canada, it was difficult for the process to be transparent. The Atkinson Housing Co-operative board did try to communicate with members over key issues, and, generally speaking, those residents involved in the decision-making process were accountable to the rest of the residents through public meetings. Over the period of the conversion more than thirty-three newsletters, in addition to by-laws, were prepared in plain language in four different languages. However, a number of residents noted the lack of consistency and the infrequency of the distributed information. In addition, some residents felt that the language used in the material was very dense despite the attempt at using plain language.

All major conversions to some form of tenant self-management have had a leader calling for and sustaining the momentum for change. When Sonny Atkinson passed away, there was a leadership vacuum in the community. Some residents expressed concern that they could not live up to the legacy left by Sonny Atkinson, and the presidents who followed went hesitantly into the position. There has been a chronic problem in identifying leaders in the community, and those who are singled out have been reluctant to become involved. Therefore, a program to develop new leaders must be part of any future conversion process in order to identify future board members. The existing committee structure can be used for this purpose as well as for promoting greater youth involvement.

Foster Inclusive Practices of Different Ethnic and Cultural Groups

The initial outreach efforts were made in the languages that were predominant in the community, including Portuguese, Chinese, Somali, Vietnamese, and English. Despite the lack of resources, the Co-operative Housing Federation of Toronto provided translators at the community meetings in four different languages. However, a number of residents noted that they still did not understand what was going on at meetings.

The lack of involvement on the part of certain ethnic groups in community activities has shown the need for particular attention in outreach activities. The challenge is to bring people together despite their differing backgrounds and experience. This requires not only additional funding – for outreach, translation of materials, and translation services at meetings – but also particular expertise in managing divisions. A key step in the needs assessment phase should be to identify the language needs and cultural diversity in the community.

Ensure the Availability of Resources for the Conversion

A limitation of the conversion was the lack of adequate funding to support the complex community development process. While funds were initially allocated by the Metropolitan Toronto Housing Authority for community outreach and education for the referendum, their deficiency once the conversion proceeded created complications. Almost all of the interviewees stated that there was insufficient funding to support the kind of community development required. While some funds were raised privately or from charitable organizations, the Co-operative Housing Federation of Toronto did much of the work gratis. In fact, the CHFT was placed in a position of bearing the bulk of the liability for the conversion, both financial and professional. Future co-operative conversions need to be adequately funded to undertake training and education.

An issue was whether the Co-operative Housing Federation of Toronto had sufficient understanding of the needs of public housing residents. Co-operatives usually include a mix of incomes, and many have up to 70 per cent of their residents paying rent geared to income. Public housing projects, however, consist of 100 per cent lower-income households, requiring deeper subsidies, and they accommodate more newly landed immigrants than do other forms of social housing (non-profits and co-operatives). The federation is used to dealing with residents who have chosen to live in a co-operative, whereas in a public housing conversion the residents already live on the property and are trying to choose a management model that will meet their need for greater control over their living environment. The Co-operative Housing Federation of Toronto was not experienced in dealing with public housing communities and learned many lessons through this experience.

In future co-operative conversions, community development activities need to apply a broader notion of participation and development. The co-operative sector tends to focus on training in the "mechanics" of operating a co-operative, particularly for the board and its committees. The challenge in public housing communities, however, is that such communities often have needs that are more complex than those found in typical co-operatives. For this reason, there is a need to concentrate on broader community-building exercises. This means building upon the existing strengths in the community (including services and leadership), identifying areas for development, and developing a training and education program to address the identified needs. For future conversions of public housing, it is recommended that there be explicit government support throughout the process. The government must be prepared to facilitate the conversion process in order to overcome many of the bureaucratic delays that were found in the Alexandra Park experience. In addition to the explicit support, a considerable amount of funding is required for such matters as the initial feasibility study and education and training.

Celebrate the Achievements

As Alexandra Park's conversion was the first of its kind in Canada, there was very little celebration of the successful outcome. The time involved in completing the conversion process seemed to reduce any excitement among the residents that something groundbreaking was occurring within their community. Excepting for the board of directors and some member volunteers, there were few examples of celebrating the innovation of becoming a housing co-operative. The absence of showcasing successes during the conversion process demonstrated the entrenched scepticism that the conversion would be completed. This scepticism helped to fuel both the divisions among the residents and the lack of faith in the board of directors by the housing corporation. Thus, the final key event – the transfer of management authority – was simply viewed as just another day.

Future conversions should focus on the social aspect of the conversion by encouraging social gatherings that celebrate achievements – a gathering as large as a festival or simply a community meeting. Celebrations can be empowering and can act as unifying or consciousness-raising events. They help to sustain momentum and the faith that a complex community-change process can lead to a beneficial outcome.

Implications and Applications of the Framework for Community-Based Control

The outcomes associated with the framework for community-based control rely on the successful completion of various activities intended to build on and enhance a community's strengths. Community assets ensure that the strategies that build and demonstrate capacity reflect a community's abilities rather than its deficiencies. The capacity strategies are intended to influence the change from a consciousness that is naive to one that is critical. As social change is a lengthy process and often occurs in discrete steps, capacity strategies can be planned to strengthen a community's critical consciousness and can be designed to lead to gradual organizational or community change. For example, meaning making and knowledge creation through technical assistance can lay a foundation for stable social change. Issues are thereby understood at a much deeper level, and solutions reflect the needs of the community.

The framework for community-based control illustrates the process that a community can undertake when aiming to gain control over operations and decision-making responsibilities. The process highlights the different constituents and strategies that can be adapted to fit different community settings. The factors and occurrences that contributed to the Alexandra Park conversion may not usually be found within public housing projects; thus, the framework is not intended to be prescriptive. A key strength of the framework for community-based control is that the components are attended to by the development of strategies that are based on the real experiences found within a particular community. Accordingly, one may use the framework as a "road map" to which community developers can refer as they work with residents to undertake greater control over their community.

The framework for community-based control can serve as a reference guide and an initial blueprint for future conversions in other communities. The framework can be used to develop targeted community development strategies that are intended to achieve different community-determined goals. For example, it is important to achieve a foundation of support before proceeding to the formation of governance structure, which, in turn, would affect what is outlined in the negotiated agreements. On a broader level, the Atkinson Housing Co-operative experience and the framework for community-based control are valuable in light of the significant changes that were made in 2000 to the ways in which social housing is delivered in the province of Ontario. In the next section I examine the policy implications of the Atkinson experiment and how the framework for community-based control dovetailed with policy direction in the changing climate of social housing within the province of Ontario.

The Atkinson Housing Co-operative remains unique in Canada, but it is being watched closely by different jurisdictions. There are indications that Ontario and other provincial governments are interested in encouraging the conversion of more public housing projects into one of the three forms of social housing – municipal non-profit, private non-profit, and co-operative. Changes to housing policy in Ontario in the early 2000s, which has resulted in the convergence of these three models of social housing (Sousa and Quarter, 2003), have made the Alexandra Park conversion experiment an integral case for future policy development. Inspired by the conversion, the local housing corporation for the City of Toronto has explored the transformation of existing public housing stock and has developed a policy framework for converting its projects into some form of tenant-management arrangement (Toronto Community Housing Corporation, 2004). The new framework is the direct result of the lessons learned from the experience of the Atkinson conversion. According to the policy document, the framework contains four steps that would guide a future conversion process from initial interest to eventual transfer of management responsibilities (Toronto Community Housing Corporation, 2004).

The first step is demonstrating local interest by a core group of residents. This step is analogous to the work of the Alexandra Park Residents' Association in exploring the co-operative option. The second step involves having the community work with a third party, such as the Co-operative Housing Federation of Toronto, to educate the residents and poll them on their aspirations. At least half of the residents would be required to vote, and at least two-thirds would have to vote in favour of initiating the change process. In other words, this step involves having a referendum to determine resident support for seeking greater community control, which is analogous to the 1995 referendum at the Alexandra Park housing project.

The third step is to establish a member-driven board of directors that would include five residents of the community, a representative of the local housing corporation, and up to five independent members who are knowledgeable in social housing. This board would be in place for three years, and during that time the focus would be on building capacity for management of the community. During the three years the new community organization would resemble the private non-profit housing model. The board structure is influenced by the arrangement at Atkinson, in particular the need for non-resident directors, because of the divisions that occurred during the conversion.

The fourth step involves another vote within the community on whether the residents want to become a co-operative or remain as a private non-profit. This step is analogous to the second referendum, in 1998, that occurred as part of the conversion process at Alexandra Park, but in future conversions the community should have an opportunity to manage and make decisions that address their needs. The key feature of this step is that the community would not automatically revert to a typical public housing project but rather would explore other approaches to maintain resident involvement in decision-making processes.

An additional dimension of the new policy framework is that it provides greater autonomy for the new entity. According to the policy document, "expenditure control for capital items, taxes and utilities rests with the self-managed organization and not with the Toronto Community Housing Corporation, as is the current situation in the case of Atkinson Co-op" (Toronto Community Housing Corporation, 2004). The lack of control over capital expenditures has made the Atkinson Housing Co-operative rely on the local housing corporation following through on and funding major repairs. Control over capital expenditures would give greater autonomy to a community than currently exists at Atkinson and would draw it closer to the private non-profit and co-operative housing models.

The new policy framework recognizes the unreasonable length of time it took to create the Atkinson Housing Co-operative by stating that the time for the entire process, which includes capacity strategies and other community development activities, is expected to take up to five years – a timeline that is vastly different from the Atkinson experience of over ten years. It should be noted that as of 2012 no community has taken up the option outlined in this new policy.

Arguably, the use of steps outlined within the policy document can make the framework appear prescriptive and seems to contravene the fundamental principles of the asset-based community development described earlier in the book. However, the mere recognition of a need to systematically consider an overall strategy for converting future properties is something that Atkinson did not have at the time. It is my contention that the framework for community-based control can complement a government's need to be prescriptive with the reality of needing to give a community time to develop at its own pace and to provide community developers with a set of goals that can be shared with members of a community; and the different activities can be developed to meet those goals.

What is noticeably absent from the policy document is an actual implementation strategy for a conversion to proceed, thus making it difficult to estimate the overall cost of such a process. It is to be hoped that the costs of future conversions will be much different from those experienced by the Atkinson Housing Co-operative. For those reasons, a framework is needed that outlines and targets areas of community development that can be applied during the steps outlined in the policy document. The framework for community-based control developed in this study fills the gap in the policy document by detailing the key elements and factors required for a successful conversion to take place. The factor of critical consciousness in this framework is central to transforming a community's self-identity from one of residents to one of members.

In closing, the multi-stakeholder structure of the Atkinson Housing Co-operative is a novelty in the context of the social housing system in Canada, but the hybrid model is consistent with the implementation of the Social Housing Reform Act (Sousa and Quarter, 2003; Ontario, 2000). This experiment has parallels to innovations in the United States and in Western Europe to increase tenant involvement in the management of public housing. However, the Atkinson experiment is unique in that it creates a co-operative within public housing, with the potential to increase further its capacity for self-management. Although it is premature to determine the efficacy of this model, it is likely to influence the movement for increasing tenant involvement in the management of public housing.

Conclusion

The purpose of this book is to share with the reader the efforts involved in transforming a community away from government control. It is not my intention to provide evidence of whether the Alexandra Park conversion has been a successful experiment, as it would be premature to do so. The process used to create the Atkinson Housing Co-operative has demonstrated that public housing residents, a housing corporation, and the co-operative sector can develop mutually beneficial agreements that resolve issues of concern. The completion of the conversion is a step in empowering a disenfranchised community. The proposed framework is the outcome of different struggles faced by the three stakeholders over a ten-year period, and it is my hope that it can be applied and refined by residents of different communities seeking greater control over their residences.

The journey to the formation of the Atkinson Housing Co-operative was long and challenging. The absence of government policy supporting tenant self-management and encouraging resident participation in a purposeful way created varying challenges for the stakeholders involved in this conversion process. Fortunately, the absence of guidelines did not deter the residents and members of the co-operative housing sector from pursing the conversion, thereby adding significance to the experiment. The policy environment within jurisdictions that contain large housing project is suitable for other conversions to take place. The Atkinson experience has shown the necessity of incorporating a community development component to government policy that complements the bricks-and-mortar approach to developing social housing properties.

The residents faced a tremendous number of challenges in creating the Atkinson Housing Co-operative. Addressing unforeseen obstacles and great uncertainty became part of the community's culture for close to ten years. Now that the co-operative has been formed, the members have the means to improve vital aspects of the community. Although Atkinson Housing Co-operative does not have the same degree of autonomy as do other co-operatives, the hope is that with continued work and improvement those distinctions will decrease.

Finally, as a former resident, it has been a privilege to document and interpret the transformation of my community. I will always have fond memories of the exciting and frustrating work that went into creating the Atkinson Housing Co-operative. It is my hope that the information and resulting framework is a fair assessment of the conversion process. Most of all, it is my hope that other communities can learn from the Atkinson experience by being aware of the challenges and by appreciating the potential for living in a co-operative community.

Afterword: Pursuing the Co-operative Dream

The framework for community-based control reflects the process that the Alexandra Park residents took to becoming a housing co-operative, but more data is needed in order to make it an analytical tool for understanding the complexity associated with housing conversion processes. However, it can be used as a lens to identify and explain some of the successes as well as some of the challenges that have occurred over the ten years at the Atkinson Housing Co-operative since the conversion. For instance, the first five years were focused on community development strategies aimed at building and demonstrating the capacity to manage a multimillion-dollar budget, which is crucial for a co-operative community to function. The community has elected boards annually through a democratic process, with all of the elections being contested. There has been more responsive management since the board has had sole authority over the hiring of the management company. There have also been significant efforts to encourage greater youth involvement in the decision-making processes in order to prepare new board members.

The many residents involved, I included, did not fully comprehend the magnitude of what it meant to be a member of a co-operative and associated with a broader movement. Consequently we felt that the community would be improved by having the housing authority transfer control to the co-operative. However, shortly after completion of the conversion, the members quickly realized that the social ills faced by the community were systemic and could not be addressed solely by a change in management structure. For example, there continues to be pervasive drug dealing, and efforts to resolve the ethnic divisions are an ongoing project. The Atkinson Housing Co-operative is a little "United Nations" with many languages and cultural groups. Melding such a

diverse community into a cohesive co-operative is a formidable challenge. Furthermore, all the members involved in leading the conversion process have either moved away or reduced their involvement to
only attending community meetings. Thus, developing new leadership
capacity is challenging because those involved are not close to the historical context that initiated the conversion process.

The exciting and demanding efforts that started and finished the conversion created the expectation of the stakeholders that there would
be immediate improvements across all areas and transformation into a
healthier community. The persistence of chronic problems such as drug
dealing and ethnocultural divisions has fuelled the original naysayers
who felt that the community could never meet the expectations associated with becoming a co-operative. In addition, the ongoing feeling
that the leadership is neither prepared nor responsive to the community's needs has given some credibility to the opposition.

These concerns notwithstanding, follow-up interviews and participant observation reveal that there is a general sense of satisfaction in
some vital areas within the Atkinson Housing Co-operative but that
there continue to be some misgivings about whether the members actually live in a co-operative or in a public housing project with a change
in management (Sousa, 2007). In these interviews I explored a series
of issues that seemed critical to having a successful conversion: community identity, safety and security within the community, forms of
leadership, and the level and quality of participation.

Community Identity

When transitioning towards community-based control, it is essential that the members identify with a collective that is based on trust
and reciprocity. As many people living in housing co-operatives can
attest, one of the principal factors associated with the success of their
organization is ensuring that the membership is aware and supportive of the board's decisions and activities. In essence, a membership
with a consciousness grounded in co-operative ideals, often referred to
as a co-operative identity, will contribute greatly to the success of the
organization. A co-operative identity is revealed in a number of ways,
including an engaged and informed membership, a knowledgeable
and responsive board of directors, and the expression of co-operation
through community-oriented activities and by-laws. Sousa and Herman (2012) describe how a weak co-operative identity can increase the

likelihood of disunity. In the case of the Atkinson conversion, the community developers relied on active resident engagement throughout the conversion process. In spite of much ongoing community development work since the conversion, it appears that the members are ambivalent about identifying with the co-operative.

Member reaction to the co-operative has been mixed. Some state that they have seen a difference: "Before it was like you don't really know about what was going on. No information was given to you. With the co-op, they seem like they try to get everybody to be part of it." Others have claimed that nothing has changed: "It doesn't look like a co-op. This looks like project housing to me. I haven't seen changes except for the name; that's the only differences: before it was government housing, now it's a co-op." Part of the confusion could be attributed to growing pains, which is part of establishing a collective identity. However, the members of Atkinson were long-time residents of public housing, and, for many, perceiving themselves differently could be challenging.

An important part of co-operative identity is management by the membership, and Atkinson still faces challenges in this domain. Cultivating member engagement has included developing an active governance system. People are not always happy with the result, but that is true of democracy in general. A challenge in any democracy is for the leadership to engage the citizenship so that it does not feel disenfranchised. For residents of public housing in particular, a large change is required that includes the willingness of the residents to work at developing new skills associated with building community and managing responsibly. Arguably, the leadership of Atkinson has fallen short in this regard, but with more investment in education that shortcoming might be addressed.

In my interviews I asked the question "What does living in a co-operative mean?" Most of the individuals found it challenging to see where their involvement in the decision making made a difference to the overall community. However, some interviewees, particularly the younger residents, did appreciate the potential associated with member control. In 2010, Sheik offered the following insights: "I think the residents have more of a say and have more control, and their opinion actually matters because it's not just a government thing. The residents are actually making the decisions and not the government. If you are a project, the government doesn't necessarily care. People actually care what happens in their co-op. Basically it's important because people need to look out for themselves. So, if you are faced with a decision that will affect you personally and right away, then you are going to want to be part of that decision. And you are going to make a better decision if you live here than if you don't live here and know what's going on."

Although many residents still view the Atkinson Housing Co-operative as a public housing project, there have been efforts to institute small yet visible improvements, including efforts to integrate youth by developing more recreation spaces. According to Ahmed in 2009, "the basketball courts, the playground went in, there is improved lighting, the roads have been repaired. There are all kinds of things that are going on around here. There are supposed to be cameras going in here. Lots of stuff that you can see." The key point not addressed in his statement is that the board made the decisions to build all of those additions to the community. Unfortunately, the decisions were not always based on member consultation. In 2008, long-time member Diane explained to me that the additional recreational activities had created additional challenges such as youth attempting to damage the playground and using it for gang activities: "The playground area is a problem. The people's homes who face the area have to take responsibility for it. If they see something happening, they gotta get out there and say something. They have to be educated to do so. And the basketball courts. They're pulling the wires off the fences and stuff. And I'm thinking, 'How long did it take to get this stuff in here for you and now you have these nice courts to play in. Have some decency to respect the area so you have a nice area to play in.'"

Figure 9 is an image of one of the basketballs courts, and it can be seen how close the courts are to people's homes.

Once these concerns had been shared with the board, with the help of the property management company the members created a set of rules that included clear hours of operation, and a community basketball house league was formed.

Some Atkinson members who are co-op savvy, having either visited or lived in such communities previously, reflected on the aesthetics of the property. In fact, they expressed reservations about the quality of Atkinson's facilities compared to those that they had experienced elsewhere. While commenting on a photograph he had taken at a housing co-operative that was not too far from Atkinson, former board member Steve stated in 2007:

We're going to one of the co-ops. And my daughter was like, 'Party,' when we went in. The picture here is for the fencing. It's just plain wood, but what a difference. There are many benches. And all the green. There are many

Figure 9. New Basketball Courts. The new basketball courts resulted from the partnership between the Atkinson Housing Co-operative and the Co-operative Housing Federation of Toronto. Originally a tennis court, they are seen as an achievement for the community but have caused some tensions with those living just outside the fences. Photo taken by the author.

flowers. She really liked it. Where we live [at AHC], a lot of us sit outside, and we bring our chairs, and it makes it look really messy. Which, I mean, we all bought the same colour of chairs. I enjoyed having a little walk here. It's not even a big place where we passed through. There are two co-op parts. Again, a lot of green. You don't see much cement.

More grass, again, they took out the cement. Another gazebo and chairs together. Everything is coordinated. No garbage. And this one, which is in front of an apartment building, which shocked me, was that when people have a barbecue and whoever doesn't have a barbeque shares it. And there's a garbage bin right there. And no garbage anywhere.

There is broad recognition of the challenges and what can be done realistically to deal with them, but while some members express hope, others are finding it difficult to look towards a brighter future because of the frustration associated with rectifying long-standing issues. For instance, Bob, who was involved in the conversion process, stated in 2006: "We are still dealing with the same issues. Nothing's changed. We are not a community. It depends on where you live. OK, we are friends, everyone sticks together, but the whole place itself, we are not a co-op. We are far from it. We live in a project. The kids have an understanding what a co-op is about and what a co-op is supposed to be looking like. But you get a clear message when they are saying, 'We are co-op? Sure doesn't feel or look like a co-op.' This is basically project housing, and that's the sadness of it."

While in general the statements seem to support the notion that very little has changed with respect to becoming a co-operative, a key difference is that the members are now free to make fundamental decisions that will shape their community. The example of the new playground is instructive, because it provides the members with a sense of responsibility and an understanding of what should be involved in maintaining not only the activities but also the sense of neighbourly obligation. This is a fundamental departure from previous practice, and this knowledge could and should be seen as an asset rather than a liability.

Safety and Security

An issue that drove the initial effort to call for tenant-self management and eventual co-operative control was safety and security. The earlier key event of the residents' response to the violent attack on a mother and her son became the driver for the residents to mobilize against the instigators. The concerns and subsequent action blossomed into the call for local control over decision making, which helped to rally the residents against a non-responsive housing authority. In spite of the co-operative giving the members greater control over their community, concerns for safety and security recur continually. Specifically, drug dealing and vandalism still are pervasive. There is little indication that the safety concerns have improved since the project converted to a co-operative. Nevertheless, discussions with residents in 2008 suggest that there is an appreciation that the problems are complex. The description of the underlying causes is consistent with the historical portrayal described in chapter 4: "You've got a lot of gangs from surrounding areas competing for turf and the right to sell their drugs in here. They actually take shifts. They are being smart about what they are doing and putting it in blue bins so they don't get caught with it on them ... Another problem in here is vandalism. It's the start of everything – graffiti and such. A lot of kids in here have no respect for this place as a community, and it has to stop somewhere. You can't be doing it. If you take care of the little things early, it doesn't have a chance to spread."

For Atkinson members, improving safety and security has been their priority since 2003. In the past, hiring a security company would have been arranged and approved by the government housing authority, Toronto Community Housing Corporation, without consulting the residents of the housing project. Since the formation of the co-operative, the board of directors oversees all hiring of management and contractors. The co-operative has instituted a rigorous hiring process for a security company that is expected to be primarily receptive to the uniqueness of the community's circumstances. The board has hired different security companies over the last ten years, but the expectation that the security presence would be sensitive to the special needs of the community was not always met. This rigour in hiring is a reflection of the community's increased control in determining who is best suited to protect the members.

The co-operative has lacked sufficient financial resources to meet the challenge, however. The security officers were on site for such limited times that the drug dealers became aware of their patrol patterns. It was quickly realized that an alternative solution had to be found. The Toronto Community Housing Corporation and the Atkinson board of directors decided to introduce security cameras in strategic locations throughout the community, but the co-operative did not have the funds to purchase or install them. The board had to lobby and negotiate with the housing corporation for over two years to get the necessary funds to install the cameras.

While these situations demonstrate the ongoing challenges of community safety, they also reflect the will of the co-operative to address the concerns, arguably a positive characteristic. The board has developed a stronger working relationship with the local police division. Until 2008 it had a security committee engaging with the membership and making recommendations to the board of directors. The primary reason the security committee is no longer functional is that its leader burned out and no one has stepped forward to assume this vital role.

Member Engagement and Leadership Development

While the history of the community has involved a strong residents' association, a significant obstacle encountered during the conversion process was the maintenance of two bodies to represent residents or members – one for the co-operative and another associated with Alexandra Park.

It was hoped that eventually the two would merge, but the acrimony that arose in 2000 lingers to this day. Efforts to resolve the conflicts have largely been unsuccessful; thus, the residents' association continues to manage the community centre, and the Atkinson board is responsible for everything else. One of the consequences of this duality is member confusion about where to commit their efforts.

The existence of two representative bodies and the subsequent confusion can be addressed through community development activities, but the dearth of funds for developing a comprehensive community development strategy continues to profoundly affect the community. Once the conversion was completed in 2003, there was an absence of funds for further community development activities. A selling point that had led to the government supporting the completion of the conversion was the idea that the co-operative would be more efficient and reduce the costs of managing the property. The Atkinson Housing Co-operative experiment was a by-product of a conservative agenda that involved the offloading of services in the early 2000s. However, there have not been any cost savings, and the co-operative pays a monthly fee of over $80,000 back to government for capital repairs and other non-operational costs such as utilities. The hope was that member engagement would result in improved efficiencies, but that type of improvement does not magically appear.

One of the themes highlighted in this book is the importance of leadership development and training as part of the conversion process and after its completion. As indicated in the final key event, there were two controversial conditions that the Toronto Community Housing Corporation wanted to see in place in order to support the conversion process. The first was the presence of three non-member directors who would be selected by the housing corporation and the Co-operative Housing Federation of Toronto. The second was the ongoing involvement of a third-party organization that would support the community. This second condition continues to stand, but the condition for non-member directors has changed. Although I was personally against the idea of having non-community members involved in the decision making, I did appreciate the merits of their role. For instance, they provided important insight on financial decisions as well as on the legal implications of some board actions. However, by two years after the conversion, achieving a meeting quorum was a challenge, and over time those individuals were not able to continue the commitment. For these reasons, the board, the Toronto Community Housing Corporation, and the Co-operative Housing Federation of Toronto decided to withdraw the condition of having non-community board members. I was surprised at the withdrawal of the first condition, which in my view has had a negative effect on the board's capacity to prioritize key matters such as finance and maintenance. As a result there has been an increased reliance on the property managers to provide "impartial" insight, but as they are employees of the co-operative, their voice could and should be muted.

In order for the work on member engagement and leadership development to continue, funds have been raised from the Atkinson Foundation, and the Co-operative Housing Federation of Toronto continues to do much of its work on an unpaid basis. The target of those funds has been community development activities that are intended to build a stronger understanding of living in a co-operative. However, there has been no systematic program to develop new leaders. In fact, following the passing of Sonny Atkinson there has been a lack of consensus on what constitutes a good leader. Atkinson's style might have been inappropriate for a co-operative, but he was very effective in galvanizing the residents, something that has been lacking since his death. Another issue related to leadership in the co-operative has been the engagement of members, or, as Linda stated in 2009: "The trouble I had with the leadership was I couldn't see it. I wanted to see leadership playing in the community. I was hoping to see someone raking their lawn or something. That's more leadership to me. Not everyone has time to commit to being a board member. Just deciding to move in here, you are becoming a member, not only a tenant."

An exciting outcome of the conversion has been that some members are recognizing that leadership in a co-operative involves not only electing a president and a board of directors but also participating in many facets of the community, as indicated in comments from some of the residents in 2008:

> The people that live in the community don't necessarily know how to go about it. But I agree that leadership is everyday in life like the commitment of a mother taking her child to school every day. Or like a man playing ball with his kid, that's more leadership for me. It's taking the initiative and taking your time to be a responsible citizen.
>
> I think participation can be a lot of things. Depends on the comfort level of the person. It could be just talking over the fence in the backyard with your neighbour. Or it could be going to meetings. It's not one specific thing for an entire community. There are different ways to participate.

Some of it is just like childcare. For single parenting, it can be more difficult to participate. I find that flyers don't have a very effective form of outreach. It lets people know what's going on, but it's not face-to-face outreach.
Yet, our resources – flyers are realistically the only way we can do outreach.
There is just not enough money. We don't have an outreach worker any-
more. I find face-to-face outreach much better.

In a co-op, participation should have to do with actually building the
community. But the way that I see it, there is something to do and people
come and do it. I think there is no participation because I don't really think
there is anything to do here.

These are very positive realizations of the potential impact that
engagement and leadership development could have in the community.
However, there are indications that members feel alienated from the
decisions that are being made. Several interviewees are critical of the co-
operative's governance and indicate that it is not working for the benefit
of the broader membership. Linda, a member of the board, summed up
this concern in 2007:

You have a board up there with myself included. Two of the most important committees aren't functioning or up and running. Why aren't they
running? The board can't get off their butts and say the community has a
say on the maintenance and finance. The community needs to see a financial report, and they can go over it and say, 'You explain to me why you
have spent this much money here. And why the maintenance isn't being
done over here.' They won't do that because they are afraid of the results
and they may be bombarded with people wanting answers to some very
serious questions. They don't want to face that. And if they don't want to
face that, they should get off the board.

Linda goes on to describe a challenge that the membership has in
accessing the board: "People too often take that stance and don't put it
in writing. A written letter demands a written response. And if you get
a written response, and they said they're going to do this and this, you
have it for proof."

A related point has been the absence of information regarding the
board's activities and decisions. Bulletin boards have been placed in
strategic locations around the community, but they are not updated
regularly. In addition, the members consistently express the view that
they are unaware of the outcomes of various meetings, especially the

board meetings. Some say that they find out the crucial decisions too late. Another challenge has been ensuring that all groups can communicate with each another. Sandra's description in 2006 provides some insight on the issue: "I wish all the people in this block would be so friendly. It may be because their language is different. Some of them pass and say hello; some of them don't talk. We should communicate more to the people that do not speak English. When they sent those flyers, they should print them in different languages, like English, Spanish to people who speak Spanish, then everybody can communicate with each other and be more active. It has a long way to go here. I think we are reaching there."

The Atkinson Housing Co-operative was founded on a strong sense of pride and on the involvement of an engaged resident population. The issues and concerns expressed by the residents are serious, but they are not insurmountable. It should be noted that when the level of engagement was at its highest in the 1990s, the context was different in that the focus was on mobilization against a problem, which brought people together. Managing a housing complex represents a different challenge, and the understanding of what it means to participate needs to change as well. Fortunately there are indications that such a realization is beginning to dawn within the community.

New Initiative: Neighbourhood Revitalization

A trend has emerged across Canada over the last ten years that has seen public housing providers address the problems found in these communities by razing the housing and developing the area into a mixed-income neighbourhood through the physical transformation of a property. The example of Regent Park in downtown Toronto is a case in point (Toronto Community Housing Corporation, 2012b). While this is a very expensive approach, for example, close to a billion dollars for the Regent Park effort, the neighbourhood where the Atkinson Housing Co-operative is situated is planned to go through a similar process (Toronto Community Housing Corporation, 2012c).

Efforts to improve the neighbourhood, which is still referred to as Alexandra Park, through revitalization of the property have been driven by the local municipal councillor, Adam Vaughan. He has publically stated that there is great potential for a mixed-income community to be the means of addressing the social ills. This mixed income will start with private investment in new condominiums and later involve new housing for the members of the Atkinson Housing Co-operative. As an agency of the municipal government, Toronto Community Housing Corporation undertook a broad consultation process in response to Vaughan's interest. The consultation included many stakeholders, including the Atkinson board. Once it became clear that the Atkinson Housing Co-operative would feel the greatest impact of the revitalization plan, members of the board wanted to ensure that their role changed from consultation to partnership where there was meaningful and accountable engagement. According to the former president of the co-operative in 2011, Fathi Sheik Hassan, "TCHC had asked the board to come to their meetings, but as the developments accelerated, we realized the need to meet with TCHC, so we made TCHC representatives come to our board meetings as a standing agenda item to update us ... We requested that they do the presentation to us first, and then go to the community, so at least we could say the board is behind this. But if they were proposing things and we had objections, we would raise concerns about this. And then we'd bring it to the community as well."

Members of the board became strong advocates for the co-operative, and as a result they sat on the planning design committee established by the housing corporation. With that success in hand, the board held a community meeting to discuss the revitalization proposals. The members wanted there to be zero displacement during construction. The notion of displacement is a very common element within revitalization efforts, which means that residents need to move away from their homes while the property is being rebuilt. In many cases the residents do not have a say about where they will have to move, and they may never be given the chance to return to the community, which was the experience of many when the property was first developed in 1969. At the community meeting there was complete unanimity, and now the members will not have to move during the construction, which is envisioned to take place over fifteen years.

The zero-displacement principle was heralded as a success across the community, but there are significant associated implications. For instance, new houses will have to be built in order for the members to occupy them. While this seems to be rather a small price to pay, the City of Toronto requires that these projects be self-funded, which means that another funding source has had to be identified. It will be the revenue generated from the new condominiums. In other words, the members will have to wait until the new condominiums have been built before the income from those properties can be used as leverage to build the

Atkinson Housing Co-operative's new housing. The frustrating point for someone like me was that the co-operative's board realized only then that the implications of the decision for zero displacement were much bigger than had been originally envisioned. For example, there will have to be significantly higher density and a critical number of condominium owners ready to live in an area that has been stigmatized by its social ills. It is uncertain whether that level of private investment is possible or feasible. Clearly these are complex issues that require a much more thorough research analysis. Nonetheless, this example reveals that there is mobilizing potential within the community and demonstrates the increased cohesion and the understanding of the potential outcomes of member-based community decisions.

Sowing the Seeds of Change

While the outcomes of the Alexandra Park conversion are not ideal, they are hopeful. The new entity has not met all expectations, but there have been some improvements and hopes that the change process will continue. There are lessons that can be gleaned from this experience. The Atkinson Housing Co-operative will continue to evolve, and the members will face many challenges and receive many rewards. One of the challenges continues to be a government mindset that seems unable to acknowledge the potential of the Atkinson conversion. Despite the lack of explicit government endorsement, the Atkinson Housing Co-operative is attracting much attention. At least one other conversion of public housing (in Winnipeg) has been attempted, and others are being contemplated.

An additional challenge is to build bridges so that members realize that mutuality cuts across race and ethnicity. Regardless of group affiliation, everyone wants to live in a community where inclusiveness is not an ideal but a practice. At Atkinson this challenge has proved formidable, and there is still work to be done. The solutions are not always easy, and it will take time and effort to see results. As has been emphasized in this book, the Co-operative Housing Federation of Toronto was a critical support to making the Alexandra Park conversion go forward. The role of the federation should not be underestimated. Their role was similar to that of a coach, and it is not clear that this type of conversion could proceed without such support. As noted, most of the Co-operative Housing Federation of Toronto service was uncompensated, and it is unrealistic to expect that similar support could be obtained

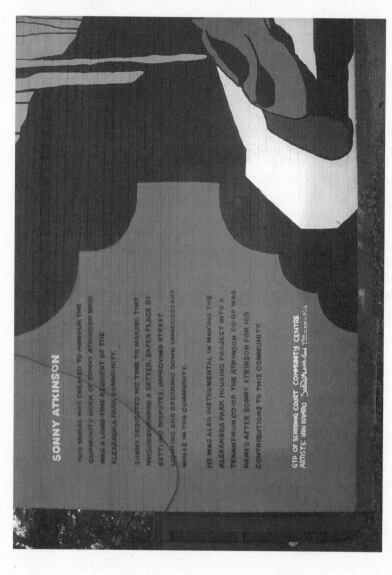

Figure 10. A Portion of the Mural Dedicated to Sonny Atkinson. The mural shows Sonny Atkinson knocking down the walls, and the text in the lower section recognizes Sonny's effort to open the community to the broader neighbourhood. Reproduced by permission of the Scadding Court Community Centre.

for future conversions without compensation. For a conversion of this sort to achieve its potential, there must be not only a coach but also an ongoing program of community education. These are costs that to some extent clash with government's desire to save rather than to spend. However, there are also long-term savings to society from having a well-functioning community.

In conclusion, as indicated in this afterword, the Atkinson Housing Co-operative continues to struggle to build a strong sense of community that is consistent with being a co-operative. Progress has been slow, but there have been successes. The co-operative is viable, and most of the members contribute to it in a variety of ways, including voting in elections, beautifying the neighbourhood, and participating in committee meetings. There is dissatisfaction, and there are ongoing concerns about resident safety, an issue that was a driver for the co-operative's formation. Nevertheless, the members of the co-operative continue to actively struggle with these issues.

As a co-operative, the members have the social and structural means to ensure that change is sustainable. While there is an absence of financial capital for efforts to further develop the community, there is no shortage of human and social capital to contribute to the success of the new entity. There is a strong belief that the community can prevail, or, as Bob stated in 2008, "it doesn't matter what kind of obstacles are showing up in your way, if you stand together as a community you can move those obstacles. Like they say, you can move that mountain. There is nothing that you cannot move in this community."

In addition to the forward-looking mindsets that many members exhibit, there is also recognition of the need to remind themselves that the original purpose of converting into a co-operative was to open the community to the wider neighbourhood. The reference point is on the cover of this book: a photograph of a mural that recognizes and is dedicated to Sonny Atkinson. What is poignant is the short piece written by the individuals who painted the mural, which can be seen in figure 10.

Sonny wanted to live in a safe community and expose, as socially constructed, the limitations of public housing. To Atkinson, the limitations of public housing could be knocked down like those barrier walls. Even though Sonny is dead, Atkinson Housing Co-operative lives on as a symbol of his vision, a symbol that continues to evolve.

Appendix: Methodology and Research Design

The appendix outlines the specific details associated with the research framework and the information-collection procedures that enabled me to explore and explain the conversion of the Atkinson Housing Co-operative. The stated aim of this study, to create a community-development framework, was achieved by drawing on the experiences and events that contributed to the conversion of the Alexandra Park housing project into the Atkinson Housing Co-operative. Since a conversion of this sort had never been successfully completed before, a qualitative framework was determined to be the most appropriate research paradigm. Research that utilizes a qualitative framework relies on participants' perspectives, when exploring different social issues, in order to gain insights into how people think about their living conditions either within their community or within the broader society (Stringer, 1999). Insider knowledge is essential for the research process and is integral to a researcher's understanding and subsequent interpretations. According to Miles and Huberman (1994), a successful and comprehensive qualitative research process balances insider and outsider perspectives (also known as *emic* and *etic*, respectively) at all stages of the research process. The results form the foundation of a rich descriptive understanding of the insights that arise out of the interaction of various psychological and sociological constructs that can have an impact on the construction of the knowledge and meaning of individuals who are often considered to be on the margins of society (Kirby and McKenna, 1989).

A limitation of qualitative enquiry is that the perspectives can be open ended and subjective, which can be challenging when it comes to interpretation of the data. In essence, the relativistic nature of qualitative information can make the information collected seem unwieldy and unfocused (Miles and Huberman, 1994). In this study I minimize the impact of relativism by using a conceptual framework to guide the information-collection process and the subsequent analyses; however, the potential for emergent themes required a restructuring of different elements of the conceptual framework.

In order to determine the underlying factors that were involved in the process of converting into the Atkinson Housing Co-operative, a case study approach was used. Although not exclusively a qualitative approach (Yin, 2003), case studies frequently utilize qualitative data. Yin (2003, 13) defines *a case study* as "an empirical inquiry that investigates a contemporary phenomenon within its real-life context, especially when the boundaries between phenomenon and context are not clearly evident." An advantage of the case study approach is that a researcher can apply a variety of information-collection techniques, and the data from these differing techniques serve as a check of credibility and transferability, a point to which I return later in this appendix.

Yin (2003) describes two types of case-study-research design – single case and multiple case – and two forms within each of those types. In a single-case design there is a single unit of analysis within one site and a single context being explored. In a multiple-case design the investigation takes place on different sites and in different contexts. According to Yin (2003), the rationale for the multiple-case design is either to test a prediction that the results in the different cases would be similar or to understand results that are perceived as being contradictory but could be explained in a comparative analysis of the phenomenon under investigation. Yin (2003) states that each type of case-study design can take on two forms, holistic and embedded. The holistic form is most appropriate for examining the global nature of a phenomenon. However, if the unit of analysis of a given case study divides a particular phenomenon into several subunits, an embedded design is developed. The advantage of the embedded form is the potential to make extensive comparative analyses of much more complex phenomena. Although this study documents a single case, occurrences prior to and throughout the conversion process required the recognition that individual meaning-making was embedded in a participant's understanding of the community's historical context.

Research Process

In this study I used a multi-method research framework in order to determine the underlying factors associated with converting a public housing project into a housing co-operative. The primary means to identify and interpret these factors was acquired from historical accounts provided by individuals and by an analysis of existing documentation and public records. The research process integrated aspects from the different approaches found in qualitative enquiry that conduct research within a natural setting. Specifically, I applied strategies taken from action research, ethnography, and naturalistic observations in order to collect and interpret the information. In all instances I took on the role of ethnographer, where I immersed myself in the life of people in order to place the phenomena studied in their social and cultural context (Lewis, 1985). In this section I go into greater detail on the sampling strategies and information-collection techniques.

Participant Selection and Recruitment

The first step in the research process was to determine who would be appropriate for participation in the study. This determination had to ensure that the individuals and groups who had had a role in different areas of the community's development into a co-operative would be involved in some capacity. Potential participants were differentiated according to their relative role or stake in the operation and management of the community, which involved distinguishing their status as either primary or secondary stakeholders. Clarkson (1995, 106) states that "a primary stakeholder group is one without whose continuing participation the corporation cannot survive as a going concern," whereas the presence of a secondary stakeholder group is not integral to the survival of an organization. Distinguishing between the two types of stakeholders was intended to determine the relative roles that the participants had played in the community's development.

In this study the primary stakeholders include members of the board of directors and regular residents of the Atkinson Housing Co-operative; the Co-operative Housing Federation of Toronto; and Toronto Community Housing Corporation (including the previous Metropolitan Toronto Housing Authority and Metropolitan Toronto Housing Corporation). The resident sample consisted of individuals who had resided in the community for an extended period of time. Since public housing is a public asset that is owned and managed by a government agency, it is integral that the government's voice be included in the study. The secondary stakeholders include local support agencies and organizations with a peripheral interest in the conversion process. According to community development literature, the surrounding neighbourhood can have an impact on a particular community. In the context of public housing, the surrounding neighbourhood includes support agencies and concerned individuals. In this study I refer to the surrounding neighbourhood, secondary actors, as a source of information on the conversion process from public to co-operative housing. The staff of the Alexandra Park Residents' Association and of the Atkinson Housing Co-operative are also referred to as secondary stakeholders.

Following are some characteristics of the sample: the ages range from 20 to 75 years; the size, representing all stakeholders, consists of 43 individuals, of which 18 are male and 25 are female. Please see the table for

Table 1. Characteristics of the Final Participant Sample

Stakeholder	Number interviewed	Role in community	Gender	Age range
Primary Stakeholders				
Atkinson board	4	Members of the board of directors	1 female, 3 males	20–65
Alexandra Park Residents' Association board	4	Current and former members of the board of directors	3 females, 1 male	35–73
Residents/members	15	Interested in the conversion process and with different roles in growth of community	12 females, 3 males	35–75
Government housing representatives	4	All involved in conversion process	2 females, 2 males	40–60
Local politicians	3	Supported initiative at the municipal and provincial levels	1 female, 2 males	50–60
Secondary Stakeholders				
Co-op sector resources persons	4	Supported community development and conversion process	1 female, 3 males	40–60
Support agencies	3	Provided education and conflict resolution	1 female, 2 males	45–55
Staff from community centre and housing agency	6	Implemented services and programs	4 females, 2 males	30–65

a listing of the characteristics of the final participant sample, including the role that each stakeholder group had in the community's development into a co-operative.

RECRUITMENT PROCEDURES

A non-probability or purposive sampling approach was the primary technique to solicit participation. Purposive sampling involves selecting participants based on specific characteristics and roles within a particular context (Sommer and Sommer, 1997). In this study, in order to select appropriate individuals to participate in the research, a set of inclusion criteria was created. The criteria ensured that the selection resulted in participants who best represented a particular stakeholder and were knowledgeable about the community. The inclusion criteria were based on factors associated with an individual's or a group's involvement in the community's activities and in the conversion process.

The resident sample selection consists of individuals who have resided in the community since 1998 or earlier and are knowledgeable about the conversion process. The year 1998 was chosen because it was the year that the Atkinson Housing Co-operative was registered as a non-profit corporation and the residents became directly involved and informed about the conversion process. The inclusion criteria for the other groups were based on their involvement and knowledge in the conversion process as well as on their association with different community-building initiatives that had occurred over the years.

Although different members of the community had been aware and supportive of this research, when the sampling strategy had been finalized, I introduced the research to the community by formally approaching the board of directors and the membership at a community meeting. In both cases there was a lot of interest in the research, but, most of all, the members felt that documenting the growth of the community would help to develop an institutional memory that has long been neglected. According to one resident, "having a former resident actually interested in listening to us" added more to their descriptions than would having an outsider conduct the research.

INFORMATION-COLLECTION TECHNIQUES

In this study I used four information-gathering techniques to generate an understanding of the underlying factors that led the community to become a housing co-operative. The techniques included participant observation of key meetings, informal gatherings, and planned community events; a semi-structured interview with a sample of residents and other key participants involved in the conversion process; an analysis of documents relating to community and the conversion process; and an analysis of various statistics kept by the community and by the government. These research methods were applied to the collection of information related to the series of key events in the community's transition to a housing co-operative.

As a member of the board of directors I have been informally conducting participant observations of the conversion since 1995. A participant observer can take either an active or a passive role in the phenomena being observed (Spradley, 1980). The overall purpose is to achieve a deeper understanding of the tacit knowledge or information that exists within a community (Spradley, 1980). The researcher becomes both an insider and an outsider as the means to contextualizing the various experiences being observed. Over time, the researcher is able to build a knowledge base that accounts for both points of view in order evaluate an experience objectively.

A second research method was the analysis of documents associated with the community's history and with the conversion process. Examples of documents and policies include the following:

- Correspondence
- Media coverage
- Minutes of meetings of the board, the community, and between the community and the government
- Community newsletters and posters
- Community event and meeting posters
- Provincial legislation including the Social Housing Reform Act, the Co-operative Corporations Act, and the Tenant Protection Act
- Waiting list and tenant selection policies
- The Atkinson Housing Co-operative by-laws
- Legal agreements between the co-operative and the government that outline where control has been given and where it has been taken away

The third research approach involved a review of information, both quantitative and qualitative, on the characteristics of the community. There were three objectives to reviewing this information. The first objective was to examine patterns of resident involvement over time – for example, an examination of meeting minutes to determine whether there had been a change in the number of residents participating in committees or community activities over the years. The second objective was to qualitatively examine the organization and execution of different community initiatives. The third objective was to identify strategies related to conflict resolution and problem solving. Following are examples of information that was collected:

- Number in attendance at different meetings, events, and activities
- Presence of volunteer opportunities
- Number of volunteers participating in activities
- The activities in which residents preferred to be involved
- Number of residents involved on committees
- The rate of resident turnover
- Crime statistics in the community
- Maintenance logs in order to determine the frequency of problems
- The content of community information bulletins or newsletters

A fourth approach was conducting semi-structured interviews with residents and non-residents who had been involved in or were knowledgeable about various aspects of the changes and events that had occurred within the community. The interviews took place with key participants in the conversion process (community leaders and government representatives), long-time residents, and knowledgeable figures involved in the administration of Ontario's social housing system. In some cases, there was resistance to being interviewed individually, so an ad hoc focus group was held during the resident programs that were operating in the community centre. For example, I met with five women who were considered to be community elders and who met on a weekly basis for arts and crafts. They felt that the best way to discuss the community was as a group. The added benefit of meeting with this group was that it resulted in publicly honouring the stories of people who felt like they had been silenced during the conversion process. Furthermore, they expressed appreciation at being able to openly discuss specific issues associated with building the community, and not just the conversion, with someone who was involved in the process. I was humbled by their statement and certainly appreciated the extent of their trust. In the next section I describe the interview procedures including the protocol.

INTERVIEW PROCEDURES

The interviews took place at various locations, including coffee shops, the community centre, a park, at kitchen tables, while walking through the community, and at the head office of the housing corporation. An interview protocol was developed, and the elements of the conceptual framework guided the questions. The focus of the interviews was the impact of the different events and activities on the lives of the residents. The interview consisted of seven sections:

1. Background information
2. Goals of the conversion process
3. Role in the conversion process
4. Views of the conversion process
5. Event information
6. Details about the event
7. Additional information

Participants were informed of the nature of the research and why they were being asked to participate. They were given informed consent forms, which emphasized that their responses would not be evaluated as right or wrong. The participants were told that the study was examining the factors that had contributed to Alexandra Park becoming a housing co-operative. Finally, each person was given a copy of the interview protocol prior to the interview.

With the participants' permission, the interviews were recorded using a digital recorder, and I took notes. The interviews were subsequently transcribed, and the participants were informed that they would have the opportunity to review the transcript, but no one made that request. The interviews lasted for one to two hours, and some follow-up interviews were required. Information collection was completed once there was evidence of theoretical saturation.

Interpretation, Analysis, and Establishing Trustworthiness

The analysis consisted primarily of interpretations of each event. The underlying theme in the written account was determining the impact of these events on the conversion process. A standard format for describing the case studies was constructed using elements from Miles and Huberman's (1994) description of within-site analysis of qualitative information. Each case study review focused on three main points: what happened; why was it significant; who was involved and what was their role. Specifically, the case study format had the following main headings:

- Event description, including background factors leading up to the event
- Relationship and relevance of the event to the conversion process

The transcripts were subsequently coded to determine whether the presence of the five elements of the conceptual framework could explain how this community had converted into a housing co-operative. Although the elements guided the interpretations of the events, I applied a grounded theory approach to delve deeper into the information collected (Guba and Lincoln, 1988). Martin and Turner (1986, 23) state that "grounded theory seeks to develop theory that is grounded in data systematically gathered and analyzed." Although a set of categories was prestructured, by using a grounded theory I was not bound to a priori assumptions, and new meaning and knowledge from the participant's perspective could be generated. Furthermore, the use of grounded theory ensured that additional factors that had contributed to the community's development were identified – factors that can result in a reconceptualization of the conceptual framework.

In qualitative research, asserting the reliability of the findings is not an appropriate goal because social processes and phenomena can vary from one context to another (Rolfe, 2006). According to Guba and Lincoln (1988) and Sommer and Sommer (1997), the transferring of information into different settings is the primary goal. Guba and Lincoln (1988) state that validity is achieved by determining the trustworthiness of the information rather than its reliability and generalizability. In this study I utilized the four different methods of data collection in order to determine that the credibility, confirmability, dependability, and transferability were not the result of researcher bias alone, which can be a problem in single-case studies (Yin, 2003). Thus, every attempt was made to conduct interviews that focused on the events, and any "facts" were verified through a triangulation process with existing documentation and information provided from the other methods (Annells, 2006; Webb, Campbell, Schwartz, and Sechrest, 1965).

Ethical Considerations

The building of trust became an integral part of the information-collection process since participants tended to feel quite vulnerable when discussing their experiences of living in the community. The interviewees were assured that the information would be kept strictly confidential, and prior to the analysis of the information, anything that would have easily identified a participant was blocked out. Written summaries contain pseudonyms to disguise the identities of all participants. In a few instances the interviewees preferred to be named and for their organization to be named as well.

This study was presented as low risk for the participants, and the questions in the interviews did not involve any emotional threat. Since the roles of the residents and the individuals from various organizations differed, two different information letters and informed consent forms were created. For residents, the information letters and consent forms reflected their participation as residents and members of the Atkinson Housing Co-operative. For participating organizations, such as the housing authority or the housing corporation, an information letter was given to the organization, and the representative who was interviewed was given an informed consent form.

The participants were informed that they could withdraw or have their participation excluded from the study at any point. Furthermore, they were informed that they could choose not to answer any particular question or stop the interview at any time. The participants were informed that no reimbursements, remuneration, or other compensation would be provided. I conveyed to the participants that the study should benefit the community and themselves in that it would focus on an innovation in which they were involved. The participants were also informed that should they decide not to participate or not to answer particular questions, there would be no adverse consequences to them. The transcripts were subsequently coded and locked in a cabinet, and the recordings were destroyed. A summary of the research findings was made available to each participant upon completion of the study.

Notes

1. Canadian Public Housing Policy and Programs

1 The local housing authority became known as the local housing corporation following the devolution of all housing responsibilities from the Province of Ontario to the municipalities in January 2001. In 2002 the local housing corporation became known as the Toronto Community Housing Corporation.

3. Exploring the Circumstances That Led to the Conversion Process

1 A detailed description of the methodology used to collect the information that informed the writing of the key events is provided in the appendix.

4. Formalizing the Conversion Process

1 Efforts were made to hold the sessions in the first language of those attending.
2 Using these four principles as guidelines, the final agreement can be a template for other communities wishing to convert into a co-operative.
3 Parking and laundry revenue is considered a small percentage of the overall revenue.
4 As stated earlier, the local housing authority was a provincial agency, which became known as the housing corporation after devolution in 2001. The Toronto Community Housing Corporation is a municipal agency responsible for maintaining and managing the social housing stock in Toronto, Ontario.
5 This process is known as "rotating" and is common in housing co-operatives. Since the size of the board is actually greater than the number of contested positions in a given election, new co-op members are potentially brought onto the board while institutional memory is preserved (since a number of experienced board members' positions are not up for re-election). As such, this approach ensures continuity and the presence of some experienced individuals on the board of directors at all times.
6 There is no formal record to explain Mr Latchman Ramkhalawan's resignation.

References

Alexandra Park Community Centre. (1985). *Constitution*. Toronto: Alexandra Park Community Centre Archives.

Alexandra Park Residents' Association (APRA). (1971). *Constitution*. Toronto: Alexandra Park Community Centre Archives.

Alexandra Park Residents' Association (APRA). (1975). *Co-management Agreement with the Ontario Housing Corporation*. Toronto: Alexandra Park Community Centre Archives.

Alexandra Park Residents' Association (APRA). (1985, December 5). *Minutes of Board Meeting of the Alexandra Park Residents' Association (APRA)*. Alexandra Park Community Centre Archives, Toronto.

Alexandra Park Residents' Association (APRA). (1986a, February 10). *Minutes of Board Meeting of the Alexandra Park Residents' Association (APRA)*. Alexandra Park Community Centre Archives, Toronto.

Alexandra Park Residents' Association (APRA). (1986b, September 16). *Minutes of the Annual General Meeting of the Alexandra Park Residents' Association (APRA)*. Alexandra Park Community Centre Archives, Toronto.

Alexandra Park Residents' Association (APRA). (1987). *Constitution*. Toronto: Alexandra Park Community Centre Archives.

Alexandra Park Residents' Association (APRA). (1988). *Members' Handbook*. Toronto: Alexandra Park Community Centre Archives.

Alexandra Park Residents' Association (APRA). (1989, September 27). *Minutes of Board Meeting of the Alexandra Park Residents' Association (APRA)*. Alexandra Park Community Centre Archives, Toronto.

Alexandra Park Residents' Association (APRA) (1990a, March 12). *Minutes from the General Meeting of the Alexandra Park Residents' Association (APRA)*. Alexandra Park Community Centre Archives, Toronto.

Alexandra Park Residents' Association (APRA). (1990b, August 13). *Minutes of Board Meeting of the Alexandra Park Residents' Association (APRA)*. Alexandra Park Community Centre Archives, Toronto.

Alexandra Park Residents' Association (APRA). (1990c, December 11). *Minutes from the Security/Drugs Committee*. Alexandra Park Community Centre Archives, Toronto.

Alexandra Park Residents' Association (APRA) (1991a, February 6). *Minutes from the Meeting of the Alexandra Park Residents' Association (APRA)*. Alexandra Park Community Centre Archives, Toronto.

Alexandra Park Residents' Association (APRA). (1991b, February 12). *Minutes of Board Meeting of the Alexandra Park Residents' Association (APRA)*. Alexandra Park Community Centre Archives, Toronto.

Alexandra Park Residents' Association (APRA). (1993a, November 27). *Minutes from the Meeting of the Alexandra Park Residents' Association (APRA)*. Alexandra Park Community Centre Archives, Toronto.

Alexandra Park Residents' Association (APRA). (1993b, December 4). *Minutes from the Meeting of the Alexandra Park Residents' Association (APRA)*. Alexandra Park Community Centre Archives, Toronto.

Alexandra Park Residents' Association (APRA). (1994a, May 4). *Minutes of Board Meeting of the Alexandra Park Residents' Association (APRA)*. Alexandra Park Community Centre Archives, Toronto.

Alexandra Park Residents' Association (APRA). (1994b, March 15). *Minutes of Board Meeting of the Alexandra Park Residents' Association (APRA)*. Alexandra Park Community Centre Archives, Toronto.

Alexandra Park Residents' Association (APRA). (1995, January). *Alexandra Park Co-operative Times Newsletter*. Alexandra Park Community Centre Archives, Toronto.

Alexandra Park Residents' Association (APRA). (1999, June 21). *Minutes of Community Meeting of the Alexandra Park Residents' Association (APRA)*. Alexandra Park Community Centre Archives, Toronto.

Alexandra Park Residents' Association (APRA). (2000, January 10). *Minutes of Board Meeting of the Alexandra Park Residents' Association (APRA)*. Alexandra Park Community Centre Archives, Toronto.

Alexandra Park Residents' Association (APRA). (2001a, September 19). *Constitution*. Alexandra Park Community Centre Archives, Toronto.

Alexandra Park Residents' Association (APRA). (2001b, October 15). *Minutes of Community Meeting of the Alexandra Park Residents' Association (APRA)*. Alexandra Park Community Centre Archives, Toronto.

Alinsky, S. (1971). *Rules for Radicals: A Practical Primer for Realistic Radicals*. New York: Vintage Books.

Amer, L. (1990, July 24). *Letter to Jean Augustine Re. Co-operative Conversion*. Alexandra Park Community Centre Archives, Toronto.

Anderson, G. (1992). *Housing Policy in Canada*. Vancouver: University of British Columbia, Centre for Human Settlements.

Annells, M. (2006, October). Triangulation of Qualitative Approaches: Hermeneutical Phenomenology and Grounded Theory. *Journal of Advanced Nursing, 56* (1), 55–61. http://dx.doi.org/10.1111/j.1365-2648.2006.03979.x Medline:16972918

Appleby, T. (1990a, April 12). Police visits rare at popular Toronto drug den. *The Globe and Mail*, pp. A1, A16.

Appleby, T. (1990b, July 9). Residents organize vigilante group. *The Globe and Mail*, pp. A1, A3.

Appleby, T. (1990c, September 22). Big drug sweeps net small hauls. *The Globe and Mail*, p. A1.

Atkinson, S. (1993, April 1). *Letter to Rosario Marchese Re. Co-operative Conversion*. Alexandra Park Community Centre Archives, Toronto.

Atkinson, S. (1994a, January 13). *Letter to Minister Gigantes Regarding the Demonstration Project to Test the Co-op Self-Management Idea*. Alexandra Park Community Centre Archives, Toronto.

Atkinson, S. (1994b, September 7). *Letter to Ron Hikel Regarding Funding*. Alexandra Park Community Centre Archives, Toronto.

Atkinson Housing Co-operative. (1996). *Business Plan*. Toronto: Alexandra Park Community Centre Archives.

Atkinson Housing Co-operative. (1999, November 11). *Minutes of Community Meeting of the Atkinson Housing Co-operative*. Atkinson Housing Co-operative Archives, Toronto.

Atkinson Housing Co-operative. (2000, March 23). *Minutes of Board Meeting of the Atkinson Housing Co-operative*. Atkinson Housing Co-operative Archives, Toronto.

Atkinson Housing Co-operative. (2001a, January 20). *Minutes of Board Meeting of the Atkinson Housing Co-operative*. Atkinson Housing Co-operative Archives, Toronto.

Atkinson Housing Co-operative. (2001b, May 29). *Minutes of Board Meeting of the Atkinson Housing Co-operative*. Atkinson Housing Co-operative Archives Toronto.

Atkinson Housing Co-operative. (2001c, June 26). *Minutes of Board Meeting of the Atkinson Housing Co-operative*. Atkinson Housing Co-operative Archives, Toronto.

Atkinson Housing Co-operative. (2001d, July 23). *Minutes of Board Meeting of the Atkinson Housing Co-operative*. Atkinson Housing Co-operative Archives, Toronto.

Atkinson Housing Co-operative. (2002a, March 11). *Minutes of Board Meeting of the* Atkinson Housing co-operative. Atkinson Housing Co-operative Archives Toronto.

Atkinson Housing Co-operative. (2002b, April 3). *Minutes of Board Meeting of the Atkinson Housing Co-operative.* Atkinson Housing Co-operative Archives, Toronto.

Atkinson Housing Co-operative. (2002c, November 9). *Minutes of Board Meeting of the Atkinson Housing Co-operative.* Atkinson Housing Co-operative Archives, Toronto.

Atkinson Housing Co-operative. (2003a, January 13). *Minutes of Board Meeting of the Atkinson Housing Co-operative.* Atkinson Housing Co-operative Archives, Toronto.

Atkinson Housing Co-operative. (2003b, February 10). *Minutes of Board Meeting of the Atkinson Housing Co-operative.* Atkinson Housing Co-operative Archives, Toronto.

Atkinson Housing Co-operative. (2003c, March 5). *Minutes of Board Meeting of the Atkinson Housing Co-operative.* Atkinson Housing Co-operative Archives, Toronto.

Atkinson Housing Co-operative. (2003d, March 12). *Minutes of Board Meeting of the Atkinson Housing Co-operative.* Atkinson Housing Co-operative Archives, Toronto.

Atkinson Housing Co-operative. (2003e, March 20). *Minutes of Board Meeting of the Atkinson Housing Co-operative.* Atkinson Housing Co-operative Archives, Toronto.

Atkinson Housing Co-operative. (2003f, April 1). *Final Operating Agreement between the Atkinson Housing Co-operative and the Toronto Community Housing Corporation.* Atkinson Housing Co-operative Archives, Toronto.

Augustine, J. (1990, July 13). *Letter to Liz Amer Re. Public Housing Design.* Alexandra Park Community Centre Archives, Toronto.

Bacher, J. (1993). *Keeping to the Marketplace: The Evolution of Canadian Housing Policy.* Montreal: McGill-Queen's University Press.

Barnes, A. (1997, January 1). Good neighbor 'Sonny' Atkinson. *The Toronto Star*, p. A18.

Bass, B. (1990). From transactional to transformational leadership: Learning to share the vision. *Organizational Dynamics, 18* (3), 19–31. http://dx.doi.org/10.1016/0090-2616(90)90061-S

Bauman, J.F. (1994). Public housing: The dreadful saga of a durable policy. *Journal of Planning Literature, 8* (4), 347–61. http://dx.doi.org/10.1177/088541229400800401

Bennis, W., and Nanus, B. (1985). *Leaders: The Strategies for Taking Charge*. New York: Harper and Row.

Berkowitz, B., and Cashman, S. (2000). Building healthy communities: Lessons and challenges. *Community*, Fall/Autumn, 1–7.

Best, R. (1996). Successes, failures, and prospects for public housing policy in the United Kingdom. *Housing Policy Debate, 7* (3), 535–62. http://dx.doi.org/10.1080/10511482.1996.9521232

Bourdieu, P. (1986). The forms of capital. In J.G. Richardson (Ed.), *Handbook of Theory and Research for the Sociology of Education* (pp. 241–58). New York: Greenwood Press.

Brooks, S., and Miljan, L. (2003). *Public Policy in Canada: An Introduction*. Toronto: Oxford University Press.

Burnette, L. (2001, June 25). *Letter to the Atkinson Housing Co-operative Board from the Board Liaison*. Alexandra Park Community Centre Archives, Toronto.

Burns, J.M. (1978). *Leadership*. New York: Harper and Row.

Canada Mortgage and Housing Corporation. (1991). *Evaluation of the Federal Co-operative Housing Program*. Ottawa: Canada Mortgage and Housing Corporation.

Canada Mortgage and Housing Corporation (CMHC). (2004). History of CMHC. Retrieved from http://www.cmhc-schl.gc.ca/en/corp/about/hi/index.cfm.

Carder, C. (1994). MTHA embraces new community-building outlook. *Toronto Star*, July 23, p. A1.

Carter, T. (1997). Current practices for procuring affordable housing: The Canadian context. *Housing Policy Debate, 8* (3), 593–631. http://www.knowledgeplex.org/showdoc.html?id=2281

Chandler, M.O. (1991). What have we learned from public housing resident management? *Journal of Planning Literature, 6* (2), 136–43. http://dx.doi.org/10.1177/088541229100600202

Chatterjee, A. (2001, April 20). *Letter to Latchman Ramkhalawan Regarding the Need for an Intervention*. Alexandra Park Community Centre Archives, Toronto.

Chavis, D., and Pretty, G. (1999). Sense of community: Advances in measurement and application. *Journal of Community Psychology, 27* (6), 635–42. http://dx.doi.org/10.1002/(SICI)1520-6629(199911)27:6<635::AID-JCOP1>3.0.CO;2-F

Christenson, J., Fendley, K., and Robinson, J. (1994). Community development. In J. Christenson and J. Robinson (Eds.), *Community Development in Perspective* (pp. 3–25). Ames: Iowa State University.

City of Toronto Development Department. (1971, February 25). *Alexandra Park.* Research and Information Division, City of Toronto.

Clarkson, M. (1995). A stakeholder framework for analyzing and evaluating corporate social performance. *Academy of Management Review, 20* (1), 92–117.

Cohen, D., and Prusak, L. (2001). *In Good Company: How Social Capital Makes Organizations Work.* Boston: Harvard Business School Press.

Coleman, J. (1988). Social capital in the creation of human capital. *American Journal of Sociology, 94* (s1), S95–S120. http://dx.doi.org/10.1086/228943

Cooper, M., and Rodman, M. (1992). *New Neighbours: A Case Study of Cooperative Housing.* Toronto: University of Toronto Press.

Co-operative Conversion Committee. (1994, May 19). *Minutes from the Meeting of the Co-operative Conversion Committee.* Alexandra Park Community Centre Archives, Toronto.

Co-operative Housing Federation of Toronto (CHFT). (1994, September 16). *Alexandra Park Conversion to Atkinson Co-op Education Plan Submitted to the Housing Authority.* Alexandra Park Community Centre Archives, Toronto.

Co-operative Housing Federation of Toronto (CHFT). (2002). *Alexandra Park Conversion to Atkinson Co-op: A Community Development Plan.* Atkinson Housing Co-operative Archives, Toronto.

Co-operative Housing Federation of Toronto (CHFT). (2003). Co-operative Housing Federation of Toronto. www.coophousing.com. (02/21/03).

Co-operatives Secretariat. (2009). *Various Kinds of Co-operatives.* Retrieved from http://coop.gc.ca/COOP/display-afficher.do?id=1232133235546and lang=eng

Dahl, R.A. (1961). *Who Governs?* New Haven, CT, and London: Yale University Press.

Dahl, R.A. (2000). *On Democracy.* New Haven, CT: Yale University Press.

Dennis, M., and Fish, S. (1972). *Programs in Search of a Policy.* Toronto: Hakkert.

Dobelstein, A. (1993). *Social Welfare: Policy and Analysis.* Chicago: Nelson Hall.

Dreier, P., and Hulchanski, D. (1993). The role of non-profit housing in Canada and the United States: Some comparisons. *Housing Policy Debate, 4* (1), 43–80. http://dx.doi.org/10.1080/10511482.1993.9521124

Ellis, S.J., and Noyes, K.H. (1990). *By the People: A History of Americans as Volunteers.* San Francisco: Jossey-Bass Publishers.

Epp, G. (1996). Emerging strategies for revitalizing public housing communities. *Housing Policy Debate, 7* (3), 563–88. http://dx.doi.org/10.108 0/10511482.1996.9521233

Fine, B. (1999). The developmental state is dead – Long live social capital? *Development and Change, 30* (1), 1–19. http://dx.doi.org/10.1111/1467-7660.00105

Fisher, R. (1999). Social action community organization: Proliferation, persistence, roots and prospects. In M. Minkler (Ed.), *Community Organizing and Community Building for Health* (pp. 53–67). New Brunswick, NJ: Rutgers University Press.

Franklin, B. (2000). Demands, expectations and responses: The shaping of housing management. *Housing Studies, 15* (6), 907–27. http://dx.doi.org/10.1080/02673030020002609

Freeman, L. (1998). Interpreting the dynamics of public housing: Cultural and rational choice explanations. *Housing Policy Debate, 9* (2), 323–53. http://dx.doi.org/10.1080/10511482.1998.9521297

Freire, P. (1972). *Pedagogy of the Oppressed.* Harmondsworth, UK: Penguin.

Freire, P. (1973). *Education for Critical Consciousness.* New York: Seabury Press.

Friedman, L. (1968). *Government and Slum Housing: A Century of Frustration.* Chicago: Rand McNally.

Gadd, J. (1995, November 2). Public unit tenants seek to form co-op. *The Globe and Mail,* pp. A1, A8.

Giddens, A. (1984). *The Constitution of Society: Outline of the Theory of Structuration.* Cambridge: Polity Press.

Giddens, A. (1994). *Beyond Left and Right: The Future of Radical Politics.* Stanford, CA: Stanford University Press.

Gigantes, E. (1993, October 27). Assisted Housing. In Ontario Legislative Assembly. *Legislative Debates (Hansard).* 35th Parliament, 3rd Session. Retrieved from http://www.ontla.on.ca/web/house-proceedings/house_detail.do?Date=1993-10-27andParl=35andSess=3andlocale=en#P225_69653

Goldblatt, M. (1991). *Public Housing to Co-operative Conversion (PHCC): Proposal; Demonstration Process for Public Housing to Co-op Conversion.* Toronto: Alexandra Park Community Centre Archives.

Goldblatt, M. (1994a, July 11). *Letter to the Alexandra Park Residents' Association Regarding the Outreach Worker.* Alexandra Park Community Centre Archives, Toronto.

Goldblatt, M. (1994b, November 2). *Letter to the Alexandra Park Residents' Association Regarding the Education Committee.* Alexandra Park Community Centre Archives, Toronto.

Government of Canada. (1944). *Final Report of the Sub-committee on Housing and Community Planning. Advisory Committee on Reconstruction.* Ottawa: King's Printer.

Gramsci, A. (1971). *Selections from the Prison Notebooks.* London: Lawrence and Wishart.

Granovetter, M. (1973). The strength of weak ties. *American Journal of Sociology, 78* (6), 1360–80. http://dx.doi.org/10.1086/225469

Guba, E.G., and Lincoln, Yvonne S. (1988). Naturalistic and rationalistic enquiry. In John P. Keeves (Ed.), *Educational Research, Methodology, and Measurement: An International Handbook* (pp. 81–5). Oxford: Pergamon Press.

Hague, C. (1990). The development and politics of tenant participation in British council housing. *Housing Studies, 5* (4), 242–56. http://dx.doi.org/10.1080/02673039008720689

Hancock, T. (1996). Healthy, sustainable communities. *Alternatives Journal, 22* (2), 18–23.

Haworth, A., and Manzi, T. (1999). Managing the "underclass": Interpreting the moral discourse of housing management. *Urban Studies (Edinburgh, Scotland), 36* (1), 153–65. http://dx.doi.org/10.1080/0042098993790

Hawton, J. (Talk Show Host). (1990, July 12). Call-in show. Radio Broadcast. Toronto: CFRB.

Hellyer, P. (1969). *Report of the Federal Task Force on Housing and Urban Development*. Ottawa: The Task Force.

Henslin, J. (2003). *Sociology: A Down-to-Earth Approach* (6th ed.). Boston: Allyn and Bacon.

Howlett, M., and Ramesh, M. (2003). *Studying Public Policy: Policy Cycles and Policy Subsystems* (2nd ed.). Toronto: Oxford University Press.

Huang, M. (1992, August 31). War on drugs succeeding: Residents see results in Alexandra Park. *Toronto Star*, p. A7.

Hughes, E. (1998). Leadership development program serves as a change agent in community development. *Journal of Extension, 36* (2). Retrieved from http://www.joe.org/joe/1998april/iw2.php.

Hustedde, R. (2009). Seven theories for seven community developers. In R. Phillips and R.H. Pittman (Eds.), *An Introduction to Community Development* (pp. 20–37). New York: Routledge.

International Co-operative Alliance (ICA). (2013). *Statement on the Co-operative Identity*. Retrieved from http://ica.coop/en/what-co-op/co-operative-identity-values-principles.

Jacob, A. (1999). The Quebec experience. In H. Campfens (Ed.), *Community Development around the World: Theory, Practice, Research, Training* (pp. 90–101). Toronto: University of Toronto Press.

Kanungo, R., and Mendonca, M. (1996). *Ethical Dimensions of Leadership*. London: Sage Publications.

Kingston, S., Mitchell, R., Florin, P., and Stevenson, J. (1999). Sense of community in neighbourhoods as a multi-level construct. *Journal of Community Psychology, 27* (6), 681–94. http://dx.doi.org/10.1002/(SICI)1520-6629(199911)27:6<681::AID-JCOP4>3.0.CO;2-W

Kirby, S., and McKenna, K. (1989). *Experience Research and Social Change: Methods from the Margins*. Toronto: Garamond Press.

Klein, J. (1969). Alexandra Park: Urban renewal. *Canadian Architect, 13* (9), 5–20.

Koebel, T., and Cavell, M. (1995). *Tenant Organizations in Public Housing Projects: A Report on Senate Resolution No. 347.* Prepared for the Virginia Housing Study Commission by the Virginia Centre for Housing Research.

Koebel, T., Richard, S., and Robert, D. (1998). Public-private partnerships for affordable housing: Definitions and applications in an international perspective. In T. Koebel (Ed.), *Shelter and Society: Theory, Research, and Policy for NonProfit Housing* (pp. 39–70). Albany: State University of New York Press.

Kretzmann, J.P., and McKnight, J.L. (1993). *Building Communities from the Inside Out: A Path toward Finding and Mobilizing a Community's Assets.* Chicago: Center for Urban Affairs and Policy Research, Northwestern University.

Lane, V. (1995). Best management practices in U.S. public housing. *Housing Policy Debate, 6* (4), 867–904. http://dx.doi.org/10.1080/10511482.1995.9521 208

Lapointe, L., and Sousa, J. (2003). *The Conversion of Alexandra Park to Atkinson Housing Co-operative: An Evaluation of the Process.* Report prepared for the Canada Mortgage and Housing Corporation.

Leavitt, J., and Saegert, S. (1990). *From Abandonment to Hope: Community Households in Harlem.* New York: Columbia University Press.

Lewis, B. (1996, June 12). Letter from Lewis and Collyer to Mark Goldblatt. Alexandra Park Community Centre Archives, Toronto

Lewis, I. (1985). *Social Anthropology in Perspective.* Cambridge: Cambridge University Press.

Ley, D. (1993). Co-operative housing as a moral landscape: Re-examining "the postmodern city." In J. Duncan and D. Ley (Eds.), *Place/culture/representation* (pp. 128–48). London: Routledge.

Lomas, J. (1998, November). Social capital and health: Implications for public health and epidemiology. *Social Science and Medicine, 47* (9), 1181–8. http://dx.doi.org/10.1016/S0277-9536(98)00190-7 Medline:9783861

MacPherson, I. (1979). *Each for All: A History of the Co-Operative Movement in English Canada, 1900–1945.* Toronto: Macmillan of Canada.

Maier, F. (1969, July 19). Bitterness and fear in Alexandra Park. *The Globe and Mail,* p. 5A.

Martin, P.Y., and Turner, B.A. (1986). Grounded theory and organizational research. *Journal of Applied Behavioral Science, 22* (2), 141–57. http://dx.doi.org/10.1177/002188638602200207

McCarthy, J.D., and Zald, M.N. (1977). Resource mobilization in social movements: A partial theory. *American Journal of Sociology, 82* (6), 1212–41. http://dx.doi.org/10.1086/226464

McKenzie, B., and Wharf, B. (2010). *Connecting Policy to Practice in the Human Services* (3rd ed.). Toronto: Oxford University Press.

McKnight, J.L. (1995). *The Careless Society: Community and Its Counterfeits*. New York: Basic Books.

McKnight, J.L., and Kretzmann, J. (1999). Mapping community capacity. In M. Minkler (Ed.), *Community Organizing and Community Building for Health* (pp. 157–72). New Brunswick, NJ: Rutgers University Press.

Melnyk, G. (1985). *The Search for Community: From Utopia to a Co-operative Society*. Montreal: Black Rose Books.

Metropolitan Toronto Housing Authority (MTHA). (1994, June 21). Report of 164th regular meeting of the Metropolitan Toronto Housing Authority. Alexandra Park Community Centre Archives, Toronto.

Metropolitan Toronto Housing Authority (MTHA). (1995). Tenant Income Profiles of Alexandra Park. April.

Metropolitan Toronto Housing Corporation (MTHC). (2001a, March 31). MTHC Quarterly Report.

Metropolitan Toronto Housing Corporation (MTHC). (2001b, August 15). MTHC Report of the Board of Directors. Alexandra Park Community Centre Archives, Toronto.

Miceli, T., Sazama, G., and Sirmans, C. (1994). The role of limited-equity cooperatives in providing affordable housing. *Housing Policy Debate, 5* (4), 469–90. http://dx.doi.org/10.1080/10511482.1994.9521175

Miceli, T., Sazama, G., and Sirmans, C. (1998). Managing externalities in multi-unit housing: Limited equity cooperatives as alternatives to public housing. *Journal of Policy Modeling, 20* (5), 649–68. http://dx.doi.org/10.1016/S0161-8938(97)00071-9

Miles, M., and Huberman, M. (1994). *Qualitative Data Analysis: An Expanded Source Book* (2nd ed.). London: Sage.

Ministry of the Attorney General. (1994, September 1). *Letter to Sonny Atkinson Regarding Funds for Consultation Process*. Alexandra Park Community Centre Archives, Toronto.

Minkler, M., and Wallerstein, N. (1999). Improving health through community organzation and community building. In M. Minkler (Ed.), *Community Organizing and Community Building for Health* (pp. 30–52). New Brunswick, NJ: Rutgers University Press.

Moloney, P. (1990, August 31). Brick walls hiding drug deals start to come tumbling down. *Toronto Star*, p. A6.

Murdie, R. (1992). *Social Housing in Transition: The Changing Social Composition of Public Sector Housing in Metropolitan Toronto*. Ottawa: Canada Mortgage and Housing Corporation.

Murray, B.L. (2003, April). Qualitative research interviews: Therapeutic benefits for the participants. *Journal of Psychiatric and Mental Health Nursing, 10* (2), 233–6. http://dx.doi.org/10.1046/j.1365-2850.2003.00553.x Medline:12662341

National Housing Act (NHA), R.S c. N-11. (1985).

Newman, O. (1972). *Defensible Space: Crime Prevention through Urban Design.* New York: Macmillan.

Newman, O. (1996). *Creating Defensible Space.* Washington, DC: U.S. Department of Housing and Urban Development.

O'Neil, P. (1994, February 8). *Letter to Sonny Atkinson Accepting Invitation to Begin the Discussions.* Alexandra Park Community Centre Archives, Toronto.

OECD. (2008). *Government Programs to Reduce Administrative Burdens.* Centre for Tax Policy and Administration: Paris. Retrieved from www.oecd.org/tax/taxadministration/39947998.pdf.

Ontario Advisory Task Force on Housing Policy. (1973). *Working Papers, Volumes 1 and 2.* Toronto: Queen's Printer.

Ontario. Ministry of Municipal Affairs and Housing. (2000). *Social Housing Reform Act.* Toronto: Queen's Printer of Ontario.

Ontario Housing (1977). Alexandra Park resident and OHC tenant management agreement. *Ontario Housing, 21* (1 and 2), 32–3.

Ontario Nonprofit Housing Association (ONPHA). (2002). www.onpha.on.ca. (09/25/02).

Papp, L. (1990, July 15). Protesters want walls destroyed to drive away drug pushers. *Toronto Star,* p. A21.

Peterman, W. (1989). Options to conventional public housing management. *Journal of Urban Affairs, 11* (1), 53–68. http://dx.doi.org/10.1111/j.1467-9906.1989.tb00176.x

Peterman, W. (1996). The meanings of resident empowerment: Why just about everybody thinks it's a good idea and what it has to do with resident management. *Housing Policy Debate, 7* (3), 473–90. http://dx.doi.org/10.1080/10511482.1996.9521230

Phillips, R., and Pittman, R. (2009). A framework for community and economic development. In R. Phillips and R. Pittman (Eds.), *An Introduction to Community Development* (pp. 3–19). New York: Routledge. http://dx.doi.org/10.1007/s11205-011-9833-6

Praeger, W. (1976, July 13). Recreation centre funds available group told. *Toronto Star,* p. B01.

Prezza, M., Amici, M., Roberti, T., and Tedeschi, G. (2001). Sense of community referred to the whole town: Its relations with neighboring, loneliness, life satisfaction, and area of residence. *Journal of Community Psychology, 29* (1),

29–52. http://dx.doi.org/10.1002/1520-6629(200101)29:1<29::AID-JCOP3>
3.0.CO;2-C

Prince, M. (1995). The Canadian housing policy context. *Housing Policy Debate*,
6 (3), 721–58. http://dx.doi.org/10.1080/10511482.1995.9521201

Prince, M. (1998). Holes in the safety net, leaks in the roof: Changes in
Canadian welfare policy and their implications for social housing programs.
Housing Policy Debate, 9 (4), 825–48. http://dx.doi.org/10.1080/10511482.19
98.9521320

Putnam, R. (1998). Forward. *Housing Policy Debate*, 9 (1), v–viii. http://dx.doi.
org/10.1080/10511482.1998.9521283

Putnam, R. (2000). *Bowling Alone: The Collapse and Revival of American
Community*. New York: Simon and Schuster.

Quarter, J. (1992). *The Social Economy*. Toronto: James Lorimer.

Quarter, J. (2000). The social economy and the neo-liberal agenda. In J.M.
Fontan and E. Shragge (Eds.), *Social Economy, Debates and Perspectives*
(pp. 54–64). Montreal: Black Rose.

Ramkhalawan, L. (2001a, May 28). *Letter to the Atkinson Housing Co-operative
Board regarding management problems at the community centre*. Alexandra Park
Community Centre Archives, Toronto.

Ramkhalawan, L. (2001b, May 30). *Letter to Community Centre staff*. Alexandra
Park Community Centre Archives, Toronto.

Randolph, B., Rumming, K., and Murray, D. (2010). Unpacking social exclusion
in Western Sydney: Exploring the role of place and tenure. *Geographical
Research*, 48 (2), 197–214. http://dx.doi.org/10.1111/j.1745-5871.2009.00619.x

Resident Advisory Council. (1993, January 28). *Minutes of the Resident Advisory
Council*. Alexandra Park Community Centre Archives, Toronto.

Resident Advisory Council. (1994, January 24). *Minutes of the Resident Advisory
Council*. Alexandra Park Community Centre Archives, Toronto.

Rohe, W. (1995). Converting public housing to cooperatives: The experience of
three developments. *Housing Policy Debate*, 6 (2), 439–79. http://dx.doi.org/
10.1080/10511482.1995.9521192

Rolfe, G. (2006, February). Validity, trustworthiness and rigour: Quality and
the idea of qualitative research. *Journal of Advanced Nursing*, 53 (3), 304–10.
http://dx.doi.org/10.1111/j.1365-2648.2006.03727.x Medline:16441535

Room, G. (1995). Poverty and social exclusion: The new European agenda for
policy and research. In G. Room (Ed.), *Beyond the Threshold: The Measurement
and Analysis of Social Exclusion* (pp. 1–19). Bristol, UK: Policy Press.

Rose, A. (1958). *Regent Park: A Study in Slum Clearance*. Toronto: University of
Toronto Press.

Rose, A. (1963). *Housing, Urban Renewal, and the Community Social Services.* An address to the Eleventh Annual Conference of Ontario Association of Housing Authorities.

Rose, A. (1980). *Canadian Housing Policies, 1935–1980.* Toronto: Butterworth.

Rothman, J. (1968). *Three Models of Community Organization Practice: Social Work Practice.* New York: Columbia University Press.

Rothman, J. (1995). Approaches to community intervention. In J. Rothman, J. Erlich, and J. Tropman (Eds.), *Strategies of Community Intervention* (pp. 26–63). Itasca, IL: F.E. Peacock Publishers.

Rothman, J. (2000). Collaborative self-help community development: When is the strategy warranted? *Journal of Community Practice, 7* (2), 89–105. http://dx.doi.org/10.1300/J125v07n02_05

Saegert, S., and Winkel, G. (1998). Social capital and the revitalization of New York's distressed inner-city housing. *Housing Policy Debate, 9* (1), 17–60. http://dx.doi.org/10.1080/10511482.1998.9521285

Sarick, L. (1998, June 5). Alexandra Park takes control. *The Globe and Mail,* p. A10.

Schuguerensky, D. (2004). The tango of citizenship learning and participatory democracy. In K. Mundel and D. Schugurensky (Eds.), *Lifelong Citizenship Learning, Participatory Democracy and Social Change* (pp. 326–34). Toronto: Transformative Learning Centre, OISE/UT.

Seeking Volunteers. (1971, December). *Alexandra Park Residents' Association (APRA) Newsletter 3,* 2. Alexandra Park Community Centre Archives, Toronto.

Sennett, R. (2003). *Respect in a World of Inequality.* New York: W.W. Norton.

Sennett, R., and Cobb, J. (1972). *The Hidden Injuries of Class.* New York: Vintage Books.

Sewell, J. (1993). *The Shape of the City.* Toronto: University of Toronto Press.

Sewell, J. (1994). *Houses and Homes: Housing for Canadians.* Toronto: James Lorimer.

Shephard, M. (1995, July 26). Townhouse tenants live in fear: Drugs, shootings plague Alexandra Park residents. *Toronto Star,* p. A6.

Shor, I. (1993). Education is politics: Paulo Freire's critical pedagogy. In P. McLaren and P. Leonard (Eds.), *Paulo Freire: A Critical Encounter* (pp. 25–35). New York: Routledge. http://dx.doi.org/10.4324/9780203420263_chapter_2

Silver, J. (2011). *Good Places to Live.* Winnipeg, MB: Fernwood Publishing.

Skelton, I. (2002). *Supporting Identity and Social Need: The Many Faces of Co-op Housing.* Ottawa: Canadian Centre for Policy Alternatives.

Smith, C. (1968, May 29). All could be lost without old spirit. *The Globe and Mail,* p. A5.

Smith, N. (1995). Challenges of public housing in the 1990s: The case of Ontario, Canada. *Housing Policy Debate, 6* (4), 905–31. http://dx.doi.org/10.1080/10511482.1995.9521209

Social Planning Council of Metropolitan Toronto. (1970). *Alexandra Park Relocation after Relocation: Part I.* Toronto: Social Planning Council of Metropolitan Toronto.

Somerville, P. (1998). Empowerment through residence. *Housing Studies, 13* (2), 233–57. http://dx.doi.org/10.1080/02673039883425

Sommer, B., and Sommer, R. (1997). *A Practical Guide to Behavioral Research: Tools and Techniques.* New York: Oxford University Press.

Sousa, J. (2007). *Building Community Capacity: Assessing Member Satisfaction in the Atkinson Housing Co-operative.* Commissioned by the Toronto Community Housing Corporation.

Sousa, J., and Herman, R. (2012). Converting organizational form: An introductory discussion. In J. Sousa and R. Herman (Eds.), *A Co-operative Dilemma: Converting Organizational Form* (pp. 1–22). Saskatoon, SK: Centre for the Study of Co-operatives.

Sousa, J., and Quarter, J. (2003). The Convergence of nonmarket housing models in Canada. *Housing Policy Debate, 14* (4), 591–620. http://dx.doi.org/10.1080/10511482.2003.9521488

Sousa, J., and Quarter, J. (2005). Atkinson Housing Co-operative: A leading-edge conversion from public housing. *Housing Studies, 20* (3), 423–39. http://dx.doi.org/10.1080/02673030500062459

Spradley, J. (1980). *Participant Observation.* New York: Holt, Rinehart and Winston.

St. Stephen's Community House. (2002, January). *Conflict Resolution Report and Recommendations.* Alexandra Park Community Centre Archives, Toronto.

Steele, A., Somerville, P., and Galvin, G. (1995). *Estate Agreements: A New Arrangement for Tenant Participation.* Manchester, UK: University of Salford, Department of Housing.

Streich, P. (1993). The affordability of housing in post-war Canada. In J. Miron (Ed.), *House, Home and Community Progress in Housing Canadians, 1945–86* (pp. 257–70). Montreal: McGill-Queen's Press.

Stringer, E. (1999). *Action Research: A Handbook for Practitioners.* Thousand Oaks, CA: Sage.

Sullivan, E. (1990). *Critical Psychology and Pedagogy.* New York: Bergin and Garvey

Taylor, M. (2003). *Public Policy in the Community.* London: Palgrave, Macmillan.

Thomas, G. (1976, July 12). Residents demanding fund centre turn sod. *Toronto Star,* p. C1.

Toronto Community Housing Corporation (TCHC). (2004). *Report of the Self-Management Committee (TCHC:2004–102)*. Toronto.

Toronto Community Housing Corporation (TCHC). (2011). Investing in Building. Retrieved from http://www.torontohousing.ca/revitalization.

Toronto Community Housing Corporation (TCHC). (2012a). About reporting your income. Retrieved from http://www.torontohousing.ca/about_reporting_your_income.

Toronto Community Housing Corporation (TCHC). (2012b). Regent Park. Retrieved from http://www.torontohousing.ca/investing_buildings/regent_park.

Toronto Community Housing Corporation (TCHC). (2012c). Building a Plan in Alexandra Park. Retrieved from http://www.torontohousing.ca/investing_buildings/alexandra_park.

Toughill, K. (1991, October 14). Tenants' drug war runs into brick wall. *Toronto Star*, p. A1.

Tunstall, R. (2001). Devolution and user participation in public services: How they work and what they do. *Urban Studies (Edinburgh, Scotland), 38* (13), 2495–514. http://dx.doi.org/10.1080/00420980120094632

Vakili-Zad, C. (1993). Tenant participation and control in public housing in Canada. *Habitat International, 17* (2), 91–103. http://dx.doi.org/10.1016/0197-3975(93)90007-Y

Vale, L. (2002). *Reclaiming Public Housing: A Half Century of Struggle in Three Public Neighbourhoods*. Boston: Harvard University Press.

Van Dyk, N. (1995). Financing Social Housing Canada. *Housing Policy Debate, 6* (4), 815–48. http://dx.doi.org/10.1080/10511482.1995.9521206

Van Laar, C. (1999). *Increasing a Sense of Community in the Military: The Role of Personnel Support Programs*. New York: Rand Corporation.

Van Ryzin, G. (1996). The impact of resident management on residents' satisfaction with public housing: A process analysis of quasi-experimental data. *Evaluation Review, 20* (4), 485–506. http://dx.doi.org/10.1177/0193841X9602000406

Wandersman, A., Goodman, R., and Butterfoss, F. (1999). Understanding coalitions and how they operate: An "open systems" organizational framework. In M. Minkler (Ed.), *Community Organizing and Community Building for Health* (pp. 261–78). New Brunswick, NJ: Rutgers University Press.

Warren, M. (1991). *Using Indigenous Knowledge in Agricultural Development*. World Bank Discussion Paper no.127. Washington, DC: World Bank.

Webb, E.J., Campbell, D.T., Schwartz, R.D., and Sechrest, L. (1965). *Unobtrusive Measures: Nonreactive Research in the Social Sciences*. Chicago: Rand McNally.

Weber, M. (1947). *The Theory of Social and Economic Organization* (T. Parsons, Trans.). New York: Oxford University Press.

White, N. (1993, July 23). Co-op fight could make history. *Toronto Star*, p. A1.

White, N. (1995, April 23). Tenants turn project into co-op. *Toronto Star*, p. A16.

White, N. (1996, March 3). Co-op fight could "make history": Activist aims for tenant-run public project. *Toronto Star*, p. A6.

Wilkinson, P., and Quarter, J. (1996). *Building a Community-Controlled Economy: The Evangeline Co-operative Experience*. Toronto: University of Toronto Press.

Wolfe, J. (1998). Canadian housing policy in the nineties. *Housing Studies, 13* (1), 121–33. http://dx.doi.org/10.1080/02673039883524

Wolfe, J., and Jay, W. (1990). The revolving door: Third sector organizations and the homeless. In G. Fallis and A. Murray (Eds.), *Housing the Homeless and Poor: New Partnerships among the Private, Public, and Third Sectors* (pp. 197–226). Toronto: University of Toronto Press.

Wright, L. (1994a, July 23). Co-op move afoot at MTHA. *Toronto Star*, p. A6.

Wright, L. (1994b, November 13). Tenants win okay to run own co-op: Public housing group gets $40,000 in start-up funds. *Toronto Star*, p. A7.

Yin, R. (2003). *Case Study Research, Design and Methods* (3rd ed.). Newbury Park, CA: Sage Publications.

Index